The Software Craftsman

The Software Craftsman

PROFESSIONALISM, PRAGMATISM, PRIDE

Sandro Mancuso

PRENTICE
HALL

Upper Saddle River, NJ • Boston • Indianapolis • San Francisco
New York • Toronto • Montreal • London • Munich • Paris • Madrid
Capetown • Sydney • Tokyo • Singapore • Mexico City

Many of the designations used by manufacturers and sellers to distinguish their products are claimed as trademarks. Where those designations appear in this book, and the publisher was aware of a trademark claim, the designations have been printed with initial capital letters or in all capitals.

The author and publisher have taken care in the preparation of this book, but make no expressed or implied warranty of any kind and assume no responsibility for errors or omissions. No liability is assumed for incidental or consequential damages in connection with or arising out of the use of the information or programs contained herein.

For information about buying this title in bulk quantities, or for special sales opportunities (which may include electronic versions; custom cover designs; and content particular to your business, training goals, marketing focus, or branding interests), please contact our corporate sales department at corpsales@pearsoned.com or (800) 382-3419.

For government sales inquiries, please contact governmentsales@pearsoned.com.

For questions about sales outside the United States, please contact international@pearsoned.com.

Visit us on the Web: informit.com/ph

Library of Congress Cataloging-in-Publication Data

Mancuso, Sandro.
  The software craftsman : professionalism, pragmatism, pride / Sandro Mancuso.
    pages   cm
  Includes index.
  ISBN 978-0-13-405250-2 (pbk. : alk. paper)—ISBN 0-13-405250-1 (pbk. : alk. paper)
 1. Computer software—Development.   2. Software architecture.   3. Quality of products. I. Title.
QA76.76.D47M3614 2015
005.3—dc23

                                                2014040470

ISBN-13: 978-0-13-405250-2
ISBN-10: 0-13-405250-1

Text printed in the United States on recycled paper at RR Donnelley in Crawfordsville, Indiana.
First printing, December 2014

This book is dedicated to my parents, Luiz Carlos and Marisa Mancuso, for all the sacrifices they've made so that I could have better opportunities in life. It was a very long and difficult road I shall never forget.

CONTENTS

FOREWORD

In 1973 Roberta Flack sang "Killing Me Softly." You've no doubt heard it in elevators or on your grandmother's radio station. It's a soft, lilting ballad about a woman who goes to a concert and hears a young man sing a song that she so strongly identifies with that she ponders whether the young man had found and read her letters. She even professes her belief that he feels her pain when he strums his guitar, and is singing the story of her whole life.

The book you are holding feels that way to me. Sandro Mancuso's career has been very different from mine. He is a bit younger than I. He and I have lived our lives and worked our careers on different continents and in different cultures. We share neither nationality nor ethnicity. I've met him only a few times, and each time it was never for more than a few minutes. In short, about the only thing we have in common is that we are both programmers. But that, it seems, is enough.

Within the pages you are holding you will find a fascinating alternation between autobiographical anecdotes that chronicle the author's vast experience and authoritative recommendations based on those experiences. If you are a programmer, you will feel these stories and recommendations resonate within you. You will say to yourself, as I did, "Been there. Done that." And you may hear the strains of that song echoing in your mind as he strums your pain.

And strum your pain he will, because this book is about pain. It is about the pain that you and I and, indeed, all programmers experience. It is the pain of feeling constantly constrained to do a poor job. It is the pain of feeling trapped in an *un-profession*. It is the pain of *wanting to do better* and not knowing how.

This book also contains the antidote for that pain. Indeed, I believe it contains the *cure*. You see, this book is all about software professionalism. Not just the professionalism of the programmer, but also the professionalism of the whole software organization. This is a book about Software Craftsmanship.

In these pages the author lays out a plan, a strategy, a set of attitudes, and a suite of principles that every programmer, programming team, and software organization can use to haul themselves out of the mire of mediocrity, to make themselves more professional, more productive, and more proud of the work they do.

The scope of this book is incredibly wide. Topics range from design patterns, pair programming, and Test-Driven Development to how to conduct and evaluate interviews, how to respond to tight deadlines, how to write job descriptions, and how to relate to coworkers and managers.

In short, this book is an encyclopedia on the behavior, attributes, and structure of an organization striving to grow in professionalism and adhere to the principles of Software Craftsmanship.

If you are the type of programmer, team lead, or manager who craves to be able to go home after a long day of work, look in the mirror, and say, "Damn, I did a good job today!" then this is the book for you.

—*Robert C. Martin*
August 2014

PREFACE

Back in the mid-1990s, two years after I started my professional career, a large international company in São Paulo, Brazil, announced that they would be hiring 60 developers in one go. Their selection process would take a few weeks and was divided into four phases: a three-hour-long technical test; two weeks of training in their proprietary technology followed by a test; a full day of group dynamics; and a round of final interviews. They announced it in a major newspaper and around 900 developers applied. I was working for a small software house at the time, a place where I was very happy, but I felt that I was ready for something bigger. Since the first phase would be on a Saturday, I decided to apply. Fewer than 300 developers passed to the next phase, and I was one of them. I was happy and confident but worried as well. I had to resign from my current job in order to move forward with the selection process because I would need to take too many days off for the remaining phases. Back then, my financial situation was not great and I could not count on any monetary support from my family. It was quite hard to resign from a job I liked in order to pursue a dream job that I had no idea I would get. Also, I had no idea how I would pay my bills if I didn't get that new job. But I had to do it. I had to try. That was the type of company I wanted to work for. That's what I wanted for my career.

I was 21 years old, and although I was young, I already had quite a few years of coding experience—I started coding when I was 11 and started my professional career when I was 19. The problem is that the mix of youth and a bit of experience can easily lead to arrogance. And by no means was I an exception. Think of an arrogant, young developer you know. I could beat anyone hands down. I used to think I was awesome, better than any other person who studied with me at university, and better than the vast majority of the developers who worked with me in my previous jobs.

After going through all of the four phases, the international company announced that they could not find 60 developers at the level they were expecting. They hired just 32, and I was one of them. I was over the moon and more cocky than ever. In my first week there, I was placed in one of the teams responsible for delivering one of the business modules of the system. For the first few weeks, while speaking to developers from different business modules, I heard them talking about this *other* team, a team that was supposedly the best team in the company. They were the "architecture" team, responsible for the core of our system and for providing all infrastructure code used by the business teams.

The architecture team was led by this incredible guy who, besides doing all the *management* work, was also a fantastic developer. He was a busy man, but he would always find some time to code, check in code against his name, and review the code written by his team. I heard their team was always working on interesting things and that their code was really good. That's exactly what I was looking for. I wanted to be working with the best.

After a few long weeks, I decided to speak to the *manager* of the architecture team, this guy that I heard so much about. I didn't really know what to say or what to expect. I was only certain of one thing: I had nothing to lose. In the worst-case scenario he would say that he was not interested to have me on his team. One day I saw him alone in the coffee area. I was shaking. I approached him and introduced myself. "Hi, I'm Sandro." He looked at me and shook my hand with a smile. "I'm Namur. Nice to meet you." He was calm and relaxed. "I want to work for you," I nervously said after a few awkward seconds. He was a bit surprised but apparently took it in a very positive way. We then started talking about the selection process, why I applied, what I was expecting from the job. He also asked me if I had pet projects, technologies I was interested in, if I wrote code outside working hours, and some other random things that I don't remember. After around 30 minutes of conversation he asked me when I could start. I was shocked. I was not expecting that at all. I was expecting to schedule a meeting, have a formal interview, and so on. It took me a long time to realize that he spent the entire conversation measuring my passion for software development. He was analyzing whether I cared about doing things right. He was not worried about my current technical knowledge. "I'll speak to my manager and hopefully it will be as soon as possible," I said. After a few weeks I was sitting among my new teammates.

My first day was a Monday. In the morning, Namur came to talk to me and assign me a task. He explained one part of the application and what I had to do, and he said he would sit with me again on Friday to check what I had done. I was thrilled. That was my chance to shine. I had to show him why I deserved to be there. I stayed in the office until almost midnight, slept a few hours, arrived very early on Tuesday, and around two o'clock in the afternoon, I was done. I had finished my first assignment in less than half of the time I had been given. I was feeling great. Well, I always knew how good I was, but being able to do that in that team, in a totally unknown code base, was a huge achievement.

I rushed to Namur's office and with excitement I said, "It's done. I finished it. And it is *working*." He stopped typing and turned to me. "Making things work is the minimum I expect from someone who is paid for it," he calmly said. "When you say that something is finished, it is implied that it works." That was like a big slap in my face. My smile faded away a little bit but I thought, maybe it is just his way of saying things. Maybe he is having a bad day. No, he definitely did not mean to be rude. "Sit here and let's see what you've done," he continued. I sat there and watched him typing in the command line, checking in the code from source control, and opening my single *.pas* file containing all my code. He opened the file using this horrible black and green editor on the command line. That was the first time I had seen vi. We were using Delphi back then and Delphi was very famous for its amazingly powerful integrated development environment (IDE). For me, seeing someone opening Delphi files on vi (a Unix text editor) was very alien. "Come close so we can have a look at it together," he said. I had written about 200 lines of code. He positioned the cursor on the first line and started looking at the code line by line. Every five lines he would stop and say things like, "Do you know what happens when we allocate and deallocate memory? Can you see here? You are allocating memory in one method and deallocating it in another method. This is a potential risk of memory leak. Have you heard about temporal coupling? Can you see this block of lines here? If you thought a little bit harder, you could reduce these eight lines to two. Do you know what happens when you have a `try/catch` block this big? What about the names of this variable and method? What do they mean? Have you ever thought that some of your colleagues, when needing to change this code, may not have the same amount of information and context as you have now? How would you feel if you knew nothing about this part of the code but you had to maintain it? What about this hard-coded bit here? Have you ever thought that if we wanted to change where it points to, we would need to open it, change it, recompile it, and redeploy the entire application? Why do you have this piece of code duplicated all over the place? Wow! This is a big method. Do you know how much we would need to keep in our heads if every single method were that big? What about making them smaller and naming them according to their behavior?" He went on and on.

At some point he stopped and started staring at a few lines of code. He spent a few minutes there, occasionally moving the cursor one page up and down again. Back in the 1990s, a developer would be considered a senior developer if she could write code that no one else could understand. "Wow! She must be really good. I have no idea what her code does." And I made sure to have some cryptic code in there, trying to show how clever I was. At some point he figured out what the code was doing. I was expecting a compliment, at last. "Do you know how disrespectful this is?" he said calmly. "We work on a very large system, with many teams and developers working on the same code base. Can you imagine how hard it would be to understand the code if everyone decided to show off how smart he or she is? Imagine thousands, if not millions, of lines written like that." And that was a second slap in my face.

It was just 200 lines of code, and I could not answer any of his questions or find a good response to the points he had raised. Line by line he looked at the code, criticized it, and explained to me how it could be better. Once we reached the end of the file, I was ashamed and extremely annoyed. He was still very calm, as if we had been looking at some random code written by an absent stranger. "Have you understood everything I said? Do you agree with all the *suggestions*?"

Without saying a word, I just nodded. "Do you feel you could write this code in a better way now?" Without looking at him, I just nodded. "Do you feel you can apply the things we discussed as we move forward?" Once again, I just nodded. He then pressed a few keys and deleted the entire file with all my code in it. "Excellent. Since you still have three days left, do it again."

I was shocked. I didn't know how to react to that. I stood up and slowly walked to the door without saying a word. "Sandro," he called me when I reached the door. I stopped and looked back at him. "*How it is done is as important as getting it done.*" And with this, he turned back to his computer and started typing again in that horrible green editor.

I was frustrated. In fact, I was furious. I left his office, went straight downstairs, and then outside the building. Who the hell does he think he is speaking to me like that? What a bastard. I can't work for a guy like that. That's it. I'm done with this company. I'm resigning. After a few cigarettes, feeling a little bit calmer, I started reflecting on what had happened. Namur had spent over one hour going through my code and explaining to me how it could be improved. He listened to me on the few occasions I expressed my view and calmly showed me that either I was wrong or there were better ways. I realized that for the first time since I wrote my first line of code, I had found someone who took the time to show me how to write good code. I had found someone who, besides being far better and more experienced than I was, really cared about helping others become better. I had found someone who cared about producing great, quality software. I had found someone who took the time to teach me. And more than that, I had found my first mentor.

After a few more cigarettes, I pulled myself together and went back inside a different person. That day I learned I was not as good as I thought I was. I learned how to be humble. I learned that I had a lot more to learn. I learned that just getting things done was not enough, especially when you are working in a team. I learned to be respectful to my peers and clients, not leaving crap code behind. I learned that a great professional cares about his or her work.

For two and a half years I worked with my mentor and some of the best developers I have ever met. That experience shaped me not just as a professional, but also as a person. Although we never used the term, I realized more than a decade later that that was my first encounter with Software Craftsmanship. I learned a lot from all those guys. Technically speaking, it was a great experience, but that was not the most important thing. What was really important to learn was the attitude that my boss and all the other developers had toward their career. The last words he said during our first code review session changed me forever. Ten years later, I founded the London Software Craftsmanship Community (LSCC) (http://www.meetup.com/london-software-craftsmanship) and Namur's words, "*How it is done is as important as getting it done*," were some of the first words I put on the website. Later I also had LSCC t-shirts printed with those words on them. Those words did not just make me a better professional, they also made me a better person.

ABOUT THIS BOOK

After decades and many different methodologies, software projects are still failing. Although there are many reasons why they fail, there are a few things that cannot be ignored: managers see software development as a production line; companies do not know how to manage software projects and how to hire good developers; and many developers still behave like unskilled, unmotivated workers, providing very poor service to their employers and clients. With the advent of Agile methodologies, the software industry took a big step forward, but the percentage of failing software projects is still incredibly high. Why are all these projects still failing? Why are we so bad at delivering successful projects? What is missing?

Although the term "Software Craftsmanship" has been around for over a decade, it was not until recently that it emerged as a viable solution for many of the problems faced by the software industry today.

Software Craftsmanship proposes a very different mindset for developers and companies. Although Software Craftsmanship is not a methodology, it strongly recommends the adoption of certain technical practices and disciplines, mostly the ones defined by Extreme Programming. With a great synergy with Agile and Lean principles, Software Craftsmanship promises to take our industry to the next level. Professionalism, technical excellence, and customer satisfaction are the main focus of Software Craftsmanship. One of its main focuses is changing the perceptions that software developers are like workers on a production line and that software projects can be run as if running a factory.

How can we become better developers? How can we deliver better software projects? With real stories and practical advice for developers and companies, this book is relevant to all software developers and every professional directly involved in a software project.

ACKNOWLEDGMENTS

My career has been a great journey, from a small town in Brazil to the biggest city in Europe. Having worked for many different companies and on both sides of the Atlantic, I met a lot of tremendous people who, in one way or another, helped to shape the person and the professional I am today.

First I would like to thank Professor Maria Cecilia Capelache. When I told her I would need to quit the university for financial reasons, she immediately offered me a job, which helped me to continue my studies. Even today I feel she gave me the job more to help me than because she really needed another developer on her team. She taught me the difference between all the academic things we learn at university and the real world of software development. If I had quit university I probably wouldn't be writing this book today.

Later I met Luiz Fernando Ferreira, one of the owners of a small software house, who gave me my second job. Although I was their first employee, I was never treated as such. From day one I felt I was working with an old friend. For his friendship, which has continued into today, his transparency during the good and bad times, and amazing support when the time came for me to move on, I am forever grateful.

Moving to a big international company and working under my first mentor changed my life. I'll be eternally thankful to Eduardo Namur for making me understand that how it is done is as important as getting it done, for making each one of us feel we were a big family, for instilling in me to be the best I could be, and for exposing me to the principles of Software Craftsmanship before the term had even been coined.

Alexandre Ehrenberger, a former manager who became a great friend and inspiration, was my biggest supporter when I decided to move to London. He had lived in Canada for six years and helped me understand what I needed to do in order to achieve my dream of moving to London. For his friendship, advice, encouragement, support, and for showing me that with a lot of hard work dreams can come true, I'm very thankful.

I knew that if I wanted to move to London I had to do two things. One was to learn Java, which I solved by studying hard and finding a job where I could work with it. The other one was to improve my English. I would like to thank Ana Maria Netuzzi, a lovely lady, for all the years of private English lessons, for being a friend, and more often than not, for being my psychologist, listening to all my personal problems and giving me valuable life advice.

Once in the UK and after a short period working for a small software house, I joined a startup. This startup had many talented developers and for the second time in my career I felt I was working with people who really cared about what they were doing. They helped me to step up my game, but most important, they were my first friends in the UK. They not only made me a better developer but also made me feel accepted in the UK. To Chris Webb, Greg Cawthorn, David Parry, Russell Webb, Simon Kirk, and James Kavanagh, thank you.

Joining Valtech was a big step forward in my career. It was there that I had my first contact with Agile and Extreme Programming (XP), and it is by far the place where I have learned the most. Although I could not name all the amazing people I met there, I feel the need to name a few. First I would like to thank Akbar Zamir for being a great mentor and a friend. The most important thing he taught me was to open my mind to new things. He made me see how much I did not know. Akbar convinced me to try Test-Driven Development. He also introduced me to Domain-Driven Design (DDD) and taught me a lot about Agile, XP, diplomacy, pragmatism, and professionalism. Thanks, Akbar. I learned a lot from you. There were a few other people in Valtech who had a huge influence in my career. They are David Draper, Kevin Harkin, Andrew Rendell, and James Bowman. Thank you for teaching and helping me so much.

UBS was my first contact with really huge enterprise systems and a place that forced me to reevaluate all my beliefs when it comes to software development. There I had the pleasure to work with a great team. They really helped me see things differently. One of the best things about UBS was the opportunity, once again, to work with Mashooq Badar (ex-Valtech and today my partner at Codurance), one of the best developers I've ever met and also one of my best friends. Mash was responsible for bringing me to UBS. Mash also brought in Balint Pato to one of our projects, and a strong bond was formed. I would like to thank Mash and Balint for all of our discussions, enthusiasm, passion, friendship, professionalism, and for teaching me so much. You guys are awesome and true craftsmen. Portia Tung was another great person I had the pleasure to meet and work with at UBS. She is probably the best Agile coach I've met. Her contagious passion in making our working environment *a place where we belong*, and her willingness to share her deep knowledge on how to make large organizations more agile, made my experience at UBS even better. Thanks, Portia, for your friendship and for teaching me how to bring people together. To Robert Taylor and Alexander "The Machine" Kikhtenko (a.k.a. Sasha), thank you for being amazing software craftsmen. It was an absolute pleasure to work with you guys.

David Green. Where do I start? He is a true craftsman, a friend, and one of the most talented developers I've ever met. I still remember all the awesome evenings we spent in the pub discussing our projects, craftsmanship, and how to make software development better. Dude, I learned a lot from you. David and I cofounded the London Software Craftsmanship Community (LSCC) and without him LSCC would probably not exist today.

In October 2013, I started Codurance, a consultancy company based on Software Craftsmanship principles and values, with Mashooq Badar. Codurance was a massive step forward in our careers. For the first time we have the opportunity to run a business the way we think a business should be run. This experience would not be so great without Samir Talwar. Samir is not just the first craftsman we hired; he also is a friend and an extremely talented craftsman. Codurance and LSCC would never be the same without him.

Last but not least, I would like to thank all the passionate developers from the LSCC. I would never be able to learn so much in such a short period of time if not for your willingness to sacrifice your own personal time to share your knowledge with others. A big thanks to Gonçalo Silva, Samir Talwar, Tom Brand, Tom Westmacott, Emanuele Blanco, Carlos Fernandez Garcia, and Chris Jeffery for their amazing job organizing LSCC. LSCC would never be such a cool community without you.

In relation to this book, I would like to thank Micah Martin and Tyler Jennings for their contributions related to the history of Software Craftsmanship. Thanks, Kevlin Henney, for the great tips on how to better structure the book and for convincing me to throw away the original Chapter 1 and write a brand-new one. Thanks, Gianfranco Alongi and Mani Sarkar, for proofreading parts of the book. A special thanks to Samir Talwar and Andrew Parker for their amazing job finding hundreds of grammar mistakes and typos, and for their valuable suggestions on how to make the book better. There were also many other people who contributed to this book, sending me suggestions and typos. Thank you all.

ABOUT THE AUTHOR

Sandro Mancuso has coded since a very young age but only started his professional career in 1996. He has worked for startups, software houses, product companies, international consultancy companies, and investment banks. In October
2013, Sandro cofounded Codurance, a consultancy company based on Software
Craftsmanship principles and values.

During his career, Sandro has worked on various projects, with different languages
and technologies and across many different industries. Sandro has a lot of experience bringing the Software Craftsmanship ideology and Extreme Programming
practices to organizations of all sizes. Sandro is internationally renowned for his
work in spreading Software Craftsmanship principles and is a renowned speaker
at many conferences around the world. His professional aspiration is to raise the
bar of the software industry by helping developers become better at—and care
more about—their craft through sharing his knowledge, skills, and experiences.

Sandro's involvement with Software Craftsmanship started in 2010, when he
founded the London Software Craftsmanship Community (LSCC), which has
become the largest and most active Software Craftsmanship community in the
world, with more than 2,000 craftsmen. For the past four years he has inspired
and helped developers to start and organize many other Software Craftsmanship
communities in Europe, the United States, and other parts of the world.

PART I

IDEOLOGY AND ATTITUDE

SOFTWARE DEVELOPMENT IN THE TWENTY-FIRST CENTURY

I remember the early years of my career, back in the 1990s. After three years, I considered myself a senior developer. I could mix assembly with Pascal and impress my friends. I could code fluently in at least four programming languages. Most important, I could write cryptic Delphi code—using very few lines of code and obscure Windows application programming interfaces (APIs)—that very few developers were able to understand.

That's how seniority was measured back then. If you couldn't understand a piece of code, normally it was because you were not senior enough. And writing code that no one else could understand would make you a senior developer straightaway. It was very common to hear managers and developers say, "We cannot change this code right now. We need to wait for Henry Hacker to come back from holidays. It's his code and no one else can understand it."

After seven years in the industry, I was done being a senior developer. It was time to move on with my career. I didn't want to be called a developer or, God forbid, a programmer or coder anymore. I made my decision. From that point onward I would call myself a software architect. Why shouldn't I? At that time I worked for a big consultancy company and our projects were large Java Enterprise (J2EE) applications. We were also using Rational Unified Process (RUP), drawing use cases, class, and sequence diagrams before writing the code.

After some time working for this big consultancy company, I was promoted and moved to the architecture team, where we would never dare to model our classes without first consulting our *Design Patterns* book. Besides knowing the Gang of Four (GoF) design patterns and the Core J2EE patterns extremely well, I also knew Unified Modeling Language (UML) and Rational Rose, and I had a few Java certifications. I had more than enough skills, experience, and credentials to be called a software architect. Life was good.

My job, as an architect, was to speak to business analysts, understand the functional and nonfunctional requirements, and create diagrams that specified exactly what developers had to do. I also had to think hard—very often consulting my crystal ball and checking the wind direction with my finger—to come up with the right abstractions that would enable our systems to grow without impacting anything else. Because I didn't have the details of all the features that would be added to the system in the next five years, it was almost impossible to predict how exactly the system would grow. The solution to this problem was let's add abstractions and design patterns all over the place. Today, we call it overengineering and stupidity. Back then we called it architecture and seniority.

After a few months on the architecture team, I realized that I was still far more connected to my former teammates in the development team than I was with the other architects. I was constantly having lunch with the developers, talking to them about code, and asking them to show me how they were implementing different parts of the application. I also realized that I was spending far more time than usual coding in my spare time; now I know that it was because I was not writing any code at work and I had a need to fill that gap somehow.

After almost one year just creating diagrams and documentation, I had enough. I told my boss I wanted to move back to the development team. He was shocked. He just could not understand what I was saying. "You are doing an excellent job as a technical architect. Do you know how many developers would like to be in the architecture team? Do you know how many of them would like to be in your place?" he asked me. Of course I knew. I was a developer before. I knew that many of them wanted to become *architects*. "So this will be a very easy problem for you to solve then," I told my boss. "You have many developers you can choose from to switch places with me." One week later I was back in the development team. Life was good (again).

Today, I realize how important that decision was. I remember that I spent weeks trying to figure out if moving back to the development team was the right thing to do. On one hand I had the "status" of being an architect in a large company: seniority, recognition (we don't see junior architects, do we?), power (you tell people what to do), superiority (compared to other developers), visibility (by senior management), career advancement, and wider responsibility (looking at the bigger picture). On the other hand I had happiness. I was not happy being an architect, creating diagrams all day, and discussing long-term goals that very rarely survived the test of time. I then made my decision: I chose happiness. Being able to write code every day made me happy. From that point onward, I promised to myself that I would only choose jobs and positions that would make me excited to wake up in the morning and go to work.

Decisions like that can change our careers completely and permanently. If I had decided to remain on the architecture team, without writing code, I would probably struggle a lot to become a developer again. The longer we stay away from coding, the harder it is to get back to it.

The point here is not about architects versus developers. Today, I don't even think that what I was doing back then was architecture. What I'm saying is that we should choose our career path according to our passion, to what we love doing. It doesn't matter if it is architecture, software development, testing, business analysis, management, or something else. They are all necessary and important.

In the rest of this chapter we will be discussing what seniority really means and also the new reality faced by developers in the twenty-first century.

SENIORITY

Unfortunately, the notion of seniority hasn't changed much in the last 20 years. Software developers are normally considered senior according to the number of years they have worked in the industry and not according to their knowledge.

There is a huge difference between having ten years of experience and having one year of experience repeated ten times. Ten years spent working on different projects, with different technologies, and for different companies is different from ten years working for the same company, on the same project, and with the same people and same technology.

Over the years, I learned that seniority is transient and relative. It is transient because clients will demand different types of systems as technology evolves. Having fifteen years of experience working with Clipper in a traditional waterfall fashion will not get me a senior position in a modern company developing mobile applications in an Agile fashion. Seniority is not a badge we can wear for the rest of our lives after completing five years in the industry. Seniority is also relative. When trying to identify how senior a developer is, we need to ask ourselves the following questions: senior compared to whom? In which technology? In which context?

There is no such thing as a senior or junior developer. Developers may be very experienced in developing enterprise Java applications for large organizations but totally inexperienced in writing games in JavaScript. They can be extremely experienced working in a very collaborative and Agile environment but totally inexperienced in dealing with all the bureaucracy and political challenges of a large corporation.

A NEW REALITY

Good programming practices and techniques can be applied in many different environments and types of systems, but coding is just one of the things that modern developers do. Seniority is not just about writing code or being very familiar with a language or framework. Modern developers need to know how to speak to customers, automate tests and deployment, make technological choices that may affect the entire business, work in distributed teams, help clients to define and prioritize requirements, report progress, manage changes and expectations, present products to potential clients or partners, help with pre-sales activities, estimate time and costs, interview new team members, design and evolve the software architecture, deal with nonfunctional requirements and service level agreements (SLAs), understand business goals, make decisions based on trade-offs, keep an eye on new technologies and better ways to do things, worry about the value delivered to their customers, and many other things.

Some say that good developers have been doing all of the above for decades. Well, this may true for some developers, but it is definitely not true for the vast majority of them. In the past, the roles and responsibilities of the people involved in a software project were far more specific than they are today. Developers were not involved in the design and architecture of the applications, very rarely had access to end users, and would never be trusted to do business analysis.

The days when software developers are specialized in only one thing are numbered. The old attitude we had—if it is not coding, it's not my problem—is now unacceptable. Companies started to get leaner, flattening their hierarchies and replacing many one-trick-pony professionals with generalizing specialists. Companies are looking for developers who, besides being great at writing code, can also help in many other areas of the business.

In the past two decades, with the Internet, mobile devices, cloud services, and general technology evolution, everything changed. Clients want more things faster, and companies are becoming far more aggressive with their software offerings. Being able to change the software fast, with quality, and increase the value provided to clients became a massive competitive advantage. Companies whose core businesses heavily rely on software—like Amazon, Google, Twitter, Facebook, and many others—quickly became the dominant players in the market. Clients are replacing bureaucratic service companies with rigid processes and deep hierarchical structures with smaller and more agile service companies. The waterfall approach combined with a traditional management style cannot cope with the fast pace of the market anymore. The Lean startup model—get it out there quickly, get feedback, iterate—completely changed the game.

The scale of projects changed as well. Today, we rarely see an application that does not integrate with other applications. We don't usually see new projects built using a client-server architecture, with fat clients deployed in each machine, having a huge monolithic database as an integration point. Modern applications are built using many technologies, with multiple integration points, and developed in an iterative way. Where we had applications only being used by internal employees, we now have applications used by millions of people around the world. For many companies, the cost of bugs in production became expensive enough to push them out of business, or cause massive damage to their reputation.

This new reality in the software industry forced an evolution of the software development profession. Companies are demanding professional software developers and not just cheap coders who do whatever they are told to do.

Fortunately, our industry is evolving, leaving behind the Industrial Revolution inheritance—command and control, deep hierarchies, managers versus factory workers—and moving toward a more agile and collaborative environment. The role and responsibilities of a software developer became wider and more important, making developers proud to be developers instead of aspiring to do something else in order to move forward with their careers. The problems encountered on projects with a fixed and rigid plan, and strictly defined process, are being reassessed. Flat hierarchies with talented and empowered professionals are becoming the norm. The need for agility and well-crafted software has never been higher.

In 2001, a huge revolution in the software industry happened: Agile. Companies all over the world started adopting and embracing the Agile methodologies and mindset, changing their processes and internal structures. However, even with significant improvements in their processes, companies were still unhappy with their delivery capabilities: not responding to change fast enough, low-quality software, bugs, high maintenance costs, unhappy customers, and difficulties in hiring good developers. Developers are still struggling to maintain, test, and add new features to the software they work with, especially if they are new to the project. Why do we need Software Craftsmanship? What is it anyway? Are we really professional software developers? Why was Agile not enough?

In the following chapters I'll answer all these questions. I will explain in detail what Software Craftsmanship is and what is expected from a professional software developer. But before I do that, let's first understand what Agile is.

AGILE

Back in February 2001, seventeen influential people in our industry decided to get together in a ski resort in Utah to discuss alternatives to heavyweight and document-based approaches to software development. Each of them had been working and experimenting with different techniques and approaches to software development, and they decided that it would be a good idea to get together and share what they were doing. The idea was to learn from each other and try to come up with better ways to deliver software projects.

They were Kent Beck, Mike Beedle, Arie van Bennekum, Alistair Cockburn, Ward Cunningham, Martin Fowler, James Grenning, Jim Highsmith, Andrew Hunt, Ron Jeffries, Jon Kern, Brian Marick, Robert C. Martin, Steve Mellor, Ken Schwaber, Jeff Sutherland, and Dave Thomas.

They represented methodologies and techniques like Extreme Programming (XP), Scrum, the Dynamic Systems Development Model (DSDM), Adaptive Software Development, Crystal, Feature-Driven Development, and pragmatic programming.

After many discussions, the Agile Manifesto was created and the Agile Alliance was formed.

Agile is not a single thing. Agile is a combination of methodologies and techniques that, according to the context, can help teams and companies to adapt to the ever-changing nature of software projects and also reduce the risks associated with them. The Agile disciplines and methodologies can be divided into two main groups: process-oriented and technical-oriented.

In this chapter I discuss what it means to be Agile, as well as the Agile Manifesto and the problems that many organizations face when adopting Agile.

PROCESS-ORIENTED AGILE DISCIPLINES

These disciplines affect how teams and organizations work, collaborate, and organize. They normally prescribe and/or suggest, among many other things, the types of meetings the teams should have, the roles people should play, ways in which to capture requirements, how to measure work velocity, how to work in an iterative way, how to plan and divide work, and also how to demonstrate progress and get business feedback.

Process-oriented disciplines help teams to keep the focus on what is really important and valuable to the business. Using these methodologies is a great way to make sure the team is *building the right thing*.

TECHNICAL-ORIENTED DISCIPLINES

These disciplines are more specific to the challenges of developing, growing, maintaining, and delivering the software itself. They normally prescribe or suggest technical practices and techniques. Test-Driven Development, pair programming, continuous integration, and simple design are a few examples of these practices and techniques. Technical-oriented disciplines help teams to focus on the quality of the software they are producing and help teams to make sure they are *building the thing right*.

WHAT IS IT TO BE AGILE?

> [Being Agile means] adapting successfully
> to new circumstances.
> —Tom Gilb

We don't *do* Agile. Either we *are* Agile or we *are not*.

Agile methodologies are all about quick and short feedback loops. The quicker and shorter our feedback loop is, the more agile we can become. Every time we receive some feedback, we have an opportunity to react to it, and the act of reacting (or not) to new information is what makes us more (or less) agile. Narrowing the feedback loop helps us to make problems visible sooner, allowing us to inspect and adapt quickly. Agile does not solve any problems; it exposes them. The faster we demo a screen or any other feature to a user, the earlier we will get feedback on it. I'm using *user* here as a general term. It can be a product owner, sponsor, or an end user. Getting feedback from multiple sources is extremely important. Knowing if a feature is commercially viable sooner helps us to mitigate the risks of our investment.

A GAME CHANGER

Agile was a huge step forward in our industry. Its acceptance by the wider community, immediately after its creation, was massive. The fast pace of change in modern software projects is frustrating and costs a lot of money for companies. Agile was an antidote for that. The mindset changed. Where before we had many documents, big design up-front (BDUF), and bureaucracy, now we have running software from week one. Where before we were reactive to changes, now we embrace them.

Agile completely changed the way we work. The old, hierarchical, and very specific segregation of roles within a software project team started fading away. Software professionals realized that writing code is just one of the things they need to be good at. Developers, who before were just following a plan, finally understood the importance of getting involved with business and delivering value to their clients. The realization that the team as a whole was responsible for all the different aspects of a software project was a game changer. It made software professionals evolve. Instead of just being someone who could write some code according to a predefined (quite often ill-defined) plan, developers started taking an active role in planning, estimation, requirements, team organization, analysis, architecture, production readiness, prioritization, demos, and collecting feedback from users and stakeholders on a regular basis.

PEOPLE EMPOWERMENT

Software teams became flat in hierarchy. No more team leads and segregation of duties. Instead of having managers assign tasks to individuals and specify the amount of time that it should take to be done, we now have a backlog of tasks that is prioritized by sponsors and product owners with the help of the team. The team decides which task to work on next, according to priorities, and also decides who is going to do what, how it is going to be done, and how long it is going to take. This all happens as part of an iterative process where the feedback loop for all the people involved is constant.

PROFESSIONAL EVOLUTION

To fit this way of working, software professionals had to evolve. Instead of just being specialists, like in the past, companies started to look for generalizing specialists. **Being good at writing code is the minimum skill expected from software professionals.** Testing, analysis, ability to understand the business, good communication, and a more extroverted personality became part of the skill set that software professionals need today.

AGILE MANIFESTO

The following is an excerpt from the Agile Manifesto website.

> We are uncovering better ways of developing software by doing it and helping others to do it. Through this work we have come to value:
>
> **Individuals and interactions** over process and tools
>
> **Working software** over comprehensive documentation

Customer collaboration over contract negotiation

Responding to change over following a plan

That is, while there is value in the items on the right, we value the items on the left more.

Besides the Agile Manifesto, the originators of Agile also came up with twelve principles.

PRINCIPLES BEHIND THE AGILE MANIFESTO

The twelve principles include the following:

1. Our highest priority is to satisfy the customer through early and continuous delivery of valuable software.
2. Welcome changing requirements, even late in development. Agile processes harness change for the customer's competitive advantage.
3. Deliver working software frequently, from a couple of weeks to a couple of months, with a preference to the shorter time scale.
4. Businesspeople and developers must work together daily throughout the project.
5. Build projects around motivated individuals. Give them the environment and support they need, and trust them to get the job done.
6. The most efficient and effective method of conveying information to and within a development team is face-to-face conversation.
7. Working software is the primary measure of progress.
8. Agile processes promote sustainable development. The sponsors, developers, and users should be able to maintain a constant pace indefinitely.
9. Continuous attention to technical excellence and good design enhances agility.
10. Simplicity—the art of maximizing the amount of work not done—is essential.
11. The best architectures, requirements, and designs emerge from self-organizing teams.
12. At regular intervals, the team reflects on how to become more effective, then tunes and adjusts its behavior accordingly.

THE AGILE TRANSFORMATION ERA

Agile was a major revolution in our industry and, bit by bit, companies started adopting it. Consultancy companies and individuals became *specialized* in helping companies to go through the Agile journey. The role of the Agile coach emerged. Agile coaches go to companies; analyze their problems, processes, and people; and help them to change in order to become more agile. Companies started to visualize and understand where their inefficiencies were.

During these Agile transformations, Scrum, combined with a few other more specific techniques, was normally the methodology of choice. That was a great entry point into the Agile world. The notion of self-organizing teams was totally alien for many companies. Accepting the idea of having teams controlling backlogs, defining and splitting stories, estimating tasks, helping with prioritization, testing, and demonstrating implemented features at the end of each iteration was a massive step forward. Communication also improved. Team members started talking to each other and with their customers much more often—another alien thing in certain companies.

Providing an environment where people interact more with each other helped companies to solve problems and understand weaknesses and strengths of teams and individuals. Agile processes helped to unite team members, providing them with a common goal.

Agile processes definitely helped companies to move forward, not only exposing their problems but also providing a feedback loop mechanism that allowed them to react and adapt.

THE AGILE HANGOVER

> Many Agile projects are now, steadily and iteratively, producing crap code.

For a few years, companies and teams were in this Agile transformation party. Companies were *transformed*. Meetings became stand-up meetings—although some companies have them in a room, sitting down for one hour. Burn-down charts, iteration backlogs, and release backlogs became the new project management tools. Use cases became user stories. Project managers became Scrum masters. And Agile became just the new name for their old way of working. But some changes were noticeable. If you looked at photos from offices before and after the Agile transformation, the difference can sometimes be massive. We now see open-plan offices, cubicles were removed, two or more people working around a single computer, and whiteboards everywhere. Some companies even have entire walls as whiteboards, covered in colorful Post-Its. And that was what Agile meant to many companies. The number of colorful Post-Its on a whiteboard became their true measure of Agility. The more Post-Its, the more Agile they thought they were. *Very mature* Agile companies could be identified by their use of colorful and differently sized Post-Its, each, of course, representing or meaning a different thing. Anyway, everyone was happy, everyone could see the colorful Post-Its moving (some of them quite slowly, some a bit faster, some not at all), and everyone had that great feeling of empowerment and freedom. Every team member could do whatever he or she wanted—as long as his or her boss agreed. And then one day, after a few months, or years in some cases, of having fun in the Post-It party, teams and companies woke up with a massive headache—the Agile hangover.

They realized that after all this transformation, they were still not delivering software with good quality fast enough. In fact, many of the teams and companies still had the same problems they had before the Agile transformation. They were still taking a long time to deploy anything into production. They still had loads of technical debt, even in projects that they had started from scratch in an Agile fashion. Motivation was still a big problem. The dedicated quality assurance (QA) teams were still around. Many companies still had a period of testing (a few days, to a few weeks) after each iteration. Making a change in their applications was still extremely painful. Their code bases were still a mess and slowing them down. The list of bugs was not smaller than it was before. They still had applications that no one could understand and everyone was scared to touch. Debugging and log file analysis were still their main techniques for figuring out what the hell was going on. Managers were still talking about decommissioning applications just a few years after they had been written because making changes to them was too expensive and was slowing the business down.

The new applications, built in an Agile fashion, were as badly designed, complex, and buggy as the applications developed before the Agile transformation. These applications and their respective development teams were still not good enough to embrace the changes that were desperately needed by the business. For developers, yes, they had a better working process and were talking to each other more often, but besides that, in terms of the actual technical work they did, nothing had really changed. The same old problems were still there: stagnant skill set, low morale and motivation, mountains of technical debt, lack of technical expertise, unreliable release process, unstable system, late discovery of bugs, unreliable and costly tests, inefficient develop/debug/deploy cycles, long running builds, and requirements not well understood—just to mention a few. Companies then started to ask, "What went wrong? That was not what we were sold." At the end of the day, the main reason to change the whole process and adopt Agile was so that they could have a better return on the investment made in their software.

A PARTIAL TRANSFORMATION

Over the years I have seen, and was part of, many Agile transformation projects. I have seen many companies state strongly that they wanted to adopt Agile but not make much effort to actually *be* agile. They wanted a prescription: something that they could follow to magically make them better. Today, many companies and teams claim that Agile does not work. They went through this Agile transformation and were not really much better than they were before. They just forgot that in a software project, the most important deliverable is the software itself.

The problem with almost all the Agile transformations that I have seen was that they were a *partial* transformation. Consultancies and Agile coaches were hired by companies, most often, to help them change their *process*. However, these consultancies and Agile coaches did very little, or nothing, to help companies to be better at writing quality software. In general, Agile transformations were focused on process but not on technical disciplines, which means that they did very little to make developers better. Agile coaches did practically nothing to improve the skill set of people working on operations, production services, or QA. The technical disciplines, in the vast majority of Agile transformations, were totally forgotten or dismissed. There was this very naive assumption—almost unprofessional (from some incompetent Agile coaches)—that companies had developers who were great at writing code and the only thing they really wanted was to work within the Scrum framework. Having such an *amazing* software delivery capability in their companies, the only thing they needed was a better process, promoting communication and empowering people, and everything would be great. "Let's improve our process and everything else will be OK." In their minds, magically, the same old developers with the same old habits would start producing amazing software. Writing code is easy and just a detail, right? We just need a better process, don't we? Unfortunately, that was never the case.

The Agile transformations focused mainly on process; empowering people; reducing bureaucracy and waste; prioritization; visibility of work in progress; and improving the information flow. These were real and important problems that needed to be solved, and for sure, companies were far better off when they were addressed and improved. Without fixing these problems, it would be almost impossible to have a successful software project. However, the principles behind Agile were forgotten. Process became more important than technical excellence. Technical excellence, which is assumed to be in place by every process-related Agile methodology, is normally ignored by managers and ill-prepared Agile coaches.

Many people in the Agile and Lean communities love to talk about Toyota and how successful they became changing their process, reducing waste (or inventory), limiting work in progress (WIP), and all the great things they have done. That is what Agile coaches and consultancy companies like to sell to uninformed clients: the Toyota Dream. First, building cars is totally different from building software. We do not use a car if it is not totally finished. We do not go back to the manufacturer after buying a car and ask them to add an extra door to it or to move the engine from the front to the back.

When talking about Toyota, we very rarely think, "What if the cars were not good? What if no one wanted to buy them? What if they were so fragile and we had to take them to the garage every month?" An important factor to Toyota's success was, besides a good process, the focus on the quality of their cars.

Customers wanted to buy their cars because they were well built and reliable. They wanted their cars because they were a good value for money. Customers wanted Toyota cars because they had quality.

Effective processes work from the premise that, in order to achieve quality, we need to provide a great feedback system, at all levels. For a feedback system to work, we need talented and passionate professionals who care enough about what they do, raising their voices when they feel something is wrong or could be done better. Focusing purely on the process and treating software development like a production line leads to average 9-to-5 developers doing what they are told—they become factory workers. This approach makes the feedback system inefficient, compromising the entire project.

Agile Coaches

Every profession has good and bad professionals and this is no different for Agile coaches. There are the ones who fully understand the original Agile message and, when advising companies and teams on their Agile adoption, they emphasize the importance of both process and technical excellence. Although the majority will focus on process, they quite often will pair with or recommend other professionals who could help their clients with the technical disciplines. However, the average Agile coach, due to his or her lack of technical expertise, will overemphasize the process side (misleading the client) and, quite often, will not mention the technical side at all.

It is far easier to *sell* processes to senior management than convince them of the importance of technical excellence and all the effort we need to make to achieve that. Senior managers understand processes really well but fail to see the benefits of having developers play a part bigger than just writing code. They also fail to understand the importance of paying attention to the quality of the code produced by developers. As long as it works, they are happy.

Senior managers, when coming from nontechnical backgrounds, can be easily misled by bad Agile coaches. After a few months, if not years, of Agile adoption, when things go wrong, it is very easy for Agile coaches and managers to blame their developers. Yes, sometimes they are at fault, but the question here is how will the Agile transformation help them to be better?

Rejecting Technical Practices

But there is the other side as well. There are very good Agile coaches and consultancy companies out there doing an excellent job advising and helping their customers. But when it comes to XP adoption, things get ugly. Many customers immediately reject the idea of having two developers pairing together—they think it is a complete waste of money. They immediately reject the idea of investing in writing tests upfront and the benefits of Test-Driven Development. "What about our QA team?" they ask. "Developers should not waste time doing that. That's why we pay that company in Asia."

Sometimes, the rejection comes from the developers themselves. They just cannot see the point in pairing. Some think they would be exposing their lack of knowledge in certain areas. They do not want that. They cannot see the point of writing tests either, since at the end of the day they are great developers and do not make mistakes. Just mediocre developers need tests, they would say.

If you do not invest in automated tests, what's the point in having continuous integration anyway? Just to make sure the code compiles? Simple design and collective ownership also do not work for them. Managers' idea of a senior and experienced developer is about how many patterns he or she knows, how complicated the design and architecture can be, and being the only one who knows how the system works.

In cases like that, if the rejection comes from senior management, they need a bit of education and stronger evidence showing them how important it is to pay attention to the quality of the software that is being produced. When the rejection comes from developers, they also need some education, quite often achieved by experienced XP developers who could come along and pair with them and lead by example. If that does not work, consider replacing some of your developers with fresh blood, keeping the ones who are keen and open to learn new techniques and practices.

A Naive Approach to Software Projects

During all these years, I saw many naive approaches to software projects. Some companies thought that the important things for a successful software project were a business expert writing requirements, a technical leader (who doesn't code) drawing diagrams and writing documents, and a manager to supervise (micro-manage) the project. With all these important roles in place, they were ready to hire a few cheap developers—normally delegating the task of hiring to an agency or to HR. They were too busy for it. The developers were then presented with a pile of requirements and technical documents—that were prepared months in advance—and presto, software comes out the other end. One year later, developers present the software to the business, everyone loves it, and the bug-free software is deployed to production. What a perfect world. It was so easy. It's a shame that it never works this way.

In all the experiences I had where I worked in a waterfall project—with no access to the real users, no collaboration with the business, and no quick feedback loop—the testing phase ended up being far bigger than all the previous phases together. I can still feel the stress, unhappiness, and general dissatisfaction. But it can always get worse. I've seen at least a couple of very bad experiences with offshore outsourcing. I really don't know what else the managers were expecting. You take a pile of documents and throw it at some developers that you never met, have no idea how they were hired, know nothing about their skills, and expect that they will provide you with software that will satisfy all your needs. After a few years of bad experiences, I wonder how much cheaper this model really was for these companies.

Another common problem I've seen is that the people leading software projects are normally too far away from the software itself. Many are either not technical or can't even remember when they wrote their last line of code—if ever. Not having technical people involved in the decision-making process is a recipe for disaster. A software project cannot succeed without collaboration with good software professionals who, besides being skillful in crafting software, can also help the business to achieve whatever they want to achieve, giving them options, feedback, and constructive criticism.

Every software process, including Agile processes, will assume technical excellence. Without technical excellence, every software project will be a painful, frustrating, and expensive experience.

But It's Not All Bad News

Although many companies had just a partial Agile transformation, it is probably fair to say that they, at least, are much better than they were before. Improving their processes and having quick feedback loops about their businesses and delivery capabilities allow them to identify all the other problems they still have. A quick feedback loop is key for any company aspiring to be agile. Reacting to the feedback they get quickly is what makes them truly agile.

By no means am I suggesting that Agile processes are bad and that just being better at producing quality software is the answer. The point here is that companies need both. Having a good process but bad delivery capability will not make software projects succeed. Having amazing developers who can produce high-quality code but having a process that does not enable them to work well will also not make projects succeed.

The important thing is to identify where the problems are as soon as possible and act on them. It is never too late to make things better—it just becomes far more painful when you delay it.

Agile versus Software Craftsmanship

A very common misunderstanding is to think that Software Craftsmanship is here to replace Agile and that both are mutually exclusive. That's not the case at all. They complement each other nicely. Agile, in its current form, provides a different mindset for organizations and businesses. Agile methodologies focus on understanding and prioritizing activities by value, reducing bureaucracy and waste, empowering people, and providing a feedback loop. This enables companies to react quickly, hence becoming agile. Agile methodologies help companies to do the *right thing*. Software Craftsmanship is about professionalism in software development. Software Craftsmanship is an ideology, which many developers decided to adopt in order to get better at what they do. Besides promoting many technical practices and ways in which developers can get better at writing good and well-crafted code, it also promotes the idea that developers should do far more to help their clients than just writing code. Software Craftsmanship helps developers and companies to do the *thing right*.

SUMMARY

In order to remain competitive, companies need to deliver software faster and with better quality. Agile software development helps companies to shorten their feedback loop, giving them the opportunity to quickly adapt to changes and the demands of their clients. Unfortunately, during their Agile adoptions, many companies tend to pay a lot of attention to Agile processes but totally neglect technical practices.

Although the Agile Manifesto clearly states "individuals and interactions over process and tools," Agile transformations end up being all about process and tools. Simply adopting Scrum, having daily stand-up meetings, and having tools to manage backlogs and work in progress won't magically improve the quality of the software or make developers better. Improving the process without improving technical excellence is pointless.

For a full Agile transformation, we also need professional software developers who master technical practices, technologies, and tools. We need developers capable of constantly delivering quality software that is regularly deployed into production. We need developers who can deliver software that is fully tested and that can be easily changed. For a full Agile transformation, companies need to embrace Software Craftsmanship.

SOFTWARE CRAFTSMANSHIP

Before we discuss what Software Craftsmanship is, let's describe what it **is not**:

- Beautiful code
- Test-Driven Development
- Self-selected group of people
- Specific technologies or methodologies
- Certifications
- Religion

So, what is Software Craftsmanship then? This chapter presents a few definitions and discusses its origins and history. This chapter also covers the Software Craftsmanship Manifesto, with an in-depth explanation of what it really means.

A BETTER METAPHOR

In a very simplistic way, we can say that Software Craftsmanship is a better metaphor for software development than software engineering. Software Craftsmanship sees software as a craft and compares software developers to medieval blacksmiths. Apprentices would work with more experienced blacksmiths, traveling from place to place and working for different masters, learning different tools and techniques, and improving their craft until the point where they were good enough to become a master themselves. There is more to it, but bear with me for now.

WHAT DOES WIKIPEDIA SAY?

> [Software Craftsmanship] "is an approach to software development that emphasizes the coding skills of the software developers themselves. It is a response by software developers to the perceived ills of the mainstream software industry, including the prioritization of financial concerns over developer accountability."

I personally don't like this definition. It's very dry and I don't think it captures the essence of what being a software craftsman means to a software developer.

A MORE PERSONAL DEFINITION

> Software craftsmanship is a long journey to mastery. It's a mindset where software developers choose to be responsible for their own careers, constantly learning new tools and techniques and constantly bettering themselves. Software Craftsmanship is all about putting responsibility, professionalism, pragmatism, and pride back into software development.

A SHORTER DEFINITION

> Software Craftsmanship is about professionalism in software development.

This is probably the most important thing about Software Craftsmanship. If you only remember one thing after reading this book, I hope you remember this statement.

BEYOND DEFINITIONS

I prefer to think of Software Craftsmanship as an ideology or a mindset. It is something that manages to express and give a name to all the things I always believed. Many developers, including myself, may say they were doing the majority of the things that Software Craftsmanship talks about: caring about what they do; always trying to better themselves; being professional; delighting customers by helping them achieve whatever they want to achieve; learning from other developers; sharing what they know; and mentoring less-experienced developers.

If you have always valued the things above, that is great. You are a software craftsman, even if you do not like to refer to yourself as such. Many people I meet do not really like labels or do not even agree with the whole Software Craftsmanship metaphor. That is totally fine. The important things here are the things we should care about as software professionals.

CRAFT, TRADE, ENGINEERING, SCIENCE, OR ART

When I first got involved with the Software Craftsmanship movement, I remember having many discussions about what software development was. I originally liked to describe it as an art. Then, over the years, I preferred to treat it as a craft. Many people I know, including people whom I really respect, do not agree with this at all. For some, it is a trade. For others, it is engineering. Very few would say that software development is a science.

Every developer has very strong arguments why software development should be qualified as art, craft, trade, engineering, or science. When listening to all the reasons why software development is one thing or the other, many of the reasons make sense—some more than others, but they all make some sense.

Another big debate about Software Craftsmanship is the name itself. Some people absolutely hate it. They cannot see the point of comparing the most innovative and fast-changing industry to something that goes back to medieval times. And, yes, they may have a point.

Over the years, I joined some of these debates and spent a lot of energy trying to convince people why Software Craftsmanship is a good metaphor and why software development is a craft. As I was getting more involved with it, I suddenly realized that it didn't really matter. This is by far the least important thing we should be discussing. I personally like the metaphor and treat software development as a craft, but what I really find important and care about are the values that Software Craftsmanship promotes.

At the end of the day, what we all care about is raising the bar of our profession and helping developers, including ourselves, to be professional software developers and not just unskilled workers doing what they are told to do.

SOFTWARE CRAFTSMANSHIP HISTORY

Although Jack W. Reeves suggested that software development is more a craft than an engineering practice in 1992, I believe that Software Craftsmanship really begins with the book *The Pragmatic Programmer: From Journeyman to Master* by Andy Hunt and Dave Thomas in 1999. In 2001, Peter McBreen published *Software Craftsmanship: The New Imperative,* the book that introduced the majority of the ideas that were used to shape the Software Craftsmanship movement years later.

In the spring of 2002, Ken Auer hosted a Software Apprenticeship Summit in North Carolina, and invited, among a few others, Pete McBreen, Ron Jeffries, and Robert Martin (Uncle Bob). At the time, Auer was already hosting apprenticeships. The conclusion of the summit was a call to action to form a community around software apprenticeship, though it didn't get much traction. But it did change the attitude at Object Mentor, the company founded by Uncle Bob. From then on, Object Mentor started taking on apprentices. There was not much formality or process around it, but several people did go through an apprenticeship at Object Mentor.

In the autumn of 2006, Micah Martin and Paul Pagel created 8th Light as an embodiment of the Software Craftsmanship values. The 8th Light's founders called it a Software Craftsmanship company from the start, aiming to hire through apprenticeships and to cultivate disciplined talent. 8th Light employed software craftsmen, not developers, and their actions did not go unnoticed.

Around the same time 8th Light was created, Dave Hoover took a position at Obtiva (acquired by Groupon in August 2011). Shortly after 8th Light touted their apprenticeship program, Obtiva began offering apprenticeships as well. So began a friendly rivalry.

Although there were a few companies in Chicago embracing Software Craftsmanship, nothing really major happened in the field between 2001 (when Pete McBreen's book came out) and 2008. Agile was the new thing, with many disciplines, methodologies, and techniques shaking the foundations of the software development industry. Back then, there was no real need for Software Craftsmanship because many people believed that the biggest problems in our industry could be addressed by one or a combination of the Agile methodologies and practices.

In August 2008, during his keynote speech at an Agile 2008 conference, Uncle Bob proposed a fifth value for the Agile Manifesto, namely "craftsmanship over crap." He later changed his proposal to "craftsmanship over execution." Also in August 2008, he published *Clean Code: A Handbook of Agile Software Craftsmanship* and later in May 2011, *The Clean Coder: A Code of Conduct for Professional Programmers,* two of the most, if not the most, influential books in the Software Craftsmanship circle.

THE SOFTWARE CRAFTSMANSHIP SUMMIT

In 2008, seven years since the Agile summit, it became apparent that things in the Agile world were not going as well as expected. The deviation from the technical Agile methodologies like Extreme Programming (XP) and the commercialization of the process-oriented methodologies like Scrum started to bother some of the original Agile innovators.

There were already lots of talks about Software Craftsmanship in the Agile community, which led Micah Martin and Paul Pagel to organize the Software Craftsmanship Summit in order to formalize and better define it. The main goal was to put a public face on Software Craftsmanship. The invitees were all people who had expressed interest, to some extent, in Software Craftsmanship.

The summit took place on December 13, 2008, in Libertyville, Illinois, just a few kilometers from Chicago. The summit lasted for six hours and there were roughly 30 people there, including Uncle Bob, Brian Marick, Corey Haines, Dave Hoover, Doug Bradbury, and David Chelimsky.

Almost immediately after the summit, the conversation was taken to the Internet via a Google group. A few people from England and a few other countries also jumped right in and had plenty to contribute. Bit by bit, Software Craftsmanship started spreading in the UK, a few places in Europe, and later to many other countries around the world.

In March 2009, after loads of debate, a summary of the general conclusions was decided on. It was presented publicly, for both viewing and signing, in the form of the Software Craftsmanship Manifesto.

CROSSING BORDERS

On February 26, 2009, the first international Software Craftsmanship Conference was held in London. Also in London, in May 2009, Adewale Oshineye held a seminar for the aspiring software craftsman, and Enrique Comba Riepenhausen started *The Wandering Book,* a book that travels from craftsman to craftsman, capturing the current thinking, the zeitgeist, of the Software Craftsmanship movement. Software craftsmen around the world wrote their thoughts about what it meant to be a software craftsman and then mailed it to other software craftsmen. The craftsmen writing in the book would also take pictures of their entries and post them on a website. Unfortunately, after traveling around a few countries, the book was lost and the website got wiped out. It is still possible to find some information about *The Wandering Book* in a few blog posts.

In October 2009, the book *Apprenticeship Patterns: Guidance for the Aspiring Software Craftsman,* by Dave Hoover and Adewale Oshineye, was published. This book was one of the first books to inspire, with practical advice, software developers to look after their careers, pursue mastery, and love their profession.

From 2009 onward, Software Craftsmanship Conferences have been held every year in the United States, United Kingdom, and, from 2011, in Germany as well.

CRAFTSMAN SWAP

In April 2009, 8th Light and Obtiva experimented with a craftsman swap in Chicago. The *Chicago Tribune* covered this event on June 15, 2009, mentioning many of the important details about the swap. There was a mutual respect between the two companies, in terms of their technical capabilities, which made them believe they could learn a lot from each other. Many people, as a first reaction, would think this is utter madness but in reality it shows that these companies have a different way of seeing things. "I look at it as not really competing against each other but against the people out there [whose] main goal is just to make as much money as they can . . . just pushing out software really fast without thinking about how software lives over a long period of time," said Corey Haines, who helped to organize the swap and was the originator of the idea.

"Initially there were some concerns from both sides in how it would work contractually but we were all very excited," said Tyler Jennings from Obtiva. "We were expecting to cross-pollinate development practices and to give our developers an experience they couldn't get anywhere else. We chose [to send] someone who was both an experienced developer and someone we thought represented the Obtiva way well."

The developers involved in the swap worked as normal developers, pairing with other developers and doing real work. They wrote code, went to meetings, and behaved as if they were working for the other company—at least during that week. This helped them to learn new process, new development styles, new languages, new tooling, and so on.

"Every company I know that has done one wants to do another. The benefits to the company were small in the direct sense, but huge for the engineers who participated and the community," said Tyler. During the conversation I also asked him if he would recommend other companies to do the same and if he had any advice. "Yes!" he said. "It makes a ton of sense for software development companies to do these, especially if they're not in direct competition. It works especially well for consultancies, as we don't have many issues around intellectual property that most organizations do. I believe companies who do employ careful, thoughtful developers, a.k.a. 'craftsmen,' should swap regularly. There are many different ways to approach a problem successfully and it has been my experience that each group has things they do better than the others. Swaps let two companies take the best practices from each to improve their own."

In my view, this was an amazing step forward for the software industry as a whole. Initiatives like that can help software developers to get better and help companies to be more competitive, producing better products and solutions.

SOFTWARE CRAFTSMANSHIP COMMUNITIES

Although there was some noise about Software Craftsmanship since 1999, it was in 2008 and 2009 that the field flourished. Besides books and a few conferences, the Software Craftsmanship movement really gained traction with the creation of the global mailing list and a few Software Craftsmanship communities in the United States, London, and a few others in Europe.

In December 2009, Uri Lavi founded the Israeli Software Craftsmanship Community. In August 2010, David Green and I founded the London Software Craftsmanship Community (LSCC). Following SoCraTes 2011, the Software Craftsmanship and Testing conference in Germany, several Software Craftsmanship communities were founded: the Paris Software Craftsmanship Community was founded in October 2011, around the same time the Softwerkskammer started with six Software Craftsmanship communities in Germany. The Germans are now organizing more than fifteen communities around the country. Many other communities have been created around the world since.

The LSCC is currently the largest and most active community in the world with more than 2,000 developers, organizing around four to five events per month, and an annual Software Craftsmanship conference—SoCraTes UK. The LSCC also served as a model to help many other communities around the world get started.

THE SOFTWARE CRAFTSMANSHIP MANIFESTO

Trying to avoid the same anticlimactic aftermath of the 2002 Software Apprenticeship Summit, Micah Martin really wanted something to come out of the Software Craftsmanship Summit. He wanted something to be written down and a document of some kind was his goal for the summit. There they discussed, among other things, what it means to be a craftsman and what it means to be an apprentice. They also discussed who the document would be written for, what the contents of it would be, if the document already existed, and if it needed to exist at all. The initial ideas were captured on a whiteboard and although they came up with lots of good ideas, there was far too much content and it was far too unorganized. They weren't even close to a finished document. Still, before closing the summit, Micah asked everyone to sign what they had on the whiteboard.

Doug Bradbury went into action of his own accord. He posted the outcome of the summit on the Google group and solicited feedback. He got lots of it. In February 2009, Doug wrote an email called "The New Left Side," which started to get the values and wording and was refined into the actual Software Crafts-manship Manifesto. There was a debate about the Agile Manifesto and the Soft-ware Craftsmanship Manifesto that was instrumental in moving forward with the manifesto. The discussion started with "The New Left Side" by Doug Brad-bury and "Right Side, Revisited" by Scott Pfister.

The discussion revolved around the question, "Why a Software Craftsmanship manifesto?" Corey Haines addressed it by saying, "By becoming a vocal commu-nity, publishing a manifesto, beginning work on establishing principles and con-crete schools of thought, we are creating a light that new developers can see. Those who are really interested can more easily find us, talk to us about appren-ticeships, meet companies that actively engage in craftsmanship activities— apprenticeships, journeymen programs, etc. In some cases, this will introduce them sooner to these ideas, hopefully saving some from the frustrations they can face in a different situation."

It was a fascinating conversation which spawned the final language of the mani-festo. The whole discussion can be read in the Software Craftsmanship Google group. After a few weeks, Doug presented an elegant manifesto based on all the ideas discussed, with the structure of the Agile Manifesto. It was great, and the community in general approved it. Within another couple weeks they built and published a site where people could sign the "Manifesto for Software Craftsmanship."

THE MANIFESTO

As aspiring Software Craftsmen we are raising the bar of professional software development by practicing it and helping others learn the craft. Through this work we have come to value the following:

Not only working software,
> but also **well-crafted software**

Not only responding to change,
> but also **steadily adding value**

Not only individuals and interactions,
> but also a **community of professionals**

Not only customer collaboration,
> but also **productive partnerships**

That is, in pursuit of the items on the left we have found the items on the right to be indispensable.

In the manifesto, the essence of Software Craftsmanship is captured in its subtitle "Raising the Bar." The manifesto summarizes the values, frustrations, and aspirations of very experienced and talented developers. For them, projects had to stop failing because of poor management, ill-defined processes, and, of course, badly written code.

Developers are taking the matter into their own hands and are trying to change how the industry sees software development. They do that not just by proposing new and revolutionary processes but also by showing their customers that they care about what they do. Developers are showing their customers they want to work together with them in order to produce great and long-lived software, helping them to achieve whatever they want to achieve.

Not Only Working Software, but Also Well-Crafted Software

Think about a five-year-old application. Imagine an application that has no tests; no one knows exactly how the application works; and the code is full of technical and infrastructure terms instead of expressing the business domain; and classes and methods have hundreds, if not thousands, of lines. Also imagine that you need to make changes to this application, but writing tests to it is a massive undertaking. Of course, you think, you can pair with the other developers on the team. No, there is no team. You are the team. All the developers who wrote the application have left and the only thing you have is a graduate who was hired a few weeks ago to look after the application.

The main problem you have when working with applications like that is *fear*. No, I'm not calling you a coward. I'm just stating that you are a responsible developer who understands the implications of making the wrong change in a code like that. You are scared to change parts of this code because you don't understand how it works, and you have no confidence you will not break something else.

This application is *working software*, but is it good enough? Well-crafted software means that, regardless of how old the application is, developers can understand it easily. The side effects are well known and controlled. It has high and reliable test coverage, clear and simple design, and business language well expressed in the code. Adding or changing features does not take longer than it used to take at the beginning of the project, when the code base was small.

The code must be maintainable and predictable. Developers must know what is going to happen when changing the code and must not be afraid to change it. Changes should be localized and not affect other parts of the application—no ripple effects. In a few minutes, if not seconds, after pressing a button, tests will check the entire application and inform you if there is something broken.

In order to evolve applications, developers must not shy away from changing them. Using Test-Driven Development, simple design, and expressing the business language in code are the best ways to keep a healthy and well-crafted code.

Not Only Responding to Change, but Also Steadily Adding Value

Have you ever thought about how expensive software projects are? Think about all the developers working on it. Now think about all the other professionals who are also part of the project, like testers, production services, operations, business analysts, product owners, and project managers. There are also sales, marketing, and back office people. Imagine how much is spent just in salaries. Now add the cost of all the computers, furniture, communication infrastructure, office rent, marketing, sales, customer services, catering, cleaning, and everything else. Yes, they all add up. On top of that, imagine distributed teams, multiple offices, traveling, and everything else that comes with it.

Software projects are normally a massive investment and as with any normal investment, companies will want a return. The only reasons for companies to invest in a software project are to make money, save money, or protect revenue. With that in mind, it is our job to help them achieve that.

When we talk about *steadily adding value*, we are not just talking about adding new features and fixing bugs. This is also about constantly improving the structure of the code, keeping it clean, extendable, testable, and easy to maintain.

It is our job to make sure that the older and bigger the software gets, the more the company will benefit from it. We want to keep adding features to the project and making the appropriate changes to the application at the same speed that we used to have at the beginning of the project. This would allow companies to react quickly to the market regardless how old their software is. As it gets older, software should become more valuable and not a source of pain and increasing cost.

Increasing the software lifespan, and keeping the ability to change it fast enough, is our main mission. Good software design, automated testing skills, and passionate and talented developers are essential for achieving that.

A paraphrase of a Boy Scout rule (first applied to software by Uncle Bob) states that we should **always leave the code cleaner than we found it**.

The focus on high-quality software must be the number one priority if you want long-lived applications. Totally rewriting a large application a few years after it has been developed makes for a very poor return on investment. On many occasions, the decision to rewrite an application is made because of the prohibitive costs of maintaining it.

> Insanity: doing the same thing over and over again
> and expecting different results.
> —Albert Einstein

The problem is that the same bad techniques that were used to build the old application will also be used to build the new one—making the new application as bad as the old application after just a few months or years. It is our job to break this cycle, building applications with well-crafted code.

Not Only Individuals and Interactions, but Also a Community of Professionals

Sharing and mentoring are at the heart of Software Craftsmanship. Software craftsmen are passionate and always strive to better themselves. However, we have a far bigger mission: we are responsible for preparing the next generation of craftsmen.

The best way to move our industry forward is by sharing what we learned through mentoring and inspiring less-experienced developers. This is also related to the idea of apprentices, journeymen, and masters, where Software Craftsmanship masters will mentor apprentices and help them in their journey. Knowledge, ideas, successes, and failures must be shared and discussed within the community in order to move our industry forward.

I was quite surprised to hear from some developers and Agile coaches that the Software Craftsmanship community is a group of self-selected and elitist developers. A developer cannot be considered a software craftsman if he or she thinks Software Craftsmanship is about elitism, is not humble enough to learn from others, or is not willing to share his knowledge and mentor less-experienced developers. From my experience, the Software Craftsmanship community is one of the most open and friendly communities I know. By its own nature, being language agnostic, it is a community that embraces all sorts of developers, regardless of their level of seniority or technology.

Learning from each other is by far the best way for us to become better. Writing blogs, contributing to open source projects, making our code publicly available, becoming part of our local communities, and pairing with other developers are some of the ways we can contribute to the greater good of our industry.

Since 2010, Software Craftsmanship communities are being created in Europe and the United States and they run many free events every month. They welcome developers from all sorts of backgrounds, industries, and levels of experience. These communities promote an environment where developers can meet, share ideas, and write code together.

Besides external communities, this item in our manifesto also includes our work environment. Great developers want to work with other great developers. Great developers want to work for great companies. What we want is to work with people that can make us better, that are willing to share and learn from each other. We do not want mere colleagues. We want passionate and inspiring professionals that we can call friends.

Not Only Customer Collaboration, but Also Productive Partnerships

The first thing to mention here is that we do not believe in the employer/ employee type of relationship. What the contract says (you being a permanent employee, contractor, consultant, vendor, paid per day, hour, or month) are just formalities. We believe in partnership and professional behavior above all. If you are a permanent employee, you should treat your employer as your customer, the same way as if you were a contractor or consultant. Employers, on the other hand, should also expect their employees to provide a great service at all times, like a consultant and contractor is supposed to. Turning up to work on time, keeping your head down, and just doing what you are told to do is not what it means to be a professional.

Software craftsmen are not factory workers. We want to actively contribute to the success of the project, questioning requirements, understanding the business, proposing improvements, and productively partnering with our customers or employers. This is a different approach to the traditional employer/employee model and the advantages for the employers are enormous. A highly motivated team has a much bigger chance to make any project succeed. Passionate and talented people want to succeed and will always find ways to overcome problems and bureaucracy.

Software craftsmen want and need successful projects to build their reputations. We want to be proud of our achievements. Successfully delivering high-quality software and having satisfied customers are essential for a software craftsman's career.

Although extremely important, writing code well is just one of the things we need to do to help a project to succeed. We must help our clients to improve their processes, provide them with more viable options, help them to remove unnecessary bureaucracy, understand their business domain, question their requirements in relation to the value they provide, provide them with good information and knowledge, help them to plan and prioritize work, and work on things that, although they are not coding tasks, are equally important to the project. Providing value to our customers at all levels is what we mean by having a productive partnership.

The core business of many of our clients is not building software, so it is our obligation to help them run a software project in the best way possible. That's what we are paid for. Developers that say it is not their job if the task is not code-related are not real software craftsmen.

But Some Clients Are Not Ready for a Productive Partnership ...

Unfortunately, there are still companies out there that are not ready for this type of partnership. They see software development as an industrial process and the least important part of the project. For some companies, software developers are the same as factory workers, who are there just to follow orders from *smarter* people.

Some of these companies focus on getting the cheapest developers they can find and will always have nontechnical managers trying to micro-manage these developers. Some of them will not welcome or listen to developers when it comes to business decisions. Some will hire a single person, quite often with outdated development skills, to be the technical leader (or dictator).

Working for a company with this type of mentality is always very difficult for any software craftsman. We should always try our best to turn this situation around and try to prove to our clients we could help them far more if they let us.

However, in the same way that companies want to have good developers, software craftsmen also want to work for good companies. There is no point in spending all our energy and health trying to help those who do not want to be helped. There is a limit to the efforts we make to help our clients. Knowing how to select clients (or employers) is also an essential skill for a craftsman. Choosing to work for a client who is not interested in or does not value the skills of a software craftsman is pointless.

Choosing clients carefully is essential for software craftsmen to build their reputations and move forward with their careers. A partnership, by nature, is a two-way street. A partnership is a good partnership only if it is good for both parties involved. If you don't feel that the partnership with your client is good for you, it is probably time for you to find another client.

The Problem with the Manifesto

There were quite a few criticisms related to the Software Craftsmanship Manifesto. The main one is that, unlike the Agile Manifesto, the Software Craftsmanship Manifesto is almost impossible to disagree with. In the Agile Manifesto, the contrast between the left and right sides is strong, clearly indicating what is being proposed. A person who believes that documentation is very important struggles to fully accept "working software over comprehensive documentation." Companies that are used to fixed-price and detailed contracts would struggle with "customer collaboration over contract negotiation." In the Software Craftsmanship Manifesto, there is no strong contrast between the left and right sides. The right side is just an evolution of an already accepted left side. A person who already agrees that working software is better than comprehensive documentation will never disagree with the value of well-crafted software. Companies that already believe in collaboration will never disagree with productive partnership.

This is a fair point. I don't think that anyone who believes in the Agile values can really disagree with what is written in the Software Craftsmanship Manifesto. However, if no one disagrees with the Software Craftsmanship Manifesto, it is fair to assume that everyone agrees with it. If that is the case, the question we should ask ourselves is do we always work and behave according to what is written in the manifesto? Are we really practicing the things on which we agree?

In my view, the manifesto should not be read as if it was just a bunch of lines put together. We must go deeper to fully understand it.

SUMMARY

Software Craftsmanship is about professionalism in software development. It's about software developers striving to always do their best and provide good service to their clients. Software craftsmen seek productive partnerships with their clients and employers and not an employer/employee relationship. Software craftsmen understand that being a good professional means having a good reputation, and for that they need to constantly delight their clients by delivering successful projects.

Software Craftsmanship is a mindset—a lifestyle that many professional developers adopt. Software craftsmen live and breathe software. They see software as a craft and are committed to do whatever they can to master their craft.

THE SOFTWARE CRAFTSMANSHIP ATTITUDE

If we think that a piece of code we wrote some time in the past is still good enough today, it means we didn't learn anything since.

For us, software craftsmen, caring about and being proud of the work we do is a given. Constantly finding ways to become better professionals is a lifetime commitment. Satisfying and helping our customers to achieve what they want to achieve, in the most efficient way, is our main goal. Sharing our knowledge with less-experienced software craftsmen is our moral obligation.

A few years ago, I was speaking to a colleague of mine. We had joined the company at roughly the same time, hired at the same position, and worked in a project together for almost one year. Since we were working for a consultancy company, after some time we went separate ways to work on different projects and for different clients. It was only after a few years that we had the opportunity to work together again. I then asked him how things were going with him and he said, "I don't really like this company. This company sucks." I was surprised by what he said since I had been really enjoying my time in that company. So then I asked him why he was saying that. "In all these years, they never bought me a book. Never sent me on a training course, and never gave me a project using modern technologies. They never gave me a promotion either," he said. "I haven't learned anything new for quite a long time," he complained.

I was not quite sure what to think or say about his comments. I had had two promotions during that period, worked on quite a few good projects, and learned many new things. "Who owns your career?" I suddenly asked him after a few seconds of awkward silence. He didn't quite understand my question and asked me to repeat it. "Who is in charge of your career and your professional future?" I asked him again. Even after a few years since we had this conversation, I still remember the puzzled look in his eyes.

In this chapter I discuss how we can own our careers, keep ourselves up to date, practice, and discover the things we didn't know. I also talk about how to create time for all these things.

WHO OWNS YOUR CAREER?

What if the company we work for does not buy us any books? What if the company never sent us to any training course or conferences? Would that be the only way we could learn anything new? Does it really mean the company is bad?

Imagine that you need a plumber to do some work in your house. Imagine that you need a lawyer to solve any legal issues, or a doctor when you are sick, or a dentist when you have an aching tooth. You normally go to these professionals when you have a problem, so now imagine them turning back to you and saying, "Could you buy me a book? Can you send me on a training course?" What would *you* think about that? To make things even worse, imagine that you, for some really bizarre reason, decide to buy them a book or send them on a training course, and once they acquired the knowledge you gave them, they come back and charge you for their services. How does it sound to you?

These professionals need to invest in their own careers so they can do a good job, satisfy their clients, and hopefully be referred to other clients. They use their own money and time to keep themselves current. Those that don't do it end up losing clients, receive fewer referrals, and will slowly be forced out of business.

On the other hand, factory workers, for example, rely on training. Factories need to train their employees to use new machines so they can do their mechanical and repetitive work well. However, factory workers have no say in what machines the factory should buy or how they are going to do the work. They are just told what to do.

Clients pay professionals with the expectation of receiving a good service. They pay professionals to solve their problems in the best way possible. Clients don't pay professionals to learn. Clients pay professionals for their knowledge and skills. Professionals are expected to provide solutions, viable alternatives, and ideas to their clients. Professionals are expected to help their clients to achieve whatever they want to achieve in the best way possible, and that is how they build their reputation.

We all want to be treated and respected as software professionals but before we achieve that we need to start behaving like professionals. That means that we should use our own time and money to get better at what we do. We should own our own careers and be in control of what we learn and when we learn. We should be in a position that we can help our clients and employers to achieve their goals. Developers who rely only on their companies to provide them knowledge are not professional software developers. They are just factory workers in disguise.

"So companies should not be investing in their own people?" you may be asking. No, that is not what I meant. Companies should invest in their people but software professionals should not see that as their obligation. That should be seen as a bonus, a win-win situation. Companies that provide time to developers to get better at what they do are much smarter and can become far more efficient. Passionate developers will always favor these companies when choosing who they work for.

Our industry moves, possibly, faster than any other industry. Languages, frameworks, practices, and processes are all constantly evolving. Keeping up to date and constantly getting better at what you do is key for a successful career as a software craftsman.

EMPLOYER/EMPLOYEE RELATIONSHIP

In creative work, the employer/employee model is the wrong model. On one hand, we have a contractual model that states how people should be paid and that also states the legal and behavioral obligations that need to be respected by employers and employees. On the other hand, we have the type of relationship that professionals have with their clients. The old top-down, command and control style of management became very popular during the Industrial Revolution and arguably still has its merits when the majority of the workforce is doing manual or repetitive work. However, it does not work well for creative workers. This style of management can be extremely damaging to the morale of software professionals, making the company far more inefficient. Companies that are still using this style of management normally struggle to hire talented professionals and are slowly losing the ones they still have. But, of course, this is just one side of the story. Keeping our heads down, working hard from 9 to 5, and doing only what we are told to do is not professional either. That is what factory workers do. If developers want to be treated as professionals, they should start acting as professionals. A software professional must, among other things, get involved and contribute to the business, provide options and solutions, and offer the best service when it comes to the implementation, technologies, and quality of what we produce.

The relationship between software craftsmen and their clients should be seen as a productive business partnership, regardless of which contractual model we may have. Being a permanent employee, a contractor, a consultant, or a developer working for an outsourcing company should not affect at all this relationship or the attitude we have toward our clients.

KEEPING OURSELVES UP TO DATE

> We live in a world where there is more and more information, and less and less meaning.
> —Jean Baudrillard

Different people have different learning patterns and preferences, and by no means do I feel that I could describe all the possible ways a person could learn. However, the following is a small list of things we can do to keep ourselves up to date.

BOOKS, MANY BOOKS

Having our own library, physical or electronic, is essential. We are very lucky to be in an industry where so much information is produced. However, there are many different types of books, and choosing which books to read can be a very difficult task.

- *Technology-specific books* are very valuable but they *expire*. They are essential for the immediate need, when we want to learn a framework, language, or any other software we need to use. They are great at giving us a deep understanding of how things work and the knowledge acquired can usually be used immediately. They are also great when we are planning our next career steps. They can give us details of how to use the technologies that may be between our current job and our desired job. However, many of the technology-specific books get old extremely quickly. When a new version of the technology they cover is released, or a different way of doing things becomes more popular, they will not add as much value as before. Examples would be books about Java, Hibernate, Node.js, or Clojure.

- *Conceptual books* are the books that give us the foundation to advance in our careers. They are the books where we get introduced to new concepts, paradigms, and practices. The knowledge we acquire through this type of book cannot always be applied immediately; it may take a significant amount of time to digest the information and become proficient. Quite often a technology or language may be used to explain some technical concepts but usually the knowledge we get can be applied broadly. Books covering topics like Test-Driven Development, Domain-Driven Design, object-oriented design, functional programming, or modeling different types of NoSQL databases, just to mention a few examples, would fit in this category. Learning new concepts, paradigms, and practices is far harder than learning a specific technology, and it may take years until we get comfortable with them. However, conceptual books are the books that give us the foundation to learn specific technologies much quicker.

- *Behavioral books* are the books that make us more efficient when working in teams and better professionals in general. They help us learn how to deal with people, clients, deadlines, team members, and so on. Knowing some programming languages, frameworks, and practices is not enough if we want to be good professionals. We also need to learn how to deal with everything else that is not related to code but is also part of a software project or organization. Books in this category will cover the more human and professional side of software development, including topics like Agile methodologies, Software Craftsmanship, Lean software development, psychology, philosophy, and management.

- *Revolutionary books* (some call them classics) are the ones that change the way we work or even some of our personal values. They propose a different set of values and principles, quite often initially rejected or ignored by the majority of professionals. Bit by bit, they end up making their way into the mainstream. They are books that every software developer is expected to have read and are constantly mentioned in technical conversations. Very rarely does a technology-specific book become a classic. Normally the revolutionary books are conceptual, behavioral, or a combination. Books in this category define or have a great influence on the direction and evolution of our industry. A few examples would be *The Pragmatic Programmer, The Mythical Man-Month, Design Patterns (GoF), Test-Driven Development: By Example, Extreme Programming Explained: Embrace Change, The Clean Coder, Software Craftsmanship,* and *Refactoring.* It may take many years to master the content in the books in this category.

Books give us a deeper understanding of a technology or subject. Favor conceptual and behavioral books for your career progression, starting with the revolutionary ones. Read technology-specific books for your short- and medium-term plans.

Reading itself also has a learning curve. There are many different ways to read books, and understanding them can make a big difference in how fast we can read them and how much we can learn. This topic is beyond the scope of this book but I recommend you research speed-reading techniques.

BLOGS

Blogs are extremely popular and a great way to keep ourselves up to date. Quite a few very good developers I know and respect just read blogs. They have almost abandoned books. Blogs tend to fit well in the Software Craftsmanship and Agile models because they contain real experiences, personal findings, opinions, successes, and failures in short snippets. Reading blogs from more experienced professionals and subject matter experts is a good, quick, and free way for us to learn from many different great professionals at the same time. There are also great apps like Instapaper and Evernote, just to mention a few, that we can use to keep track of blogs.

Blogs can be dangerous for the uninformed though. The vast majority of blogs are written without much research or deep thought. Some blog posts are just a brain dump of half-baked ideas, rants, or random thoughts. Some developers use their blogs to keep track of their own professional progression. Some report their own experiences in real projects but that does not necessarily mean they were able to solve their problems well or even to identify their real problems. And that is OK. That is exactly why blogs are great. As long as we understand that we need to read blogs with a pinch of salt, they are fantastic.

But do not think that just experienced professionals should write blogs. All software developers should have their own blogs, regardless of how much experience they have. We should all share our experiences and findings and help to create a great community of professionals. Sometimes we may think that we are not good enough or do not have much to say. We may think that we don't have an original idea and no one will read our blog anyway. First of all, we should treat our blog as a record of our own learning and progression—a history of our thoughts, ideas, and views of the world over our careers. We should not worry too much about what other people will think about it. We should first write it for ourselves. Even if developers more experienced than us have written about the subject many times before, it is worth writing whatever we are currently learning anyway. Every year there are thousands of new developers joining our industry and they will need to learn many of the things we are learning now. Maybe for them, our blogs will be very useful since we will be writing them from the perspective of a beginner. Do not worry about being judged by more senior developers because that is not going to happen. Whenever we Google for something and the first link we click leads to something we already know, we just jump to the next link. All developers should appreciate the effort that other developers make to write and share their views with the rest of the world, for free.

TECHNICAL WEBSITES

Technical websites are also good in order to keep ourselves up to date with what's going on in the market. There are many websites that work as a digital magazine, announcing new trends and techniques. Some of these websites have technical writers writing for them every day. Some of them just aggregate the best blogs or provide a big discussion forum.

KNOW WHO TO FOLLOW

In every profession, there is a group of people that contribute massively to move that profession forward. We have many of these people, some on the technology-specific side and others on the more generic, conceptual, and behavioral side. They are all important, so know who these people are. That helps us to filter the information we have online or in physical books. For example, if we work with Java or Ruby, we should know who publishes the best material on it. We should know who is helping the language to move forward or defining better ways to use it. We should know who the people reshaping our industry are. When we hear terms like Agile and Software Craftsmanship, we should try to discover who the people behind these ideas are. Look at their history. See what they've published. Try to understand where they got their inspiration or what they are basing their ideas on. We may discover that many of the things we talk about today go back a few decades.

SOCIAL MEDIA

Learn how to use Twitter. Used wisely, Twitter can be a great tool for information gathering. Following the people described above and other fellow developers can be one of the best ways to keep ourselves up to date. Whenever someone publishes a blog post, they will tweet the link. Whenever someone finds some interesting material, they will also tweet the links. Sometimes we can follow quite a few interesting online conversations and that may be a good opportunity to join in.

PRACTICE, PRACTICE, PRACTICE

How it is done is as important as getting it done. If we want to be good at writing quality code, we need to practice how to write quality code. There is no other way. When practicing, the focus should be on the techniques we are using and not in solving the problem. Solving problems is what we are paid for and what we do at work. However, when practicing, we should focus on *how* we are solving the problem. For example, imagine you are trying to learn or get better at Test-Driven Development. This is a hard discipline to master. It is counterintuitive at first, and that is why we need to practice.

Do you remember when you were learning how to drive? I remember that every time I was driving up a hill I was praying for the traffic light not to go red. I used to think to myself, "Damn, I'll need to stop, put it in first gear, release the clutch slowly, and be careful that the car does not stall or roll backward." I also remember the first time I had some friends in the car and they were asking me, "Can you switch the radio on?" and I, nervously glancing between all the mirrors, firmly gripping the steering wheel, would tell them "no." That happened because when I was learning how to drive, I was worried about the car. I was worried about the gear shifting. I was worried about the mirrors, other cars, driving straight and staying in the lane, not driving into the other lane when turning, and so on. I could not divert my attention to switch the radio on. Now, after a few years, imagine how you drive. We do not even remember we are in a car. We do not think about the mechanics of driving a car anymore. We just focus on where we are going, what we are going to do when we arrive there; we listen to music, sing along, have conversations while driving. Driving a car became second nature and the car is now almost an extension of our own bodies.

Technical practices and new technologies are the same thing. The more we practice, the more comfortable we become, to the point where we don't think about them anymore. We just focus on what we want to do with them.

When practicing, we need to focus on writing the best code we could possibly write. If it takes us minutes or even a few hours, to write a single test but it is the best test we could have written, that is OK. We should not worry if we take a long time to name a variable, method, or class. As long as we tried our best to find the most appropriate name for it, we should feel great. We are practicing and when we do it, we should strive for perfect practice. With this approach, when facing the demands of a real software project, we can concentrate on finding a good solution to the problem and not on how to write tests or which commands to use.

KATAS

Katas are simple coding exercises. They have a simple problem domain that can be understood in a few minutes and are complicated enough not to be solved too quickly. They normally take from a few minutes to a few hours to be solved and are a perfect way to try new techniques and approaches. An example would be a kata where we need to calculate the score of a bowling game or implement tic-tac-toe. We can use these katas to practice things we think we are not very good at, like Test-Driven Development, another language, or a framework.

Katas have been criticized by certain people in the Agile community, though. Some people say that it is plain stupid to do the same thing over and over again. Well, to a certain extent there is some degree of truth to it. Usually this is said because the term comes from martial arts and that is how it is done in karate, for example. We do the same movements over and over again. That was probably the original intent when we started using the term *kata* for a coding exercise. However, solving katas with our current toolkit (the techniques and tools that we are comfortable with) does not make a lot of sense.

When doing katas, the idea is that we stretch ourselves, using practices, techniques, and technologies that we are not very comfortable with, with the intent of getting better at them. After practicing these things quite a few times, you may feel ready or at least fairly comfortable with doing that in a professional environment. Think about musicians who practice for hours, days, and months before their live performances. That is exactly what we are trying to achieve here.

Katas can be very beneficial when the same kata is done over and over again but using a completely different approach or technique each time. That allows us to experiment and compare. The correct word to define this practice, according to martial arts, is *keiko*. However, as developers all over the world have already adopted the word *kata,* we should keep using it instead of introducing another term.

We can find a good source of coding katas at codingkata.org, codekata.pragprog .com, and kata.softwarecraftsmanship.org.

Pet Projects

Pet projects are for me, by far, the best way to learn and practice. A pet project is a *real* project but without pressure. There are no deadlines, they do not need to make money, you control the requirements, and, most important, you use the technologies and methodologies you want, whenever you want, wherever you want. You are the boss. In real projects, a professional software developer would first understand the problem domain, then make technical decisions and write code. We would speak to stakeholders, product owners, users, business, marketing, and whoever else is involved and could contribute to the business idea. These conversations, in a healthy Agile environment, should happen frequently throughout the project. According to what the customer wants to achieve and the scope of the project, we would then choose the most suitable technologies to develop the project. Pet projects are exactly the opposite. First we decide what we want to learn—practices, disciplines, methodologies, and technologies—and then we find a problem to solve. It is much easier to understand why and how we can or cannot use certain technologies if we have a pet project to try them out. Pet projects allow us to play, experiment, discover, and learn in a very safe environment, giving us the experience we need to apply what we have learned to real projects.

Another important thing about pet projects is that we can experience several aspects of a real project. For example, we need to come up with an idea. Once we have an idea, we need to start refining the features and preparing a backlog. Preparing a backlog means thinking about priorities, making rough estimations, writing stories, and splitting tasks. We also need to think about tests, how we are going to deploy the application, version control, continuous integration, usability, the user interface, infrastructure code, design, and databases. As soon as we start using the application ourselves, we start changing our minds about the features (business) and also the technology choices. And that is exactly what happens in a real project. We do not need to have all that in place, but we can if we want to. We can use pet projects to learn any aspect of a real project. We can even try to write a business plan for it if we want to learn something about that. Remember, we are the bosses and we do whatever we want, as long as we are learning something. That's the whole point.

Above all, pet projects are meant to be fun. A common problem that developers have with pet projects is finding a good idea. The good news is that you do not need one. You are not starting a new business. I always advise developers to choose a subject that they are very passionate about. For example, if you like traveling, try to create a website about travel. If you like running, create an application that can capture your progress, display graphics, and so forth. If you feel you should be more organized with your own tasks, create a mobile app where you can track what you need to do. It does not matter if there are thousands of other applications that do the same. There are always different things you would like them to do. The advantage of choosing a topic you are passionate about is that you will never run out of ideas for features or improvements. Besides that, you will always want to work on it since you usually will want to use it as well. All these things will help you to be quite close to a real project, and practicing them will have an enormous impact on your professional career.

A common question is if we should transform our pet projects into a real business. The answer is, "It depends." I normally would say *no* to that since if you want to have a business, writing code and learning new technologies should not be your number one priority. I would recommend that you find some good material and get yourself familiar with Lean startup concepts before writing a single line of code. The transition from a pet project to a real business can be extremely painful and full of disappointments. Believe me, I've tried it myself. Many of us get very attached to our own applications and code base, which can blind us to what the market really wants. If we feel we should transform our little Frankenstein pet project into a business, focus on the business first and be ready to throw whatever percentage of what you have written away if that is what the business demands. Detach yourself from the code, clean it up, and leave just the bare minimum to satisfy the business needs.

OPEN SOURCE

Contributing to open source projects is also a great way to practice. There are thousands of them out there. Find a project that is related to what you want to learn or know more about, and download the source code. Start running and reading the tests, if any exist. Inspect, debug, and play with the code. If you want to contribute, start small: add some documentation, write some tests, check the list of bugs to be fixed or features to be implemented, pick a simple task, and give it a try. You can also propose and implement a new small feature to start with.

Open source projects tend to be very different from pet projects because they are usually, with few exceptions, very specific in scope. For example, it may be an object-relational mapper (ORM) framework, a library to make web service calls, transaction management, a social network integrator, and so on. Although all these things are extremely important, necessary, and useful, open source projects tend to be just one of the libraries your professional applications will use, so do not forget to look at the whole picture.

Another great thing about open source projects is to see great developers in action. Looking at how they code and solve problems can be a great way to learn how to code well. Besides all that, it is also a great way to raise your public profile.

PAIR PROGRAMMING

Pair programming is more a social activity than a technical practice. It enhances the team spirit and brings developers together. Many developers are afraid to try it or think they will feel uncomfortable when pairing with others. Many years ago, I used to think like that but I realized that, in reality, I was afraid to expose my own limitations. If that is how you feel, the best advice is to get over it. There is a limit to what we can learn on our own. Of course we can learn whatever we want because we are all very smart people, but the problem is the amount of time that it can take. In addition, we will always have a naive and biased opinion when we are doing things on our own.

When pair programming, we can learn how to use a new language or parts of the application to which we had no previous exposure, a technical practice like Test-Driven Development, a few keyboard shortcuts, or even a completely new way to solve problems. Pairing can lead to very interesting discussions. It can help us to validate our own ideas or have them challenged, forcing us to rethink why we do things the way we do. It also can be a very humbling experience. Usually, we think of ourselves as very good developers, and we like to think that all the other developers are bad. Other developers write crap code, not us. When pairing, we get immediate feedback on our code and ideas. Our pair *validates* whatever we type immediately. Whenever our pair does not understand what we are doing, or does not agree with a variable name, the use of an application programming interface (API), or a design decision, we have an opportunity to step back and reevaluate the decision. Instead of thinking that the other person is stupid (which is rarely the case), we should think that we are probably not as good as we think we are. A good developer is a developer who can write code that any other developer can understand. When our pairs don't agree or don't understand what we are doing, we should take this as an opportunity to have a good discussion. Use it to learn something new and open your mind to different approaches. If someone is questioning what we've just done, maybe it is because it's not good enough and there is a better way of doing it. We should take opportunities like that to share what we know, making everyone around us better. When teaching, we are forced to structure our thoughts, making us really understand our quite often half-baked ideas so we can make someone else understand them.

Pairing with someone from our team or a friend is great, but pairing with someone that we barely know can be even better. Usually team members and friends, after some time working and pairing together, develop a common understanding and style of coding. When pairing with people we have never paired with before, we end up potentially exposing ourselves to very different ways to solve and think about problems. The best way to find different pairing partners is attending meetings organized by our local user groups or technical communities. There are also an increasing number of developers willing to set up remote pair-programming sessions in whatever we want to work with. There are plenty of tools out there that can make a remote pairing session very smooth.

We need to keep our minds open to new ideas when pairing. Sometimes we learn, sometimes we teach, and sometimes we do both.

SOCIALIZE

> Not only individuals and interactions, but also a community of
> professionals.

The idea that software developers are introverted nerds is totally outdated. Finding other developers whom we can bounce ideas off of, pair-program, and network is almost essential for a successful career. A great and easy way to do that is to join your local user groups and technical communities and to participate in their events. They normally promote free talks, coding activities, and social events. Another great aspect of being part of a community is the feeling that we are not alone. User groups and technical communities tend to be extremely open and welcoming. We find developers from many different backgrounds, working for completely different industries, with different technologies, languages, and processes. Some developers are more experienced than others but there is one thing they all share: passion. The great thing about passionate developers is that they are constantly learning and are very happy to share what they know.

Being a member of a local user group or technical community is a fantastic way to learn and share ideas.

DELIBERATE DISCOVERY

> I'm the smartest man in Athens because I know that
> I know nothing.
> —Socrates

The biggest mistake that software professionals can make is not accepting that they don't know what they don't know. Not knowing what we don't know is also called *second-level ignorance*. Accepting that we have a lot to learn is a sign of maturity and one of the first steps toward mastery.

The vast majority of us have a natural tendency to be positive and optimistic. An example of that is how bad we are at estimating tasks. Once tasks are completed, if we compare the amount of time they took to our original estimations, we will see that the majority of them took longer than we expected. We need to accept that there is a massive chance that things will not go according to plan, which means there will be unforeseen and unpredictable problems. Unfortunately, we have absolutely no idea when, where, or how. The consequence of us ignoring this fact is that we will be caught by surprise and will not be able to handle the problems as well as we could if we knew about them upfront.

There is not a magical way to completely solve this problem but we can try to minimize it. One way of doing this is to constantly expose ourselves to situations where we can learn something new about the context we are in. This is very important mainly in the early days of a project or before building a major set of new features—when we are most ignorant about what we need to do. Spending time trying to identify and minimize our ignorance across all the axes we can think of can be time extremely well spent.

Ignorance is a constant. Imagine we could start our latest project from scratch again. Same people, same requirements, same organizational constraints, same everything, but the difference this time is that we would start with all the knowledge we already have. How long do you think it would take? Now, stop and think about it. When asking this question, usually the answers average between one half and one quarter of the original time and that's where my own answer would be as well. Ignorance is the single greatest impediment to throughput, meaning that if we reduce the level of our ignorance as fast as we can, we can be far more productive and efficient.

We should always try to create opportunities where we can learn something we don't know. "But if I don't know what I don't know, how can I create opportunities to learn that?" you may ask. Speak to random colleagues and ask them how they keep up with the progress in our industry. Go to technical community and user group events. Show your code to other people. Ask for help even when you think you don't need it. Try to figure out which aspects of your current project you and your team have not explored yet, then start discussions about it or even write a proof of concept. Aiming to remove the ignorance constraint should always be your priority in order to deliver projects more efficiently and grow as professionals.

WORK-LIFE BALANCE

So far I have been saying how important it is to look after our careers and that we should dedicate loads of time outside working hours to practice and learn. However, we all have family, friends, and other interests in life. I have a wife and two kids, whom I love to bits and want to spend a lot of quality time with. It is never easy to balance work and personal life because we spend more than 50 percent of our waking hours at work, including all the time commuting to and from it.

The most common thing I hear every time I talk about investing time in our own careers outside working hours is, "I don't have time." And if you say or agree with that, you are probably right. That's what you decided to believe and that, in turn, became your reality. But the truth is, we all have time. We are just not very good at optimizing it. Maybe we prefer to spend our time with something else that may or may not be as important as our careers.

Stop reading now and think about what you did yesterday, from the time you woke up to when you went to bed. What did you do the day before yesterday? Seriously. Stop and really think about that. Now think about how much of it was waste? How much of it was productive? By productive we can mean many things, from learning something new to spending time with our loved ones. If you took some time to rest, this is also important, especially after a busy day or a busy week. Our bodies need to recharge and we should cater to that as well. Some people genuinely do not have a lot of time. I once met a German speaker at a conference who told me he had a wife and five kids. Talking about learning and practicing outside working hours, he told me that his only alternative was to be very smart in how he uses the very limited amount of time he has. Despite his tough situation, he managed to present at a conference.

CREATING TIME

Quite often, lack of time is used as an excuse for our own laziness. People are different. Some live in large cities, some in small villages, some have family, and some live on their own. Some people have hobbies. Some love going to the gym. Some are young and love going out with friends; others are older and prefer to stay at home. Some are morning people; some go to bed very late and hate to wake up early. By no means do the following tips apply to everyone; they are just a collection of things that we can do to create time and use it to invest in our careers.

I realized that I used to waste a lot of time in front of the TV, aimlessly browsing the Internet, checking all the uninteresting things my friends publish on social networks, playing computer games, or watching sports. I decided to cut down on the number of hours spent on these things. That doesn't mean I don't do them anymore. It just means that I do them in moderation. Although they are great ways to relax and switch off, we do not need to do them every night, all night.

Your local coffee shop is your friend. Find a coffee shop near your workplace with a good Internet connection. If there isn't one, find one along the way. Even if your company has a coffee area, I would avoid that since we can be tempted to do work during this time or may be interrupted by colleagues. Take one day a week and try to get to a coffee shop one or two hours before you start working. Use this time to write code, read a technical book, blogs, or whatever you think you need to do to learn and move your career forward.

Lunchtime is another great opportunity we have to practice and learn something new. Once or twice a week just grab a sandwich and your laptop, and go somewhere quiet. It is amazing what we can do in such a small period of time when we are focused.

Check if there is a user group or tech community in your city and join them. Usually user groups meet regularly; many operate on a monthly schedule. Make a commitment to go to the meetings at least once or twice a month. Meetings tend to last between one to three hours so I'm sure the vast majority of us can plan for that. The advantage of attending user group meetings is that we usually can learn a huge amount in a very short period of time, either from a presentation or from speaking or coding with other developers. There is a limit to what we can learn on our own. Although we all feel we can learn anything, sometimes we don't know where to start. It's also worth remembering that it can be a lot faster to learn something from someone with more experience than trying to learn on our own.

Go to bed 30 minutes earlier than normal and use this time to read a book, look at blogs, or watch technical screencasts before falling asleep. This is something that works really well for me. Every single night I try to read at least a few pages, regardless of the time I go to bed.

Buy yourself a Kindle, iPad, or another e-book reader, and carry it with you at all times. Use it every time you have some dead time, like commuting or waiting for your dentist, doctor, or hairdresser appointment.

I believe every developer has a good smartphone today but if you do not have one, buy one now. Use Twitter or any other information aggregator when you have a break or dead time. This is a great way to quickly read something or keep up with the latest news and trends. Being able to go to a single place and get all the information you want is key when you want to optimize time.

FOCUS: THE POMODORO TECHNIQUE

In order to use our time outside working hours wisely, it is extremely important that we focus. A good technique is to decide beforehand what we want to do before we actually use this time slot. It is like deciding the agenda before scheduling a meeting. It does not need to be strict, but we need at least to have a good idea of what we want to achieve. Once this is done, we must ensure we can focus and get it done. One way we can achieve this is by using the Pomodoro technique. There are five basic steps to implement this technique:

1. Decide on the task to be done.
2. Set the Pomodoro (timer) to 25 minutes.
3. Work on the task until the timer rings.
4. Take a short break (normally 5 minutes).
5. Every four "Pomodoros," take a longer break (15–30 minutes).

During a Pomodoro (25 minutes), we focus on the task and nothing else. The breaks between Pomodoros are for a quick rest, coffee, checking emails, making a phone call, checking your Twitter, or whatever you feel like. We should do whatever we can to finish the Pomodoro with no interruptions but in case it needs to be interrupted (there is an important call we need to take or we really need to speak to someone), then the Pomodoro must be terminated and not paused. A new one should be created when we are ready to work on the task again. There are many Pomodoro tools available out there. Some are very sophisticated where you can keep track of all the tasks you completed, interrupted Pomodoros, and many other statistics. I, personally, prefer the simple ones but feel free to use one that suits you better.

BALANCE

Whatever you do, a sustainable pace is key. Keeping a healthy work-life balance is tough but not impossible. If you are the type of person that says, "I don't want to touch a computer outside work," you probably should think again about your career choice; maybe software development is not for you. For the majority of us, software development—besides being our job—is also a hobby, which makes it relatively easy to find enough spare time to practice and better ourselves.

Keeping our professional life healthy is essential for a healthy family life. An unhealthy professional life, where we are constantly worried about not being paid well, or that we may not find another well-paid and interesting job if we are made redundant, may seriously damage our personal lives. Being at the top of our game, with good connections and with skills that are in demand in the market, puts us in a good position not to worry too much about our professional lives and give our family and friends the attention they very much deserve.

SUMMARY

Owning our careers is hard. We need to put a lot of effort into getting to a position where we can say, "I feel confident I can find a good and well-paid job whenever I want." Determination and passion are essential for a successful career as a software craftsman. However, without focus, much of our efforts are wasted. We need to learn how to keep ourselves up to date and how to practice. We need to learn how to use our time well. The day we stop learning and practicing is the day we start losing control of our careers. The more knowledge and skills we have, the easier it is to own our careers—that means we are able to choose where, when, and for whom to work, and how much to charge for our services.

Time should never be used as an excuse for not doing certain things. Ever. We all have time. In fact, we all have exactly the same amount of time. The difference is how we choose to spend our time.

HEROES, GOODWILL, AND PROFESSIONALISM

Back in the 1990s, I got a job in a big multinational company. After two years working for small software houses and a long selection process, I had the feeling that I had found my dream job. We were creating an enterprise resource planning system (ERP) similar to SAP ERP, and our clients were governments and very large international companies. The team was extremely talented and the project was massive compared to everything I had done before. I was quite intimidated by the skills of the developers on the team. They all seemed much better than me, making me feel like I had to prove myself. I had to show why I deserved a place in that team. Our team was the *architecture team,* responsible for the development of the core components of the system, the communication infrastructure, a middleware layer, code generation (porting Natural code to Delphi), and supporting the *business teams,* who were responsible for the business features and user interface.

With more than a hundred developers working on the code base, the project felt enormous. A lot of the back-end code was being developed in a proprietary language and database, running on the mainframe, and the middleware was written in C++. The only thing I could understand a little bit was the client, written in Delphi. Also, I quickly learned that my Delphi knowledge was not adequate either.

The project had started more than ten years before I joined and the majority of the effort was to port a big part of the system from mainframe to Windows, an effort that had started around two years before I joined. There were also initial talks about moving the system to the web, a massive undertaking for the teams, since they were mostly mainframe developers that had just started learning Delphi. Developers had nothing else to compare the application to since that would be the first large web project in that department. All the pressure was on our team to make this transition less challenging.

The project was being developed in the typical waterfall fashion and during the two and a half years that I spent there, I never spoke to or even met any of our clients. I don't think any of the developers ever met a client. Managers and a few other people were constantly imposing deadlines on us; I had no idea who some of these other people were or what they did. Although I never had access to the real numbers, I learned from conversations over coffee, that the contracts contained extremely large numbers representing payments and fines, and panic was the default mode every time a client wanted a new installation or version upgrade of our software.

The company employed quite a few developers (including myself) who lived about one hundred kilometers from São Paulo (where the company was), and so they provided us with a coach bus for the commute. For that I had to wake up at 5 A.M. and be at the pickup point at 5:30 A.M. I usually would be back home around 8 P.M. Because overtime was not uncommon, quite often we had to stay late in the office and I would end up missing my coach home, having to travel via public transport and getting home way past midnight.

Things got really ugly. We had this crazy deadline to deliver one module of our system to the Israeli government. Due to the time-zone difference and the level of desperation, we had to work quite late. I decided to drive to work everyday, 90 minutes each leg, because I knew I would not be able to get on the coach. The company would not pay for my gas or road tolls, as they were already providing the free coach. In two months, we worked more than 24 hours in a row more often than I could count. On those occasions, I knew I had to be back in the office in a few hours and I was too tired to face a 90-minute drive so I slept inside my car in the company's car park. Three or four times, we were at our desks for more than 36 hours, with a sleeping break of between two to five hours inside the car. Twice I woke up with people knocking on my car's window to ask me questions. Of course we were never paid any overtime. Finally, after many discussions with the company, they decided to pay for a hotel room nearby.

Many friends from the business teams were telling me that what we were doing on the architecture team was ridiculous: working so many hours, sleeping in the car, and not even being paid overtime. "What are you doing, man? Why do you put up with it?" they would say. But in my head, I just couldn't see it. I was single, living on my own, and loving my job. Above all, I wanted to show what I was capable of and that we could save the project. We wanted to be heroes. In my head, I was learning a lot, enjoying the company of my experienced teammates, and doing what I loved the most—writing good and quality code. My teammates also felt the same way. We were all exhausted, but deep inside, we were enjoying it.

Today, when I look back, I understand how crazy that was. We were not acting professionally. We never asked why we were doing certain things. We never tried to understand what the clients really wanted so that we could potentially offer different alternatives. Although we never had access to the clients, we never questioned the requirements either. We never said that it would be impossible. We just got on with our jobs because we thought we were being professionals.

Deep down, we also wanted a bit of recognition and fame. We wanted to be seen as the guys who saved the project. The guys who did the impossible. Well, at the end, all that effort was for nothing. The deadlines were moved and no one in the business really cared about how hard we worked. We didn't become famous. We were still just a bunch of low-paid developers. We managed to deliver the majority of the things that were asked but for some reason, which was never explained, they decided to move the deadline. The salesmen and businesspeople were at home, with their families, working normal hours during the whole time. We, the developers, were the only ones working like donkeys to make people we didn't even know look good. With a very top-down, command and control structure, most decisions were invisible to us. We were just the factory workers doing the heavy lifting. But we really felt good about that. Our team was awesome and it was a pleasure to work with so many talented guys.

Today, I know that what we did was wrong. It hurts me to remember how we were treated. It hurts me to know that this situation is still very common, mainly in countries that do offshore work. It frustrates me to know that we didn't act professionally—we never questioned why we were doing certain things or what the real problem was. We never tried to provide an alternative. We allowed ourselves to be treated as factory workers. We behaved like factory workers and we enjoyed it. We really did the company and ourselves a disservice. We made loads of mistakes during those long hours, including wiping out the entire production database at 3 A.M. We created things that were totally unnecessary. We had a very poor understanding of the real issues and did not create situations where we could provide better solutions. We allowed ourselves to be deprived of a personal life and even ended up discriminating against those who decided not to sleep in the car park or *just* work 12 hours a day. We were not acting professionally because we never said *NO*.

LEARNING HOW TO SAY NO

More often than not, we have tight deadlines and a lot of pressure from our managers to meet them. Many of these deadlines are unrealistic and imposed on developers by managers who can be very aggressive in trying to make sure that things are delivered on time. Developers, mainly the young ones, tend to succumb to such pressure and end up saying they will get things done by the imposed date, either because they are afraid to go against their managers or because they want to avoid confrontation. Even knowing deep inside that it will be almost impossible to deliver all the features by the imposed date, developers end up agreeing and committing to it.

The outcome of this is usually very bad. Systems are deployed into production full of bugs, clients become unhappy, and trust disappears. Even after working really hard, many hours a day, and sacrificing time with their loved ones, developers still get the heat for poor system performance. The very same manager who pushed them to do what they knew was impossible, while he was at home enjoying his weekend with his family, will blame their incompetence. "How the hell did you break the validation on the sign-up page? Why isn't the system performing well? How on earth is the system not able to process more than 10,000 transactions per minute? How could you forget about this edge case?"

AN EPIC FAILURE

I once worked for a large telecommunications company. The marketing team wanted to announce this brand-new mobile portal we were developing. They wanted to launch it simultaneously in three different countries and their estimation was that a small percentage of their customers would use the application from day one. Even being a small percentage, the company had almost 20 million customers in the three countries combined, so we were talking about a few hundred thousand customers. We did not know it. Our manager came to us and said he wanted the application done by a certain date and although we knew it was a few months away, we were almost certain we would not be able to deliver everything he was asking for. So, in one of our first meetings, we told him that we probably would not meet the deadline he was asking for. He said we had to and he was sure that if we worked hard we would be able to pull it off. We were not happy but he was saying that we did not have an option, so we said we would do it and *try our best.*

Week by week the manager and a business analyst asked for more and more features but the deadline did not move. We, more than once, told them we were already struggling with the existing requirements, let alone taking on new ones. However, they would come back to us and say the marketing team had already started the marketing campaign in all three countries and was advertising all the features.

We told them the marketing team should get our estimations first and asked if we could speak to them in order to see if we could come up with an agreement on which features we really had to deliver and negotiate the scope of a few other features. We had a few ideas that could potentially make some features much smaller or even unnecessary. The manager said he was our contact point and he was fully aware of all of the marketing team's needs, so there was no point in speaking to them. "No, there is no negotiation, unfortunately. You need to implement everything," he said. From all the conversations we had with him, we thought our only option was to get on with it and work as many hours as we could. What else could we do?

We spent a few weeks working long hours and weekends. Of course when I say we, I am talking about the developers. The manager and the business analyst were nowhere to be seen after six o'clock and almost never available on the phone on weekends. Since the beginning of the project, we mentioned that we had to do some infrastructure work. We needed to have a production-like environment and to prepare some load-testing infrastructure. They said no and that we should just focus on building the business features because they had to demo them to the marketing team. Less than a month before the go-live date, we told them that we had to stop working on business features and focus on some technical work to guarantee that the application would behave well in production, but that meant we would not be able to deliver some of the business features they wanted. The answer was *no* again. We had to finish all of the business features. "Guys, this is the last push and I know you can do it," our manager said. We told him we wanted to speak to the people on the marketing team, people we had not met once since the beginning of the project, but yet again, the answer was no. With the deadline approaching, and with so much work already put into it, we just said, "Sure, we will do it."

The day finally came. It was a Monday morning and the application went live. Our last deployment to production had been just a few hours before. We were tired and wanted the whole thing to be over but at the same time we were extremely proud of ourselves, knowing that we had saved the project. We would be considered heroes. We even had conversations in the middle of the night, during a coffee break, about asking for pay raises and promotions.

The system went live and in less than an hour, the application went down. It couldn't cope with the load. After three hours we managed to bring it up again but after a few more hours it went down again. This cycle was repeated many times during the following five days, and we had everyone looking over our shoulders, including some guys from the marketing team (hey, we finally met them) while we were trying to figure out what the hell was going on in the system. Tests? No, we had very few. Who has time to write tests under such pressure? Even with a very small team, the code was a mess, making every change extremely painful and difficult to test because we had to re-test almost everything manually.

In summary, the company got loads of complaints from their customers. We managed to stabilize all the features after a few weeks but, of course, instead of pay raises and promotions, the development team got a bad reputation. The manager, when questioned by the marketing team, said that we, the developers, had told him we could do it and he was relying on our commitment and technical skills. He was not writing the code, was he? It couldn't have been his fault.

In one of the aftermath meetings, the marketing team told us that if they had known we could not deliver certain things and we had had our doubts the system would not support the load, they would definitely have de-scoped a few things. The reason that they had been asking for more things was that they thought we had the capacity to implement them and we had the nonfunctional requirements under control. They were never told otherwise.

In the end, the majority of us left the company almost at the same time, forcing them to hire new developers very quickly and with no time to select the best candidates. This caused them an even bigger problem because the new developers were totally unaware of all the pitfalls of the fragile system we left behind. The second version of the application was scheduled to be released in three months' time but, from what I've heard, it took almost nine months to be released.

LESSON LEARNED

In the story above, we can immediately say that the manager did not act professionally. We can say he never cared about the team and was just trying to get his own promotion while other people were doing the hard work for him. We can say it was his entire fault and he should be fired. We can also say that the developers should have stood up for themselves and told everyone how the manager behaved and how hard they worked to make the project a success. Well, we can say whatever we want, but saying anything after that epic failure was of no use. It was already too late. It didn't matter anymore.

Unfortunately, we—the developers—could have avoided the entire situation, and we should be blamed. We did not act professionally either. We should have never said we would *try* to do something we already knew was impossible. Even if we believed that it could be possible to have all the features deployed into production, we would still not have all the tests in place and all the confidence that the system would behave well. Besides not feeling comfortable to confront our manager and hating the whole situation, there was something inside us that was pushing us to accept it. Deep inside we wanted to show how good we were. We had a feeling that, although we knew it would be hard, there was a small chance to pull it off and we could be heroes. We would be recognized as the guys who made a successful marketing campaign viable. Deep inside, we wanted to give it a go.

In this situation, we should have never said we would try and never even thought about being heroes. We should have pressured our manager to speak to the marketing team from the beginning. We should have identified that our manager was not being transparent with the marketing team when he constantly asked for more features, knowing we did not have capacity. We should have documented via email every time we had a meeting where we told him we did not have capacity and that we also had to prepare the system for production load. Although very badly, our manager was trying to do his job: getting features delivered. We should have done our job better by being realistic and not accepting the responsibility of delivering something when we knew it would be of low quality and not ready for production. We should have made it very clear we would not commit to anything if we did not have a meeting, all of us, with the marketing team when new features began to be introduced. We should have made it very clear that a system full of features is worthless if it is down and cannot be used by anyone. We did not act professionally by thinking we could be heroes. We should have said *no*.

BEING PROFESSIONAL

Very often we have to deal with very hard deadlines. The best way to deal with them is to analyze everything that needs to be done and communicate all the possible risks we see and concerns we may have. We should raise our concerns and highlight all the uncomfortable and unclear points as soon as possible. Most important, we need to state how much we could confidently deliver by the expected date. By confidently deliver, I mean code that is tested and intensively tried in a production-like environment.

When developers say they cannot confidently deliver all the features by an imposed deadline, managers do not always take that seriously. A negotiation between managers and developers takes place, but with lack of negotiation skills and ill-prepared arguments, developers usually succumb to the pressure. Some managers can be very persuasive in getting developers to commit to a tough deadline. "Guys, you know how important this is. I know it will be tough but I trust you. We really need to get this done. I'm sure if you guys work hard you will be able to deliver." In order to avoid confrontation or to demonstrate a can-do attitude, developers respond: "OK. We will try our best."

When we say we are going to try, two things normally happen: the person or people we say that to will understand that we are going to deliver it. For them, "*trying*" is equal to "*yes, it will be done.*" The other thing is that we are explicitly saying that we do not normally work hard. It is almost like saying we are normally saving energy and we could use it to speed up at any point in time.

If we know it will be almost impossible to deliver all the features before a deadline, how can we tell our managers we are going to try to deliver them? What does *try* mean? Does it mean we can deliver everything if we work harder? Does it mean we are committed to work far more hours, including weekends? If yes, would that really make a difference? If not, it either means we do not normally work hard enough or that we are just lying.

In *The Passionate Programmer,* Chad Fowler says that saying yes to avoid disappointment is just lying. He even goes further to say that saying yes is an addictive and destructive habit. It's a bad habit masquerading as a good one.

We usually do not like to say no. It sounds wrong. When we say no, we feel like we have failed and do not want to contribute. We feel that we are not being good team players and the last thing we want to do is to disappoint our colleagues. We want to succeed and we want to give our best shot. Although this looks very positive, it is also very selfish. We need to remember that when we say yes, people will take that into account and make plans based on it. Our bosses will make promises to their own bosses, other teams, customers, or partners based on what we said. Not being honest and transparent may cause huge damage to the entire company. Professionalism means being honest with ourselves, with our teammates, and with our managers and customers.

Sometimes we may feel that our manager is not being transparent with her boss—or whoever is paying for the project—about the current situation of the project. We may feel she is not making other people aware of our concerns, always telling them that everything is going well. We should ask her if that is really the case. If the situation is really getting bad, we should notify her that we will escalate the issue if she refuses to notify her boss, and once her boss is notified, we will arrange a meeting with everyone to discuss what can be done. Although this may sound wrong and aggressive, we will be doing a favor to the team, to the company, and sometimes even to our own bosses. Negotiation is a skill we all need to learn. In the same way our managers are doing their jobs, we should do ours—making hard decisions and not avoiding necessary confrontations. As long as we do it in an honest and transparent way, there is a big chance that no one will get hurt and the whole team and the company will win.

PROVIDING OPTIONS

Always saying no is also not a professional attitude. Every no, ideally, should be followed by a list of alternatives. Before saying no, we need to analyze the problem and provide options. Although we may not always be able to come up with viable options, we should at least brainstorm ideas. Sometimes an incomplete idea can help other people to find a different alternative. At the end of the day, we should all focus on solving the problem, regardless of which solution we choose or who proposed it.

Saying no without providing options does not help much because the person receiving our answer will not be able to do much with it. I remember a tale I used to hear when I was younger where the boss, who had just arrived in town, asked two of his assistants to buy him an orange juice. The first one rushed outside to the juice shop around the corner, asked for an orange juice, and within five minutes she was back saying to her boss that the shop did not have oranges. The second one took around 20 minutes to come back, and before she said anything, the boss said, "I already know that the shop does not have orange juice, so why did you take so long to come back to me?" "Yes," she said. "They don't have orange juice but they have pineapple and apple juice. The pineapple juice is fresh but the apple juice is bottled. I also asked around and discovered that there is a supermarket a little bit further away where I could buy some fresh oranges and could make you a fresh juice. I can get you a pineapple or apple juice in five minutes or, if you prefer, I can make you a fresh orange juice in 30 minutes. I just need to know which one you prefer."

The first assistant, although having returned quite quickly, left the boss with nothing. He would need to figure out for himself how to solve his problem without an in-depth knowledge of the area. The second assistant gave him options and now he could make a call which one was the best alternative for him. A can-do attitude is always appreciated and, even when we say no, we should always be striving to say yes.

Sometimes there are problems that we simply don't know how to solve. When this is the case, we should say it as honestly and as quickly as possible. We should also demonstrate we are willing to investigate the problem and give our best shot at solving it, making it clear we are not making any promises besides sharing whatever we learn. Providing updates of our progress as often as we can is our best option; it enables the team to decide what to do with every piece of new information. With new information, the team can contribute with other ideas and also offer help in areas in which they might have a better understanding than we do. This behavior will make the whole team really trust us when we say we know something. Being honest, no matter how bad the situation is, is a sign of professionalism.

AN UNEXPECTED AND VIABLE OPTION

Not long ago I was working on a project for an investment bank. The project was about reporting trades to regulators. The deadline was set externally, by the regulators, so there was nothing that anyone in the bank could do about it. The penalties for not meeting the deadline would vary from steep fines to not being able to trade certain products anymore, which would cause massive damage to the reputation of the organization.

We had a very talented team and we worked hard to meet the deadlines. However, at some point we realized that we could not deliver all the mandatory requirements—we would not be able to automate the process of reporting all types of trades that were expected by the regulators.

The business was pressuring us to work extra hours, possibly weekends, since there was too much at stake. All the investment banks in the United Kingdom were going through the same process and the new regulation was all over the financial news. The business reiterated that negotiating scope or deadlines was pointless because no one could do anything about them. Either we report, or we pay fines and have our reputation damaged.

The regulators' requirements were about reporting trades that would meet a certain criteria for the first deadline. There were other deadlines already announced for trades meeting different criteria. Because we knew our application would keep growing, relaxing the practices and coding standards we had in order to meet the first deadline was not an option. This would cause us to decrease the quality of our code base, which in turn would make meeting the future deadlines for the other types of trades much harder.

Although we committed to work extra hours during the week, we told the business that we would not be working over the weekends, and adding more people to the team at that stage, as it was suggested at some point, would just make the situation worse. We kept updating the business on our progress on a daily basis, and we constantly showed them that the deadline would not be met. They could see where we were with the work by just looking at our Kanban board. We also, after two or three weeks working extra hours, told them we would not work extra hours anymore.

Needless to say, panic was starting to take over and everyone was extremely worried about the consequences of not meeting the deadline. Sticking to our decisions and not succumbing to the pressure from the business was extremely tough for us. But we did it. We knew that lowering our standards and working seven days a week would burn us out, jeopardizing the project as a whole.

To our advantage, we were running the project in an Agile fashion and we had a whiteboard where the entire team could see the work in progress, as well as everything that was blocking us and all the bottlenecks. The backlog was also shared and visible to the entire team. The visualization of the work in progress and the work to be done helped the business to understand the exact situation we were in and helped us to convince them that, even if we decided to work seven days a week, we would still not meet the deadlines.

It is a liberating feeling when we are able to say no from day one and to be transparent with the business. It frees everyone to look for other viable options. It turned out that the regulators had two ways to receive the trade reports. The first one was the automated way, where the system we were building would receive all the trade messages generated by the front office systems, and then analyze, enrich, transform, and send them to the regulators. The second was a manual upload, where banks could generate comma-separated value (CSV) files and manually upload them by using an interface provided by the regulators. Before the project started, the second option was discarded straightaway because of the high volume of trades, making it nearly impossible to process and upload them manually.

We were working against the first option but as we knew the system would not be finished on time for all the types of trades we had to report, we started analyzing how viable the manual solution was. We knew it was not an option at the beginning of the project but now it was different. As we had already automated the majority of the flows for the majority of trades, there were not many types of trades left in terms of volume. With this in mind, we analyzed how trades could be manually processed and uploaded, allocating (or potentially hiring) some people to do it full time. By comparing the costs of not reporting those trades against having some people dedicated to do the manual upload work for the flows that had not been automated yet, the latter became the most viable option for the business. With this decision, even with a few problems here and there, we managed to go live and meet the regulators' deadline.

If we had not said no and had not been transparent to our managers, we would have gone with the option of trying to be heroes and potentially not delivering some of the requirements, causing the company a massive loss. Saying *no* freed our minds to focus on different approaches and find other solutions to our problem.

The mix of automated and manual solutions described above, although not ideal, allowed us to go live and meet all the regulators' requirements. It also gave us some time to automate the manual process after we went live, without lowering or relaxing our practices and code standard. We could release all the newly automated flows in small increments and have a good degree of confidence that they would work as expected.

ENLIGHTENED MANAGERS

Good managers understand that they are part of the team and need to work with the developers toward the common goal. There is no "us and them" attitude. They must understand clearly what the current state of the project is and work with the team to figure out roughly what they will be able to achieve within a period of time.

Managers should appreciate when we say we cannot deliver some features. Although that may be bad news, that information will help to avoid a much bigger problem. Transparency helps managers and the team to prepare for tough situations. Raising the red flag as early as possible, indicating that something is wrong, allows the team and all people involved to be pragmatic and come up with alternative solutions. It frees people to be creative in order to solve the problem. If we manage to deliver what we promised when we said yes, managers will be far more inclined to trust us when we say no.

Smart people know that they do not know everything and they also know that in a team game, we need to rely on all the members of the team. As the saying goes, a team is just as strong as its weakest link. Enlightened managers understand and expect that certain things are not easy to do or may take a long time to be done. They appreciate when they are challenged and different options are suggested. This attitude shows that everyone is working as a team toward a common goal. With more information and a few proposed solutions, managers feel more confident to choose the best solution to the problem, making the people that made the suggestions stand out.

Good managers are part of the team. They stay with the team during good and bad times. If everyone is committed to work extra hours, they should be there as well, even if just to buy the pizzas, give moral support, and crack a few jokes every now and again. The team feels better knowing that everyone is in the same boat, feeling the same pain or enjoying success. This type of environment helps people to focus on doing whatever they can to make things happen. Good managers shield developers from external pressure, do whatever they can to remove any impediments the team may have, and help the team to feel comfortable and confident to get their job done. Managers should be harmony ambassadors and it is their job to keep the team healthy, happy, and united.

SUMMARY

Being professional and satisfying our clients does not mean doing everything they ask us to do. Our job is to help our clients to figure out what their real needs are and also advise them on the best way to approach them. A professional has ethics, and a code of conduct. A good professional would never do something that could be harmful to a client just because the client is paying for it. Clients very rarely understand the full impact of certain decisions on a software project, and it is our job to make them aware of it. It is our job to say *no* to our clients when they ask us for something we know is not going to work or that is not going to be done by a certain deadline. This is the same thing we would expect from a good lawyer, accountant, or doctor. We don't tell these professionals what to do or how to do their jobs. They wouldn't let us anyway. We go to these professionals with a problem (or a need) and we expect them to use their experience to explain which options we have and what their respective risks are. We expect them to give us enough information so that we can make informed decisions. But if we push them to do something that goes against what they think is right, they would simply say no. And that's exactly what we should do.

WORKING 6 SOFTWARE

One of the first things said by the nonbelievers of the Software Craftsmanship movement was that good and clean code is not enough to guarantee the success of a project. And, yes, they are absolutely right. There are innumerable reasons for what may cause a software project to fail, ranging from bad business strategy, competitors' superiority, bad project management, high costs, time to market, partnerships, technical limitations, and integrations—just to mention a few. Due to the number of important things a software project may have, organizations tend not to pay too much attention to things that are considered *less* important, like the quality of the software being developed. Some organizations believe that with a good management team, deep hierarchies, micromanagement, strict process, and a large amount of *good* documentation, the project will succeed. Many organizations see software development as a production line where the workers (developers) are viewed as lesser skilled than their "highly qualified" and well-paid managers. Software development is then outsourced to workers in cheap countries since, in their view, if they produce good requirements in well-formatted Word documents and well-crafted diagrams, quality software will simply emerge. With a strong emphasis on top-down, command and control management, software development is treated as a detail. Very rarely will companies like that be able to attract or retain good software developers, leaving their entire business in the hands of mediocre professionals.

Traditional managers and business consultants can say whatever they want about the importance of a good process and documentation, but the truth is that in a software project, the most important deliverable is the software itself. Anything else is secondary. Fortunately, our industry seems to be evolving and gradually we are all learning from our mistakes, and more companies are realizing the importance of having great people working collaboratively.

In this chapter I discuss why working software is not enough and the invisible impacts of bad software. I also discuss how a change in attitude can help developers to deal with existing legacy systems and avoid the creation of more low-quality software.

WORKING SOFTWARE IS NOT ENOUGH

In the Agile Manifesto, we have **working software over comprehensive documentation**. There are also two principles that mention working software:

3. Deliver **working software** frequently, from a couple of weeks to a couple of months, with a preference to the shorter timescale.

7. **Working software** is the primary measure of progress.

This is absolutely great and we all agree with these principles. The problem here is that over the years, the idea of working software moved away from *high-quality* working software, and many *Agile* projects are producing code that is way below the standards expected from a real Agile project. All that legacy code you need to deal with on a daily basis counts as working software. Imagine all those applications that take us a long time to add a new feature to. All those applications we are scared to touch. All those applications that are fragile or tightly coupled. And what about those applications without an extensive test suite, where we are forced to test manually? What about those applications that we need to deploy into user acceptance testing (UAT) if we wanted to test it because we cannot run it locally? They are all working software.

So, what does "working software" mean? Can we consider the applications described above as working software? Is working software enough? Is it acceptable to deliver something that took a long time to build and had to go through a long period of manual testing and bug fixing? And the story is repeated for every new feature? Has quality been forgotten or just naively taken for granted?

LOOKING AFTER OUR GARDEN

> Rather than construction, programming is more
> like gardening.
> —The Pragmatic Programmer

Code is organic, not mechanical. Like a garden, code needs constant maintenance. For a garden to look beautiful all year round, we need to look after its soil, constantly remove weeds, regularly water it, remove some dead plants, plant new ones, and trim or rearrange existing ones so they can stay healthy, looking nice and whole. With basic and regular maintenance, the garden will always look great but if we neglect it, even for a short period of time, it will require much more effort to make it look good again. The longer we neglect it, the harder we will need to work to bring it to a state we can enjoy again. Code is no different. If we don't look after it constantly, the code starts to deteriorate as changes and new features are added. Bad design choices, lack of tests, and poor use of languages and tools will make the code rot faster. Gradually, other parts of the code will also be contaminated up to the point that the whole code base is extremely ill, making it painful and costly to maintain it.

THE INVISIBLE THREAT

When starting a new project, everything is great. With a nonexistent code base, developers can quickly start creating new features without the fear of breaking or changing any existing code. Testers are happy because everything they need to test is new, meaning that they don't need to worry about regression tests. Managers can see new features delivered at a fast rate. However, the team is composed of average developers, selected by matching a set of keywords against their CVs and salary expectations, and it is structured and treated like a production line. As time goes by, things become messier, bugs start to appear (some with no apparent explanation), and features start taking longer and longer to be developed and tested. Very slowly, the time to deliver anything starts to stretch out. But this is a slow process. Slow enough that it takes months, sometimes over a year or two, to be noticed by management.

It's very common to see projects where, at the beginning, a feature of size X takes N number of days to be implemented. Over time, as more bad code is added to the application, another feature, roughly the same size X, will take much longer to be implemented than it used to take at the beginning of the project. As the quality of the code decreases, the amount of time to implement a new feature, fix a bug, or make a change increases (see Figure 6.1). The lower the quality, the higher the number of bugs, and the harder it is to test. The lower the quality, the less robust and reliable the application becomes.

Interestingly, some people say that they don't have time to do it properly, but it seems that they always find a way to justify the amount of time and money spent on long testing and bug-fixing phases. "This is how software projects are," they say. "First there is a construction phase, then there is the testing and stabilization phases. Every software project is like that, isn't it?"

Hostage of Your Own Software

When the code base gets into the situation where changes or additional features take too long to be implemented and developers are scared to touch the existing code, action must be taken immediately. This is a very dangerous situation to be in because business progress is being impeded or delayed by software instead of being helped by it.

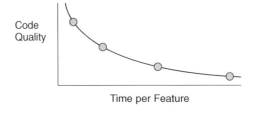

Figure 6.1 The relationship between code quality and time spent on implementing each feature over time

In order to increase business agility and have a good return on investment, keeping code quality high is paramount.

The cost of dealing with bad code can make companies less competitive—the cost of implementing new features or making the desired changes can be prohibitive. It is totally unacceptable to have bad quality code affecting business decisions.

The biggest problem here is that bad code is invisible to everyone besides the developers. Other members of the team only realize that something is wrong when it is too late. That means it is the developers' responsibility to look after the quality of the code. Sometimes developers expose the problem to project managers, but the request to have some time to *refactor* the code is often ignored by managers for various reasons, including their lack of understanding of the impacts of bad code, and the developers' inability to explain it. It is worth noting that when developers get to a point where they need to ask for some formal time to do refactoring, this means that for one reason or another, they neglected the code at some point in the past.

HIRE CRAFTSMEN, NOT AVERAGE DEVELOPERS

With the amount of literature, tools, techniques, methodologies, and the infinite amount of information available on the web, it is just unacceptable to have a team of developers that can let the code rot. Craftsmen are gardeners. They are constantly looking after the code base, quickly refactoring it without fear—they are backed by a good battery of automated tests that can test the entire application in just a few minutes. Time constraints or change in requirements will never be used as an excuse for bad code because they would have used good design principles and techniques throughout the application life span. Having an empowered team of craftsmen can be the difference between success and failure of any software project. Our industry is finally learning that quality code may not guarantee the success of a project, but it can definitely be the main cause of its failure.

THE WRONG NOTION OF TIME

No one wakes up in the morning and says, "Today, I'm going to screw up. Today, I'm going to piss my boss and my entire team off writing the worst code I could possibly write." If no one does that (well, I've met a few people that actually did, but that's another story), why are Agile projects failing? Why do we still have the same old problems?

A TECHNICAL DEBT STORY

Some time ago I was working with a development team and one of the developers was working on a brand-new feature. For the implementation of this new feature, we did not need to touch any of our existing code, except for a small place to wire the new feature into the application. After a day or two, I offered to pair with him. Naturally, since I had just joined him, I asked him to give me an overview of what the feature he was working on was about. He promptly explained it to me and showed me where he was with the code. After he finished showing me the code, I made a few observations—it was not clear to me that his code was reflecting what needed to be done. Basically, the language he used to explain the business feature was not in sync with the language that he had used in the code to implement it, and I could also see some code that was not necessary for the implementation of that feature. I also noticed that there were no tests. When I asked him about that, he said, "It is working now, and that code that is not being used, I may need that in the future." He noticed that I was not very happy with the explanation and continued: "Let's add this refactoring you are proposing, and the unit test implementation to the technical debt backlog. I need to finish this feature now and I'm almost there." How crazy is that? That was a brand-new feature. We should reduce technical debt as we go along and not create more. That was a brand-new feature for God's sake! However, this developer somehow felt that it was OK to do that. At the end of the day, we had a technical debt backlog containing improvements, didn't we? He was not the only one to think like that. That was supposedly an Agile team, with experienced developers, but somehow in their minds, it was OK to have this behavior. Perhaps one day someone would look at the technical debt backlog and do something about it. Well, we all know that will never happen.

Adding items to a technical debt backlog is a way that developers have to justify the bad code they've written without ever feeling guilty about it.

We Want to Do the Right Thing

We don't write bad code on purpose but we are constantly trying to find ways to justify it. Over time, I realized that developers have a wrong notion of time. We always think we are under pressure. We always feel we need to rush. Sometimes the pressure is put on us by the business, but more often than not, the pressure is self-imposed. When working with reasonable people, in an Agile fashion, where we have transparency in the work being done, the business tends to rely on us when we give our estimates and plan our work. They are OK with us telling them roughly how long things are going to take to be done. However, even then, we think we always have to rush to deliver the tasks we committed to. We think we never have the time to do things right.

Pressure will always be part of a software developer's life, and when we feel we are under pressure, we end up cutting corners. We don't do that because we are sloppy. We normally do that because we feel that we need to go faster. We feel that we will be doing a good job if we provide the business with the features they want as fast as we can. We feel that meeting a promised deadline with a potentially buggy solution is better than being honest and transparent, and delivering a stable solution a few days later. Fast does not mean dirty and, unfortunately, we do not always understand the implications of our own decisions.

A Busy Team with No Time to Spare

I joined a team in a very large organization. The pressure was on and the developers were working really hard to cope with it. First, it took me days to get my machine set up. The project was a nightmare to configure in our integrated development environments (IDEs). We were using Java and I was trying to get my Eclipse to import the project. The project had more than 70 Maven projects and modules, with many circular dependencies. After a few days, I finally had my local environment set.

The project was using a heavyweight Java Enterprise Edition (JEE) container, had dozens of inbound and outbound queues, and had integrations with many other systems. When pairing with one of the guys (which was uncommon, but I insisted), I noticed he was running the system in one of our testing environments, playing messages into a queue, and looking at logs. He would then make some changes in the code on his machine, package the application, copy it across to the test environment, deploy the application, play a message in a queue again, and look at the logs. It was almost as if he was in an infinite loop. He was doing this over and over again, changing bits of code, adding more logs, and checking the results in the testing environment. I asked him why he was not testing the application on his machine. He said that it was not possible to run the application locally so he had to add loads of log statements to the code, then use the testing environment to try to figure out what the application was doing. Apparently he had changed something, and the expected message was not arriving in the expected outbound queue. So, after almost two hours of changing code and XML files, and adding lots of logs to the application—those types of logs just indicate that a certain part of the code was executed—he finally found out what was wrong with the code. So he went back to his local machine, changed a few lines of code, added more logs, changed a few existing ones to print out more information, and started building the application again.

At that point I could not keep quiet anymore. "Now that you know what the problem is, why don't you write some unit tests around it?" I really wanted to ask why he didn't write the tests before his changes in the first place but I thought he probably wouldn't take that well. "What I'm doing is important and needs to be done quickly," he said. "I don't have time to write tests." Then he deployed the new version of the application into the testing environment again (note that no one else could use the testing environment while he was doing his *tests*), played an XML message into the inbound queue, and started looking at the logs again.

That went on for another two days until the problem was actually fixed. It turned out that there were some minor logical bugs in the code, things that a unit test would have caught immediately. Worse than that, any other developer working on that code would also need to spend a lot of time (hours, if not days) testing it and trying to figure out how to fix a bug. And all of this just because he *didn't have time* to write unit tests and adjust the application so it could be run locally.

We Don't Have Time but Apparently Someone Else Does

Imagine the situation above. Imagine an application with hundreds of thousands of lines of code. Now imagine ten teams with around seven or eight developers each. Now imagine these teams in five different countries working on the same application. Yes, that was the case. There were some system tests (black-box tests) but they used to take four hours to run and quite often they were broken so no one really paid attention to them. Can you imagine the amount of time wasted per developer per task or story? Let's not forget the quality assurance (QA) team, because apparently testers have all the time in the world. They had to manually test the entire system for every single change made. Every new feature added to the system was, of course, making the system bigger, causing the system tests to be even slower, and QA cycles even longer. Debug time was also getting bigger since every developer was constantly adding more code to it—code that all the other developers would need to debug to understand how it worked. Now think about all the time wasted here, every day, every week, every month. This is all because the developers didn't have time.

Dedicated QA teams are an anti-pattern. Testers should find nothing. Zero. Nada. Every time a tester finds a bug, developers should feel bad about it. Every bug found is an indication of something that we haven't done properly. Some bugs are related to bad requirements, but even then we should have done something about that; we should have helped our business analysts or product owners to clarify them. Testers can be extremely valuable to explore our applications in unexpected ways, ways that just a human could do. But testers should not waste their time executing test plans that could be automated by the development team.

Businesses want features as soon as possible, and we feel that it is our obligation to satisfy them—and it is. Businesspeople look at the system as a whole and so should we. They look at everything, not just the story we are working on or the techniques we are using to write the code. It is our job to remove (automate) all the repetitive work. I still remember, back in the 1990s, when debugging skills were a major point of discussion in any job interview. Seniority could be measured by your ability and experience in debugging code. Those days are gone. Although it is important to have debugging skills, we should be unpleasantly surprised whenever we need to resort to that, and when it occurs, we need to immediately address it, writing tests and refactoring our code so we never need to do that again.

In the years since I became proficient in Test Driven Development (TDD) and in retrofitting tests to legacy code, I probably could count the number of times I had to debug code. And that is true for many other developers I know. Developers who are experienced with test automation will very rarely use a debugger.

THE UNIT TEST TASK CARD

When breaking user stories into development tasks, I have seen many developers creating a "unit test" task card. The reason was that they wanted to assign formal time to it. No, we should never do that. Ever.

First, because unit tests are how we go about writing our code and not a separate task. We cannot say that a coding task is done if it is not tested. Unit tests are one of the best ways to make sure that code works. Usually we would just start a new task when the previous one was done, and by done we mean making sure that it works according to the specified criteria. Done means tested. If writing unit tests is the way the team agreed to verify that the code implemented works, unit tests should be part of each coding task and not a separate task.

Second, whenever we add tasks to the board, product owners have the right to *remove* stuff. Usually, when we have unit tests as a separate task, the amount of time assigned to it is almost as big as the time assigned to the coding task itself, and to the eyes of an uninformed product owner that may look like waste. The product owner, trying to do what she thinks is best for the project, may question the value of it, and may ask developers not to do it in order to finish other tasks. Although she is trying to do her best, quite often she is not in a position to understand the implications of her decision, and it is up to us to look after the quality of the software. At the end of the day, the product owner wants a system that works as intended, without any issues. It is our job to provide that, and in this case, we should factor in the time to write not just unit tests, but also any other tests that are needed to make sure a coding task is done. From a product owner's perspective, as long as the software works, it doesn't really matter what developers do to make it work.

Sometimes, even having the time, developers decide not to automate their tests. They decide they don't have time to write tests, without even considering the implications of not having tests. They just think about their own tasks, not about all the other people involved in the project and all the time they will spend testing and debugging the system. We must remember that there are many other people involved in the project and decisions like that may impact the entire project. When I hear developers saying that their code is good, that they know what they are doing, and that they don't need to write tests, I always say that they are being egocentric and selfish. Software projects are not about a single developer. Software projects are not about you. What is easy or clear for one developer may not be so easy or clear for other developers on the team, and as the system grows, everyone will pay the price of these *small* selfish decisions.

USING TIME WISELY

Our clients and employers are interested in software that satisfies their needs. They want software that can be changed almost as fast as they change their minds. It is our job to provide them with that. The way we go about satisfying their expectations is up to us. Although they may mention things like automated testing and Agile methodologies, what they really want is a good return on their investment. We need to use our (their) money and time wisely, automating whatever we can. We can always quantify how much time we are spending in repetitive tasks and show our clients how much it is costing them. Before implementing any new feature or task, we should spend some time preparing the system to accept the changes in a nice way, so we can just slide a new feature in, with no friction. We should make sure that whatever code we write can be easily tested and deployed. When estimating and planning our work, we should always make sure that we factor in all the things we need to create not only well-crafted code, but also well-crafted solutions. We won't provide a good service to our clients if we give them the false impression that we will go faster if we treat certain tasks like unit testing, refactoring, and so on, as optional tasks. The less time we waste manually testing applications, waiting for slow builds to run, debugging, trying to get our IDEs to work nicely with our totally crazy project structure, or fighting to deploy the application, the more time we have to look after the quality of our applications and make our clients happy.

A Few Months Later

The teams I mentioned above, after a lot of hard work, commitment, support from management, and a significant amount of investment, managed to turn things around and are now among the best teams in their organizations. Some of the teams managed to rewrite their entire test suite, replacing an unreliable in-house testing framework with an open source one. Their test suite used to take almost four hours to run and the tests were always broken, to a point that no one cared anymore. Their new test suite covers a much larger part of their system and it takes around 20 minutes to run.

A different team is now very close to achieving a "one-button" deployment and has an extensive test suite, with almost 3,000 tests ranging from unit to system tests, that runs in just under five minutes and with code coverage close to 100 percent.

The business, after comparing the delivery capability that these teams had in the past to the vastly improved one they have now, is sure that it was a well-deserved investment.

LEGACY CODE

> Attitude is a little thing that makes a big difference.
> —Winston Churchill

During one of my talks on Software Craftsmanship I asked who would like to work on a green-field project. Almost everyone raised their hands. Then I asked who would like to work with legacy code. Besides one or two people, everyone else kept their hands down.

It is always nice to start a project from scratch, be able to choose the technologies, use the latest frameworks, and have a lot of fun writing code without worrying about breaking existing features. It's great when we can write code without having to understand existing code. Working on green-field projects is great, mainly with an experienced and disciplined team using TDD from day one. Progress is made quickly and naturally.

However, if we are working with code written by people who are long gone, with no tests and with no documentation, we go mental. We notice we are going crazy by the number of WTFs we say during the day. We get moody and start hating our job. Frustration becomes a constant. The bad news is that changing jobs doesn't always help. In fact, it very rarely does. As soon as we start our new jobs we will face more legacy code. The difference between projects in different companies is normally just the size of the mess they are in.

A Change in Attitude

> If you don't like something, change it; if you can't
> change it, change the way you think about it.
> —Mary Engelbreit

I used to absolutely hate working with legacy code. Luckily, in the past few years, I learned quite a few things. An obvious one is that moaning, complaining, and cursing won't make my life easier or better. If we want things to be better, we need to do something about it.

When looking at legacy code, instead of moaning and getting frustrated, we should try to understand it and make it better, constantly applying the Boy Scout rule of making it better than how we found it. Improving and understanding legacy code can be massively rewarding. The process of trying to make sense of a big ball of mud seems daunting, but if we just focus on small parts of it, one at a time, and start improving them (writing tests, extracting methods and classes, renaming variables, etc.), gradually things become much easier and enjoyable.

Working with legacy code is almost like solving a big jigsaw puzzle. We don't put all the small pieces together at the same time. We start by separating the pieces into groups, often starting with the corners and edges and then separating the other small pieces by color, pattern, and so forth. Once this is done, we have a few smaller groups and we start forming a high-level model in our head. What before was a bunch of random pieces (or a big ball of mud) is now a bunch of smaller groups of not-so-random pieces. It is still not very helpful or encouraging, but nonetheless some progress is made. Bit by bit, we start working on one of these groups (parts of the code) and we start putting some pieces together (writing tests for the existing code, which will help with our understanding of the code, and refactoring it).

Once we start putting some pieces together, we start seeing a small part of our picture. We get excited because now it's getting real. It's starting to make sense and we are happy we are making progress. The more pieces we put together, the more excited we get about finishing the jigsaw puzzle. The more pieces we put together, the easier it gets to put the remaining pieces together. And that's exactly the feeling we have when working with legacy code. For every piece of code we make better, the more we want to make the whole code better. The feeling of achievement is really rewarding. What before was something we could barely read and took ages to understand now reads like a story, and every developer can understand it, with almost no effort at all. Maybe when a good part of the code is stable (covered by tests, loosely coupled, with well-defined responsibilities, etc.), we could even introduce the cool and new frameworks that we always wanted to use. We could upgrade some library versions. We could even throw a lot of code away and replace it with a framework because now that our code is clean and modularized, replacing one part of the system will not break the other. With that, we don't even need to envy our friends working on green-field projects anymore.

Another interesting thing about legacy code is that it forces us to think in a different way. In green-field projects, when developing a new feature, we write a test and start implementing it. In legacy code, sometimes we can't even instantiate a class in order to test it due to all its dependencies. A change in one place can cause an impact on other obscure parts of the application. We have two options here. We can either see all the challenges of working with legacy code as a pain in the neck or we can see them as very interesting problems to solve. I personally prefer the latter. It is easy to say that a piece of code is badly written. It is easy to complain or even laugh. But the question is: are you good enough to make it better?

PERSONAL AND CLIENT SATISFACTION

Refactoring code can sometimes be a lot of fun and also very addictive. However, although it is OK to have fun and enjoy what we are doing, we always need to remember that we are professionals and are being paid to help our clients to achieve their business goals. Companies are investing a lot of time and money on software projects. With every investment, clients want to maximize their return and we should do our part to make that happen. The more we improve and keep the software clean, the longer the client will be able to benefit from it. Stretching the life span of an application means maximizing our client's return on investment.

At the end of the day, it does not matter if we are working on a green- or brownfield project. It's our attitude toward our job that will make it more or less enjoyable.

SUMMARY

If a piece of software is expected to live and be maintained for more than a few weeks or months, neglecting its quality in order to go faster is an illusion. Many companies become hostages of their own software—their business agility (or lack of it) is totally related to how fast their software can be changed or improved. The worse the software quality is, the harder it will be to make changes to it. The longer it takes for a company to change or improve its software, the slower the company will be to react to changing market conditions.

Companies and developers need to understand that regularly taking the time to sharpen their saw is not a waste of time. In fact, it is the best way to save time and to keep moving fast.

TECHNICAL PRACTICES

What is the real business value of certain technical practices? Why should I, as a project manager or product owner, care about technical practices? As a developer, why should I care about Test-Driven Development (TDD), pair programming, and all these other Extreme Programming (XP) practices? I've been developing software for a long time and never needed them.

This chapter addresses all these questions and gives you more ammunition to convince your peers and managers to adopt certain technical practices, or at least review the value of the ones you currently use.

THE RIGHT THING VERSUS THE THING RIGHT

The feedback loop provided by process-oriented Agile methodologies enables us to regularly inspect whether the business goals are being met. Instead of freezing scope for long periods of time, companies can inspect and adapt on a daily basis. There is nothing tying them down to a ton of diagrams, documents, plans, or contracts written in a distant past. Agile methodologies embrace changes instead of fight them. However, not every company wants to adopt the existing Agile methodologies and that is totally fine. Maybe they have found their own way to establish a quick and fast feedback loop.

With a few exceptions, I believe that Agile methodologies are a better alternative to waterfall and other heavyweight, document-based methodologies. They provide a quick and short feedback loop, which helps us to make sure we are building the *right thing*. This is achieved through a combination of practices and activities: visualizing work in progress, just-in-time prioritization and planning, focusing on minimum marketable features (MMFs), backlogs, stand-up meetings, burn-down charts, user stories, acceptance criteria, scenarios, definition of done, cross-functional teams, regular demos, and everything else provided by the different types of Agile methodologies. Explaining these practices is beyond the scope of this book.

The problem is that we cannot measure the quality of our applications through the practices and activities mentioned above. Unfortunately, when companies realize that one of the biggest impediments for achieving business agility is the bad state of their code base, it may be too late. The cost of improving a big part of their code base or rewriting the whole application can be prohibitive. The "clues" that the code is deteriorating can be very difficult for the business to identify and quite easy for developers to disguise. Bad code is like a cancer, difficult to identify in the beginning, and hard to treat when it is finally discovered. And depending on when it was discovered, life can be prolonged but death is unavoidable.

So how can we make sure we are building the *thing right?* How can we get the same quick and short feedback loop on the quality and design of our code?

Although there are overlaps between Agile and Software Craftsmanship, Software Craftsmanship complements Agile by focusing on technical practices and providing a quick and short feedback loop on the quality of our code. Technical practices help us to make sure we are building the *thing right.*

CONTEXT

Software Craftsmanship, besides promoting a more professional and ethical attitude, also strongly encourages the adoption of XP practices like Test-Driven Development (TDD), pair programming, refactoring, simple design, continuous integration, and many others. These practices will be discussed later in this chapter.

Many developers cannot clearly explain why they don't use XP practices on a daily basis. After asking many developers over the years, a very common explanation is: "You don't know my company. You don't know the people I work with. These things would never work in my company. My boss would never allow us to do that. I totally buy the whole Software Craftsmanship idea but my team doesn't. You would need to be there to see and understand what I'm saying."

When speaking to other developers, of course, many times I don't know their *context,* and in theory that would make it impossible for me to draw any conclusions. They are absolutely right. I don't know their context. Not the details at least. However, after working for so many companies and on so many different projects, it is not that hard to see that, although each company has its own way of working, they also have a lot in common. Many of their problems are exactly the same. Many companies, regardless of how different they are, are unhappy about their software delivery capabilities, lack of agility, bureaucracy, and many other common problems. To solve their problems, many of these companies are looking for a magical solution that can make them better, a recipe they could easily and blindly follow. Scrum fits the bill, and many companies don't feel the need to go beyond that. Well, at least not until they realize that they also need to pay more attention to how their software is being developed.

Context *is* important. If we are adopting Agile methodologies, which may significantly change the way we work, context is extremely important. Context needs to be taken into consideration when choosing a more suitable solution to our problems. A change in the process may impact roles, responsibilities, and information flow, which makes understanding the context essential.

However, does context *always* matter?

Are there any companies that really don't care about satisfying their customers? Are there any companies that don't care about getting a good return on their investment? Are there any companies that are willing to pay for software that does not attend to their needs? Would they be satisfied if the software they are investing in is delivered in five years instead of five months? Although context is important, there are many things that are *not* context dependent.

EXTREME PROGRAMMING HISTORY

In 1996, Kent Beck introduced and combined a set of practices that originated XP. Kent became the project leader on the Chrysler Comprehensive Compensation (C3) payroll system, and he proposed and implemented some changes in their practices—some of them based on his work with Ward Cunningham in the mid-1980s.

The multimillion-dollar C3 project needed some high-caliber developers working together, as opposed to working in competition and isolation. Beck invited Ron Jeffries to the project to help develop and refine these methods. Jeffries thereafter acted as a coach to instill the practices as habits in the C3 team. The team had more notable Agile proponents, including Martin Fowler, Chet Hendrickson, and Don Wells. With a big focus on continuous integration and unit testing, they managed to keep the project on track.

During an interview, Beck describes the early conception of the methods: "The first time I was asked to lead a team, I asked them to do a little bit of the things I thought were sensible, like testing and reviews. The second time there was a lot more on the line. I thought, 'Damn the torpedoes, at least this will make a good article,' [and] asked the team to crank up all the knobs to ten on the things I thought were essential and leave out everything else."

Due to its success and unconventional practices, the C3 project was considered an anomaly, but as Don Wells moved to Ford, he was able to apply the same practices there and had the same effect. Besides unit testing and continuous integration, Don also added collective ownership to the XP practices. With the adoption of XP practices, management noticed a one-third reduction in production bugs. With a decline in production bugs, a growing suite of unit tests, and debugging time reduced to zero, productivity reached a factor of ten times. XP—after the second success case in large projects—was proved not to be an anomaly, but a viable approach.

Since the Agile summit in 2001, XP has been considered an Agile methodology. However, very rarely do companies adopt XP practices during their Agile transformation. XP technical practices are considered less important—by many Agile coaches and consultancy companies—than other practices proposed by process-oriented methodologies. The truth is, very few Agile coaches and consultancy companies are good enough to teach XP practices.

Some Agile coaches and consultancy companies say that XP practices were taken for granted during Agile transformations, and that's why they just focused on the process. I disagree. Looking at the aftermath of all Agile transformations I've seen, XP practices were not taken for granted; they were totally neglected. Were they too hard to sell? Was it too difficult to explain the value the XP practices could add to the business? Was it easier just to convince companies to *buy* Scrum? It doesn't matter anymore. What matters is that Software Craftsmanship brings the focus back to them.

PRACTICES AND VALUES

When it comes to the quality of our software and making sure we are building the thing right, XP practices provide us with many ways to shorten the feedback loop. However, practices don't magically work just because they are adopted. Adopting practices—or forcing our teams to adopt them—does not guarantee the success of a project. People are not machines we can program—imposing a set of practices on them—to obtain the expected result.

Practices are what we consistently do on a daily basis: we either do TDD or we don't do TDD; we either have continuous integration or we don't have continuous integration. Some people say, "We do TDD . . . sometimes." That doesn't help. In order to measure their benefits, practices must be adopted wholeheartedly. It is very hard, if not impossible, to know what is working or not working when practices are partially adopted and not applied consistently. We need to define a strategy and not stray away from it, until we are sure that the set of practices we adopted are (or are not) working.

Practices must be backed by values, which are shared by all members of the team, to be efficient. For example, all team members must want to be better, to improve communication, to have quicker feedback, to achieve results fast, to re- duce the number of mistakes, to do their best to provide a good service to their client, to feel bad when they can't do their best or are not learning. These are values.

But saying we have values is not enough. We recognize someone's values accord- ing to his or her actions and not by what they say. Practices are the validation of values. Practices and values have different scopes. XP practices are specific to software projects. Values are things you live by.

Software Craftsmanship, like many Agile methodologies, is all about delivering business value to customers in the smallest time frame possible: features are pri- oritized by business value; progress is measured by business value. Unfortu- nately, convincing managers of the value of adopting Scrum is much easier than convincing them about the value of adopting pair programming or TDD. "What's the **business value** of all this technical stuff?" they normally argue. "How can I *measure* the value these technical practices give me?"

A question that is often asked during our Software Craftsmanship meetings is, "How can I convince my team [or manager, company] to adopt TDD [or pair programming, continuous integration]?" Trying to *sell* technical practices for what they are is pointless. It doesn't work. Don't focus on the practices themselves when trying to convince managers or team members to adopt them. Focus the discussion on the benefit they bring and how they compare to the practices they currently have. A smaller feedback loop; a better understanding of requirements and cost; knowledge sharing; reduction of bugs; and quick and totally automated releases to production are examples of values added by technical practices.

ADDING VALUE THROUGH PRACTICES

Back to our main topic: does context always matter? Is there anything we can do to improve the chances of having a successful project? Are there practices we can adopt that can give us a quick and short feedback loop?

Let's look at the practices defined in the inner circles of Figure 7.1. Are they con- text specific? Do we really need authorization from managers to adopt them?

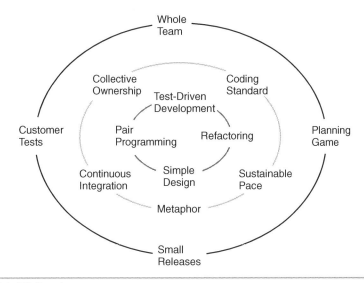

Figure 7.1 XP Practices.

Source: From www.xprogramming.com/what-is-extreme-programming/; used with permission.

Although we will discuss a few XP practices, it's not in the scope of this book to cover them all. For that, I suggest Kent Beck's *Extreme Programming Explained.* Let's take a few practices and explore the values they bring to the business.

Automated Testing

Automated testing enables us, with a click of the button, to have our entire system tested within a few minutes. It gives us confidence to deploy our application into production minutes after the last change was made. The amount of time the business can save avoiding long quality assurance (QA) phases can be measured in days, if not weeks.

The feedback loop on the correctness of our code is reduced from weeks to minutes, enabling us to correct any mistakes almost immediately. This reduction in the feedback loop also prevents us from writing more code on top of erroneous code—reducing significantly the overall bug-fixing cost.

As the system grows, testing phases become longer, since the entire system needs to be manually tested. This may also mean more testers. Writing tests before writing any production code makes us faster as the system grows. This increase in speed is due to our confidence to add new features without breaking the system. Since the entire test suite normally takes just a few minutes to run, it can be run as often as needed—reducing the need for lengthy testing phases and the number of people involved in them. Automated testing gives us measurable business value.

Test First

Test first helps us to think out our ideas; to focus on a single thing at a time; to be precise when defining the responsibility of modules, classes, and functions; and to work in small increments. It gives us assurance our code works according to our expectations. Since each test takes from a few milliseconds (unit tests) to a few seconds (higher-level tests) to run, test first gives us very quick feedback loops when writing the production code. Writing tests first helps us to just write enough code to satisfy the requirements, keeping the code simple. It reduces complexity and overengineering. That's the value it brings to the business.

Test-Driven Development

Test-Driven Development is an evolution of test first. A very common misconception is that TDD is about unit testing. TDD does not mandate the granularity to which our tests should be written. There are many different types of automated tests, with literally tens of definitions for each one of them—many overlapping or conflicting with each other. Let's not worry too much about that here. Let's just focus on the value TDD brings.

Although TDD has "test" in its name, TDD is actually a design practice. When test-driving our code, it becomes very difficult to write complex code. First, because we write just enough code to satisfy the requirements—represented as tests—we discourage overengineering and big design up front (BDUF). Second, whenever our code becomes a bit too complex and bloated, it also becomes difficult to test. Complexity in our code and bad design choices are highlighted by the complexity in maintaining and writing new tests. These tests lead us to re-analyze the design of our code and refactor to make it simpler.

The feedback loop provided by TDD on the design of our code is far shorter and more objective than when done in design review meetings. When test-driving a change or a new feature, we get immediate feedback on how maintainable the existing code is. A design review is good practice but, when compared with TDD, it falls short in two aspects. If done too frequently, it may lack objectivity and encourage overengineering. If done infrequently, the problem may already be too big to be solved quickly. Design review meetings are more effective when the agenda is well defined: bad performance of our persistence layer; a new regulator needs to be supported; integration with the company's e-commerce system. Design review meetings must be done before a big change starts and potentially a few times during the development of a big piece of work, but not more often than that. If the change is too big, it should be broken down into smaller and incremental steps. Too many design meetings are a waste of time. TDD, on the other hand, is useful for every single line of code written, highlighting problems as soon as they arise. TDD and design review meetings are not mutually exclusive and both are needed, but it is important to be able to compare the value they bring and the length of their feedback loop.

TDD offers us a quick feedback on the design, simplicity, and maintainability of our code. It provides a living and executable documentation for our applications and, as a good side effect, a rich suite of regression tests. That's value to the business. That's a quick and short feedback loop.

Continuous Integration

Teams, on average, have between four to ten developers. In larger projects, we may find multiple teams spread across different countries and time zones. Even in a small team, with just three or four developers, how can we make sure we are not stepping on each other's toes? Although teams may be working on totally different features, how can they know if the whole application will work when some code is added to it? How can we know if one of us broke a different part of the application by introducing an unexpected side effect?

One way of making sure the system is still working correctly, once all the changes made by different developers are integrated, is to have a dedicated QA team. Testers will manually execute a predefined set of test plans and will report, hopefully after a few days or weeks, if the system has any bugs or not. That would be the feedback loop.

Continuous integration, combined with TDD, can reduce this feedback loop to minutes. Every time a developer commits some code, the entire suite of tests is executed and an email is sent to the entire team whenever a test fails.

This practice needs to be combined with a "stop and fix" attitude: members of the team must stop whatever they are doing to fix a broken build, which means the problem introduced by the latest change. The advantage of following this practice is that the system is always in a deployable condition and problems don't accumulate.

In addition to that, the combination of continuous integration and TDD can make an entire QA team redundant. The best testers could be better utilized to help developers write automated tests and to help business analysts and product owners to define acceptance criteria for user stories. Good testers can also help the entire team by doing exploratory testing, which only humans can do and there is no easy way to automate.

Pair Programming

Code review is a common practice adopted by many teams in order to guarantee code quality. Code reviews are also used to disseminate knowledge of the system and good coding skills to the whole team. Like design reviews, the problem is how often code reviews are done.

Let's say code reviews happen once a week and we have a team of ten developers. That is a lot of code to be reviewed and gone through in a couple of hours, in a room full of opinionated developers. The chosen area of the code to be reviewed usually is small but important. If the code is good—which is rare, since every developer has an opinion—we are lucky and we move on. However, what if the code is not good? What if a significant refactoring is needed? Maybe the code was committed one week ago and more code may now depend on its current structure. Do we go back and change everything? Well, we should, but can you see the amount of time wasted?

In the case described above, our feedback loop is one week. Some teams do code reviews every two weeks and some don't do it at all. For those that don't do it, the feedback comes after many months, when the code is totally out of control, full of bugs, and too expensive to improve.

Pair programming has the advantage of giving immediate feedback on the quality of the code being written—a so-called four-eye check. As soon as one of the developers writes a test or names a variable, the other developer can immediately say, "I didn't understand that. What do you mean by this? What if we rename this variable *guest* instead of *notLoggedIn?* This method is now doing too much. What if we extract a private method?" The feedback on the maintainability and clarity of the code is immediate.

In order to be more effective, pairs should not stay together for too long. Rotating pairs frequently—every day or two—can improve the collective understanding of the entire system and level up developers' skills. It also helps developers to define and maintain coding standards.

That's value. That's a short feedback loop.

Refactoring

The Boy Scout rule says: "Always leave the campground cleaner than you found it." This is a value that every software craftsman must have when it comes to code.

Developers are less inclined to make improvements to code that they find difficult to understand. Because of the fear of breaking the code, developers start introducing small hacks and duplication. The bigger the mess is, the bigger it will become. This is known as the "broken windows theory." Messy applications make developers go slowly, which causes the business to slow down.

Constantly refactoring our code mitigates this risk. Developers will constantly refactor the code they touch. If this practice is accepted and established from the beginning of the project, developers will never spend too much time refactoring because the code will always be in a good state.

However, when working with legacy applications, developers need to be cautious not to succumb to the urge of rewriting the entire system in one go. In this case, focusing just on refactoring the code being changed is a better approach.

Refactoring without pragmatism can be a dangerous practice. Being professional means to understand trade-offs. Although we want to make the whole system better, we may not need to. There is no point in refactoring a piece of code that hasn't been changed in years. If we don't need to change it, chances are we should not be refactoring either. Start refactoring what changes more often. The Boy Scout rule should just be applied when we need to make a change or understand one area of the code, not everywhere.

A clean and maintainable code enables developers to go fast and reduces the chances of new bugs. That's value to the business.

ACCOUNTABILITY

Many people are still not convinced about some of these practices, even when we describe the value they bring. Time and time again, I hear people say, "They are just practices and many of them are not needed. We can easily develop good software without them."

Although this may be true, this is also a very vague statement. A quick Google search for "percent of software projects that fail" will give us many reports and statistics about projects that, one way or another, have failed. The percent of failures can range from 30 to 70 percent, depending on the source.

Whenever someone—whether a developer, a project manager, or anyone from the business—says he or she does not want to adopt any or some of these practices, we should listen. There is no reason to react badly or immediately think that person doesn't know anything. We should learn from the interaction. But after explaining the value of the practices described in the previous section, we should ask: "What do you do (or should we do) instead that gives us the same or more value than that? What do you do that is better than that?"

We should all be accountable for our own decisions—not only for the decisions of adopting certain practices, but also for the decisions of not adopting them. But this is not just about developers. Managers should also be accountable for not allowing teams to adopt certain practices. We should record these decisions and escalate the issue if necessary.

PRAGMATISM

Technologies, methodologies, and practices are constantly emerging and evolving. There is always a better way of doing things. Although we described a set of practices in this chapter, that doesn't mean they are the only practices out there or that they are suitable in every single context. Things that are considered good today may not be considered as good tomorrow. Maybe in a few years, Software Craftsmanship will be strongly encouraging the adoption of a completely different set of practices.

Being pragmatic is one of the best qualities that a software craftsman can have. We should not follow practices just because someone said so, or just for the sake of it. We should constantly look for ways of doing our job better and satisfying our customers. If that means using TDD, we should use TDD. Whenever we find something else that could give us more value and a quicker feedback loop, then we should use that thing instead of TDD.

Dogmatic thinking is bad. We should constantly ask ourselves why we are doing what we do. Is there anything better that we could do instead? Are the practices we chose a good fit for our project? What is their value? Is it time to try something else?

The best way to know if one practice is better than the other is to compare the value they both bring to the project, then compare how long their feedback loops are. Nothing else should matter. If we can't identify the value that different practices give us, maybe we should not use them. For practices that give us similar value, we should choose whatever the team is more comfortable with. It is worth remembering that nothing should be set in stone. Choosing to adopt a practice does not mean using it forever. As many Agile disciplines have taught us, we inspect and adapt. If certain practices are not giving us value anymore, we stop using them. If we find a practice that is better than what we do today, we adopt this better practice. As software craftsmen, we should always keep an open mind and choose the best technologies, tools, processes, methodologies, and practices for the job.

SUMMARY

Many developers struggle to convince their managers and other developers to adopt certain technical practices because they fail to explain the value that those practices bring to the project. Adopting technical practices doesn't come for free. There is a learning curve, and while the team is getting familiar with the new practices, they will probably be slower and get a bit frustrated because of that.

So, instead of saying to the team that they should do TDD, continuous integration, refactoring, pair programming, and other practices, we should say, "What if we could press a button and be confident, after a few minutes (if not seconds), that our entire application is working? We could reduce QA time from one week to a few minutes. We could even do it multiple times a day. What if we could immediately verify that changes made by different developers are not conflicting with each other or causing a problem in a different part of the application? That could save us a lot of time. How long does it take us to test and deploy our application to production? What if we could reduce that to minutes and do it multiple times a day, whenever a change is made? If a bug is found in production, how quickly can we fix the bug and have a new version of the application deployed? We also have a big gap in skillset within the team. How can we address that? How can we gain understanding of the different parts of the application, including its configuration, deployment, and frameworks? It would be great to reduce the dependency on certain members of the team."

Before talking about adopting practices, we should discuss what we want to achieve. What parts of our software delivery process would we like to improve and by how much? Once we define that, we can then discuss which practices we should use to achieve that.

THE LONG ROAD

Everyone wants to be good at something. The motivations may vary a little but one thing is true for all of us: mastering something gives us pleasure. We become proud of ourselves, even if no one else cares about it. However, very few of us have the focus and determination that is required to master something. Very few of us are willing to walk the long and hard road to mastery.

This chapter is about our careers and the things that really motivate us. Are we really looking after our careers? Do we really know where we are going or where we want to be? What are the things that really motivate us to do a great job? Should we see our jobs as an investment? If yes, what should be the return on our investment?

A Tale from a Brazilian Teenager

As a middle-class teenager living in a small town in the Brazilian countryside, my dream was to live in London. I could never explain why, but there was something about London that fascinated me. My parents always avoided longer conversations about the subject because they knew the chances of it happening were close to zero; our ever-struggling financial situation would never allow me to have a good education or live in a bigger city. The small town we lived in would never expose me to companies where I could become a skilled professional.

On top of that, I could not speak English and I didn't have a European passport. How could I make myself competitive in the UK job market? How could my CV stand out in a country that has some of the best universities in the world?

Even so, I was determined. When I finished high school, I had to decide which career I would follow. My options were limited because we couldn't afford the best universities. Taking into account the things I was passionate about, my limited options, and the dream to live in the UK, software engineering was the best option. As a young teenager, I spent nights having fun typing thousands of lines of BASIC on a small computer with rubber keys attached to a black and white TV in order to play some silly games. They were all character-based games and everything was square. Even a ball would be a square. Back then, that's what computer games looked like. Decision made: I would study computer science. Although still a very long shot, I knew that was the only career I could choose that was related to something that I liked and could also bring me one step closer to my dream of living in London.

After a few years working as a software developer, I finally could afford to start a very long and expensive Italian citizenship process; both my parents were Italian descendants. I had to pay a lot of money to have people going to Italy find some missing documents from old relatives, translate all of them into Portuguese, and make them legal documents in Brazil. For a middle-class Brazilian like me, that was a huge investment of money, but having a European passport was almost essential if I wanted to pursue my dream.

In 2000, with the Italian citizenship process in motion, I traveled to the UK on holidays. I was 23 years old and that was the first time I ever traveled abroad. My mission was to see if London, and the rest of the UK, was exactly what I thought it was. I also had to know exactly what I had to do in order to be competitive in the UK job market. For 30 days I traveled around the UK and spoke to a few developers, whom I contacted before the trip via an old business network website similar to LinkedIn. I realized that although I had a few years of experience as a Delphi developer, Delphi was almost nonexistent in the UK. According to the feedback I got from some of the developers I spoke to, and from searches on job websites, Java was the big thing back then. During that trip I also realized that my English was not good enough to work as a software developer in London. I could ask for directions and order a burger at McDonald's, but my English was not good enough to talk to other developers, go for interviews, or have any of the conversations we need to have when working on a software project. Talking over the phone? Forget it. I couldn't understand anyone on the phone.

After a wonderful time in the UK, and back in Brazil, I knew what I had to do: I quit my job and found a new one where I could learn Java; I hired a private English teacher who could teach me in the evenings; and I enrolled myself in a postgraduate course. As I was still a bit worried that my academic record wouldn't be enough, I decided to take a few Java certifications as well—not that they prove anything but at least I would have something on my CV that companies in London could recognize.

At that point, I realized how important my career was for me. I was not just preparing myself to move to the UK. I was preparing myself to have a successful career—according to my own ambitions and criteria—regardless of where I wanted to live. I realized that I had to move out of my comfort zone, take ownership of my career, and constantly look for opportunities where I could learn and improve. It was my life, my career, and I should own it.

For the next four years, always keeping an eye on the UK market, I prepared myself. In January 2004, a letter arrived saying that I was an Italian citizen. A few months later, with a European passport in hand, I contacted a few developers and companies in London, moved to London, and within two weeks I started my first job.

A journey that lasted more than a decade had come to an end. I was finally living in London and working as a developer. I had realized my dream and I was ready for a whole new world of opportunities. But something even deeper happened to me. When I arrived in London I was not the same teenager with a dream anymore. I was a 27-year-old professional software developer who realized that he was still at the very beginning of his journey. I realized that my career was a very long road to mastery and that a new and exciting journey was just about to start.

FOCUS AND DETERMINATION

Yogi Berra once said, "*You've got to be careful if you don't know where you're going because you might not get there.*" We, software craftsmen, value and control our careers. We understand that a career is a life-long journey that, depending on the choices we make, may or may not lead us to mastery.

Defining the direction we want to go in our careers is important. However, this is a long-term goal and many things can change. Think about your career as if you were managing a multiyear project. Once we understand the project vision—the ultimate goal—we take the most important requirements, break them down into smaller pieces, and iterate. While working on small iterations, we also keep reevaluating the project's goals and adapting when necessary. It's the same with our careers.

BUT WHAT IF WE DON'T KNOW WHERE WE ARE GOING?

It sounds simple but we do not always know where we want to go next. Actually, defining the direction we want to take our careers to can be an extremely difficult thing to do. We don't decide it once and forget. We need to constantly re-evaluate our career decisions based on not just our passion but also all the events in our personal and professional lives.

When we are not so sure where we want to go with our careers, we need to start opening doors. We need to create situations where opportunities can be presented to us. No one will knock on our doors and offer us a great opportunity if we keep ourselves isolated from the rest of the world, locked inside our houses and offices. No one will offer us a good opportunity if they don't know who we are, what we do, and, most important, how good we are. We need to go out there and speak to people. We need to show other people what we can do. We need to be available. We need to make people feel comfortable to come and speak to us. If we don't know what we want to do next, create an environment where other people and companies can present you with some options. Once you have a few doors open, and a few options available to you, you will be in a better place to decide what to do next.

Here are a few things we can do in order to create opportunities:

- Expand our technical knowledge, studying things that are out of our comfort zone, like new languages and technologies.

- Attend user groups and technical community events.
- Network with other developers and businesspeople.
- Blog about the things we are learning and doing.
- Contribute to open source projects.
- Develop projects and make them publicly available.
- Attend conferences.
- Present at a conference.

The things described above may create situations where we can receive options that we were not considering before, and this could help us decide what to do next.

JOB AS INVESTMENT

The definition of a great career in software development is very personal: each one of us has a different dream, aspiration, and different personal situation. However, the process of chasing our career aspirations is very similar. The most important thing is to treat every single job as an investment, a step toward a bigger goal. Software craftsmen invest their ever-increasing knowledge, passion, time, dedication, and professional attitude in every job they have. Therefore, like any other type of investment, we need to be clear about what we expect as a return, and we need to measure it regularly throughout the length of that investment.

After a few months of interviews and negotiations, I finally accepted a job in an investment bank. For many developers who knew me, that came as a surprise. They said, "I never thought you would work for an investment bank." Well, neither did I. I always thought that investment banks were totally hostile to Agile and Software Craftsmanship principles, making them a no-go for me. I also thought that I would be totally constrained by their bureaucracy and deep hierarchies. However, this investment bank had a need for someone that, alongside their Agile adoption, could help them to adopt good technical practices, build great new teams, and inject some passion into the existing ones. From my side, I was looking for a job where I could fill some of the gaps I had in my career. The return on investment I was looking for was experience in developing software at a very large scale, with teams spread all over the world (a context I was not familiar with), and open doors in an industry that was closed to me—usually you need to have previous experience or a financial background to be hired at a high position in an investment bank. I wanted to see how effective (if at all) my preferred software development practices and techniques would work in that context. Exposing myself to an unfamiliar environment would allow me to learn and discover different ways of doing things. That was the return on investment I was expecting from this job.

NOTE

Expecting a return on investment from jobs should not be mistaken for the selfish and unprofessional attitude known as "CV building," where developers don't care about their jobs and are there just to improve their CVs, choosing technologies and methodologies for personal reasons and not because they are fit for a specific purpose. Above all, software craftsmen are professionals who care about and respect their customers.

Knowledge is the most common return on investment expected from a job. Developers choose jobs according to what they want to learn, and they leave their jobs either when they are not learning anymore or when whatever is left to learn is not aligned with their career aspirations.

Our personal lives also play an important role in our career decisions. Sometimes we just need more money, and that's OK. If our personal lives can be significantly improved with more money, we should invest in a job that can give us a better income. Sometimes we just want more stability and security, especially if we are starting a new family or when our family is about to grow. Sometimes we are tired of traveling all the time. Sometimes we need a job where we don't work extra hours so often, so we can spend more time with our loved ones and honing our craft.

When it comes to our career, there is no right or wrong. But there is something worth keeping in mind: knowledge is forever; money, stability, and security are not. If, for whatever reason, our job is terminated, knowledge and experience are the only things we will take with us. If we always focus on learning and becoming better software craftsmen, finding jobs that can provide us with a good income, stability, and security will always be a much simpler task than if we had spent our careers just focusing on getting more money.

AUTONOMY, MASTERY, AND PURPOSE

In *Drive: The Surprising Truth about What Motivates Us,* Daniel Pink says that—assuming that money is off the table—knowledge workers are motivated by three things: autonomy, mastery, and purpose.

- **Autonomy:** It is when we are in control of what we do, how we do it, and when we do it. That should always be the case in a true Agile context.
- **Mastery:** It is when we are constantly learning and evolving—becoming better professionals and better human beings.
- **Purpose:** It is when we feel that our job is important and we are contributing to make things better—instead of just doing what we are told without understanding why.

The assumption of money being *off* the table is very important. When our basic needs are not satisfied, it is very difficult to focus and do our job well. The feeling of being underpaid always leaves a sour taste in our mouths. Even when we like the company we work for, we always end up questioning whether we are being unfairly treated.

Software craftsmen always choose jobs where they have autonomy, mastery, and purpose. They are key aspects that help any craftsman to have a successful and long-lasting career. Choosing jobs just for the money can bring our careers to a halt, making it almost impossible to put it in motion again.

For me, autonomy and mastery are absolutely nonnegotiable and deal-breakers. If I felt that I wouldn't have one of them, I wouldn't accept the job. If I already had a job and felt that I had lost one of them, I would leave the job.

Purpose is not always as clear-cut, though. It's a delight to work on projects when we know how things will be better once the project is finished or reaches some of its milestones. It makes us happy and motivated to feel that we are contributing to a greater good. However, I've been on projects where the entire project, not just features or technologies, was questionable. No one could really explain why we were doing it. Businesspeople were too busy to speak to us and no one knew who the real users were. I felt as if I was putting a lot of effort into something that no one cared about—a situation that neither myself nor the other developers could tolerate for too long.

CAREER INSIDE COMPANIES

It's always very exciting to start new jobs when we choose them carefully. I was always sure I would have a great and long career in each one of my jobs before I started. From the outside, all the companies looked great. One way or another, I always ended up a bit disappointed and had to leave.

There were a few exceptions though. One or two companies that I worked for were really great, but unfortunately, after a few years there was a misalignment between what I wanted for my career and what they could offer me.

Our careers will always be more important than any specific job or company. Pursuing a career inside a company is not the same thing as pursuing our own careers. Our careers are like long staircases and our jobs are the steps. But they are not even steps. Some steps (or jobs) are higher than others. Others are longer or shorter. Some steps are longer *and* lower. Others are shorter *and* higher. It depends on how well we do our homework before joining a company. It may also depend on changes in our personal situation or career aspirations.

If we are working for a company where we have autonomy, mastery, and purpose, and the job is aligned with our own career aspirations, then pursuing a career inside that company is the right thing to do. However, if pursuing a career inside a company means that we would be deviating from our long-term career aspirations, we should probably find another job, regardless of how much we are paid.

The problem I've seen with many people who decided to follow a career inside a traditional and large organization is that their focus changed. Instead of focusing on becoming better professionals and on what is best for the company, they focused on what they needed to do to get their promotion or bonus. They focused on following rules and orders instead of fighting for making things better. They left behind their own values to play political games. They stopped giving their honest opinion in order to avoid confrontations with people who could help them with their promotions. They started doing what was best for them to get promoted, not what was best for the company. And while they focused on the wrong things inside a particular company, our industry was still evolving, making their skills rusty or totally obsolete. All of a sudden, these people—who now have become managers and directors—realized they were now stuck in that company, potentially with a high salary but with outdated skills. They pray for the country not to go through another recession; otherwise, what would they do if they lost their jobs?

On top of that, companies that encourage this type of behavior are left with a bureaucratic and incompetent layer of managers, totally unqualified to understand the intricacies of the job done by the more qualified people below them. This is called "the Peter Principle," and its effect could be stated as "employees tend to be given more authority until they cannot work competently." In other words, through political games, misappropriation of credit, hiding incompetence by blaming others, and often unprofessional and dishonest attitudes, some people are promoted to positions for which they are totally incompetent.

People whose skills are obsolete worry about not finding another job where they can keep their salaries and personal life stability. More bluntly, only incompetent people are scared to lose their jobs. Software craftsmen are never scared to lose their jobs. For them, a career inside a company is only viable if it is aligned with their own career aspirations. Software craftsmen know that their careers are long roads, where the journey is far more important than reaching the end of the line.

SUMMARY

Delivering value to clients is the obligation of any professional who is paid to do a job. But there is far more to a job than that. Work doesn't need to be the antonym of pleasure—we just need to know what to look for when choosing a job: autonomy, mastery, and purpose. Those are the three things that a craftsman should look for in each job. Although it's not always easy to find jobs that can provide us that, they exist. Maybe we are just not ready to get these jobs yet.

The better we are, the easier it is to find jobs that give us pleasure. But to reach a point where we can choose the jobs we want, we need a lot of focus and determination while developing our careers. We need to understand where we want to be and work hard to get there. A successful career doesn't come for free. We need to craft it. Our own careers should always take precedence over a career inside a company. It's great when a career inside a company is aligned with our own career aspirations but it is often a mistake to let a company control our careers. Jobs are an investment. Carefully choosing our jobs and satisfying all our clients is the best way to construct a very successful and pleasant career as a software craftsman.

PART II
A FULL TRANSFORMATION

RECRUITMENT

The first thing to do when hiring a new person is to make sure we are not making our existing problem bigger. If we are unhappy with how our developers work or behave, there is no point in hiring more developers who work and behave in the exact same way. If we want our developers to be constantly learning, bringing innovations, adopting more efficient practices, caring about the project and quality of the code, self-organizing to solve problems, and striving to be better at what they do, why would we hire more developers who don't satisfy these criteria? Although this sounds obvious to many of us, this is not so obvious to hiring managers and the human resources department. Although every company would say that they want the best people, they have no idea what that really means. And a proof of that is how they advertise their job openings.

In this chapter we look at how to attract software craftsmen to our organizations and how to do proactive recruitment. We will also look at how to craft job descriptions and how to avoid job descriptions altogether.

AN ORDINARY JOB DESCRIPTION

The following advertisement was adapted from a job site and anonymized to protect the poor souls who wrote it. Financial institutions normally have job listings like the following:

Our Client, a Major Bank, is currently looking for a Java developer to work in their London office on a long-term contract basis.

The successful applicant for the Java Developer position will have the following skills and experience:

- Strong Java programming skills, including multi-threading and concurrency (minimum of five years' experience)
- Very good Spring background (Spring Integration, Spring Batch, MVC and IoC)
- Banking background (minimum two years)
- Low Latency High Frequency Trading systems—Foreign Exchange
- FX price (spot, forwards but also futures and precious metals)
- Front Office trading risk management and pricing in Foreign Exchange
- Strong academic background in Computer Science (preferably Masters or PhD)
- Solaris, Linux, RMDS, 29 West, Kx/Q, SQL (Oracle), Coherence
- Desirable: C#, C++, MQ messaging, Agile methodologies, distributed/replicated caches, Sybase, DB2

We offer: £80–90k base + up to 30% bonus; excellent package to include 26–30 days holiday + private healthcare for family + good pension + other benefits.

If you are interested in this Java Developer position and meet the above requirements please apply immediately.

Due to my previous experience and personal contacts, I know for sure that the companies behind job listings like these are not only looking for another Java developer. They have far bigger problems in their projects, processes, and culture, and that's what they are really trying to fix. Unfortunately, they have no clue how to solve these problems or how to hire the right people to help them.

This job listing is almost a template for investment banks. That means that the same developers who created those horrid legacy enterprise systems in one bank, and who just focused on earning more money instead of getting better at what they do, can easily find a job in another similar bank. They tick off all the boxes in the listing: they have computer science degrees, they have experience with the technologies (although don't necessary know how to use them well), and have investment bank experience. These developers are free to move from one bank to another according to who pays more. And at the same time, banks are constantly complaining that they need better people. They want to be more efficient. They want to deliver quality software. They want to reduce cost. They want people who could change things for the better. But, unfortunately, what they don't really understand is that if they want to hire better people, they will need to change their recruitment process. They will need to change how they attract great developers, starting with their job specifications. This listing immediately filters loads of great developers out just because they have no previous experience in an investment bank, a degree in computer science, or don't have (enough) experience with the specified technology.

Of course this is not just about investment banks. Many companies with similar problems also have job advertisements like that. For companies trying to change their culture, struggling with low morale, suffering with technical debt, and lacking passionate people to innovate, how useful is this job listing? If the real goal is to improve their delivery capabilities, change the way things are done—and therefore the culture of the company—this job listing is totally pointless. The listing has the wrong focus, failing to express the company's values and the attitude it expects from each candidate. Hiring people purely based on technical knowledge will not help to drive technical and cultural changes. There is no point in hiring the same type of people they are trying to get rid of.

There is also a general perception that recruitment processes take too long. Companies constantly complain that they need to interview between 10 to 30 developers in order to hire one, giving them the impression that the vast majority of the developers out there are not suitable for the job. But "developer suitability" is not the only problem here. Interviewers can't define what it means to be a good developer. Interviewers very rarely realize how bad they are at interviewing. Interviewers do not always know exactly what they are looking for or how to find it. If companies and interviewers were great at selecting good developers, they wouldn't be complaining about their existing developers. They wouldn't be saying that they need a cultural change.

When working for a large organization, I used to periodically visit teams in different departments in other countries. During these visits, my main job was to work with the developers, run technical sessions, pair-program with them, and help them to adopt more efficient practices. After each visit, I usually had to discuss my experience with high-ranking managers, who were responsible for the teams. A common question was, "How bad are they?" Before I could answer, they would usually complement the question with comments like, "I don't think the developers are very good. Everything takes forever to be done. I don't really know what they do. Tell me which ones are the worst ones so we can do something about it." I used to give them a general idea of the situation, but I never gave them any names. One of these managers really pissed me off, pushing hard for me to give him some names so he could replace the developers. My answer was, "Sorry but I can't tell you that. You called me here to help the developers and not to get them fired. I came here to make them better. I spent days with these developers and I won their trust. As I'm also a developer, I became close to them the same way they became close to me. I won't betray them. It's not the developers' fault. None of them came here one day, kicking down the front door, and saying, 'From now on I'll work here.' Regardless of how good or how bad they are, they didn't just magically appear here. They were hired. They sent their CVs, went through *your* selection process, and were hired. Your problem is not that the developers are bad. Your problem is that your selection process and whoever is responsible for it sucks. The selection process must be changed and whoever is behind it should be fired."

The identity and culture of an organization are defined by its people and not by emails sent by the chief executive officer (CEO). Delegating recruitment to HR, recruitment agencies, or vendors means delegating the identity and culture of your organization to people and companies that don't necessarily understand or care about it.

TOO BUSY TO INTERVIEW

The main mistake many interviewers make is to say that they are too busy to interview: "We can't spend too much time interviewing people. We have work to do."

We spend far more time with our colleagues than we spend with our loved ones—which makes it even more important that we trust and have great relationships with them. The truth is that if you cannot allocate enough time to interview, you can't really be serious about building a great team.

Because the vast majority of businesses rely heavily on software, developers play a big part in the success or failure of a business. Developers are the ones who build and maintain the machine that enables the businesses to stay alive.

Since hiring great developers is key, the quality of the interviewers is extremely important. Job candidates are always judged from a biased perspective: they will be considered good or bad developers according to the interviewer's own values, prejudices, and technical abilities. People that like to be in control and believe in hierarchies will not hire someone who is "better" or even at the same level as them. On the other hand, people who are always eager to learn and do things in a better way are always looking for opportunities to work with people who are better than or at least as good as them.

Although we need to allocate time to interview, the whole recruitment process—from collecting and filtering CVs to interviews and actually hiring someone—can take weeks if not months. During this time, we waste a lot of time looking at same-as-all-the-other CVs and interviewing many unsuitable candidates.

Time-boxing recruitment activities or defining a formal recruitment process is not the solution. The time wasted interviewing wrong candidates is the problem we must address. Because interviewing 100 developers to find four or five is not viable, and delegating the recruitment activity is too risky, the only alternative we have is to be more specific with our filtering criteria.

No Job Descriptions

Job descriptions are anti-patterns. Lou Adler has a series of articles on the topic at the website www.tlnt.com. He says that traditional skills and experience-based job descriptions "are anti-talent and anti-diversity, aside from being terrible predictors of future success."

Here are some reasons:

- **Absolute numbers:** They are arbitrary, misleading, and capricious. Defining that the candidate needs to have five or more years of experience in Java or a certain university degree does not make sense. Having five years of experience is different from having five times one year of experience. Many developers have worked with the same technology for a long time and never learned anything new after they were hired. A good university degree doesn't mean anything because the majority of the students are not ready to be a professional software developer when they graduate. It is what developers do at work and in their spare time, and not a university degree or certifications, that gives them the required skills.

- **Keyword matching:** Specifying acronyms and technologies encourages filtering candidates by keyword matching. Recruiters or members of the HR department, who do not understand all the subtleties of the job, become the gatekeepers.

- **Listing technologies:** Talented developers may not send their CVs because they may not have experience with all the technologies listed. As a lousy attempt to select better developers, desirable—but not needed—technologies are also added to the list. In some cases, the list of technologies is created without any correlation to the skills and experiences of those already successfully performing the job.

- **Wrong cultural fit criteria:** Companies fail to state their values, the expected attitude and responsibilities, in their job descriptions. When stated, usually it is done in a very subjective way, which makes it impossible for any developer to disagree. Eager to learn, great team spirit, positive attitude, and being smart are not good ways to define the expected profile. Not a single developer will think they don't tick off all the boxes in this list.

- **Listing the wrong requirements:** Listing the responsibilities required for the job, instead of required skills, technologies, years of experience, industry background, and academic requirements, is a far better way to attract better developers. Time and time again we see developers with all the desired skills (on paper), a university degree, and years of experience, but they can't actually do the job.

- **Wrong filters:** Job descriptions are designed to weed out the worst, not attract the best. Top developers do not apply for experience-based job descriptions.

They are usually more selective when choosing where they want to work. The company's culture, type of responsibility, and type of project are normally more important for them than the specific technologies. The approach to eliminate the clearly unqualified quite often backfires because it fails to attract the best developers.

- **No internal promotions:** Normally people get promoted into bigger jobs because of their achievements, leadership, team skills, and other important aspects related to the new job. No one gets promoted because they know the APIs of a framework or have five years of Java experience. If job descriptions are not used for internal promotions, why would they be effective to attract new talent?

There are far more reasons why job descriptions are bad but the ones above should be enough for us to avoid them.

What if a Job Description Is Needed?

Job descriptions are totally discouraged, but if one is needed, the focus should be on detailing the expected attitude and responsibilities, types of projects, technologies used (not required), and values and culture of the company.

Let's compare two job descriptions. The first one represents a very generic offer from a financial institution. The second one is from the 7digital website.

Job Description 1

Java Developer—J2SE/J2EE—Financial Software

Java Developer (J2SE or J2EE) with SQL experience required for a permanent role with a growing and extremely successful Financial Software organization.

The ideal candidate for this Java development role will possess a passion for technology and a desire to have exposure to, and learn more about the Financial Services arena.

Salary: £50,000–£60,000 plus benefits and bonus

(Continues)

Skills and Experience

Applicants must have strong core Java skills gained in a commercial environment along with the following technical skills and experience:

- 5+ years intensive Java Development (J2SE or J2EE)

- 3+ years intensive SQL (some knowledge of SQL Server and Oracle)

- Experience with web technologies (ideally HTML 5, CSS 3, jQuery, Spring MVC)

- Strong OO analysis and design experience

- Experience of the full software development lifecycle (SDLC)

- Ability to clearly communicate with peers, business analysts, and subject matter experts

The following skills would be beneficial but not essential:

- Development on high performance distributed systems (in Java)

- Experience with both real time and batch systems

- Experience with distributed technologies such as Oracle Coherence

- Experience with Spring, Hibernate

- Experience in an Agile environment (including TDD, JUnit, etc.)

The Java developer role will involve close interaction with the Systems Architect, Java Team Leaders, and other members of the development team and will demand a high level of design and coding to implement and deliver enhancements.

There will be ample opportunities for the successful Java candidate to quickly expand on their banking and funds management experience, with plenty of business exposure.

This job description was definitely created for the mass market. It defines the salary range, making every developer who applies roughly the same. They are very precise with what they need: a Java developer with SQL; five or more years J2SE or J2EE; three or more years of SQL. This shows they measure seniority by years of using a technology and not knowledge. We can note the use of old acronyms: J2EE instead of JEE. Does this mean they are using an old version of the Java Enterprise Edition or did they just not bother to update an old job description? Either way, both are bad.

As beneficial but not essential, they have "Experience in an Agile environment (including TDD, JUnit, etc.)" Here they mix Agile environment with Test-Driven

Development and JUnit as if they were the same. The "etc." after JUnit is reinforcement that they don't really care much about Agile or Extreme Programming practices. It is just a bunch of *stuff*.

It is implied they have a hierarchy instead of a self-organizing team when they mention "close interaction with the Systems Architect, Java Team Leaders."

At the beginning and at the end of the job description, they emphasize the opportunity to learn more about the business: financial services, banking, funds management. Since I've been in the banking industry before, I know that there is a very subtle message there. It implies that, with the opportunity to understand more about the business, you can progress in your career and become a manager.

Last but not least, when they say the ideal candidate "will possess a passion for technology," I could not see anywhere in the job description how this passion is appreciated, valued, and aligned with the company's software development culture.

JOB DESCRIPTION 2

We're small, fast, innovative, and bursting at the seams with people passionate about music and technology. We're growing at a rapid pace and seeking enthusiastic, creative, intelligent, and fun individuals to join us in a variety of roles. In return, we can offer you a fun but hardworking environment where you can instantly see your contribution to the company's success.

DEVELOPER (SENIOR)—DEVELOPMENT TEAM

We are looking for smart, self-motivated software developers to join our truly exceptional development team. Good working TDD experience is essential for this role.

About You

- You care about software; you have a passion for what you do which you can clearly convey by your actions rather than just waffly personal statements on your CV.

- You have an eye for software design and can talk eloquently on a range of topics due to your experiences and also from reading and experimentation.

- For you it's more than a job.

(Continues)

TDD

Among other things we're strong advocates of TDD. We think it represents such a particular mindset we'd only consider you for a senior position if you have significant working experience with it. If you do have working experience with TDD, great! We want to know more. How much? How did you do TDD? How have you used TDD on a recent project? What problems have you faced? The more the better!

The Role

Our teams are cross-functional, self-organizing, and highly autonomous. No architects, project managers, or middle management. You'll be working directly with our Product Managers and stakeholders in a highly collaborative manner. This approach requires a huge amount of teamwork and maturity and is not right for everyone, but we believe it's the best way to create great software.

Among other things, Pair Programming, TDD/BDD, Refactoring, and Continuous Delivery are deeply embedded and we're constantly striving to improve the way we work. We know typing is not the bottleneck, so among other things:

- Have around two sessions a week spending time doing things like Katas, Dojos, and discussing practices and technologies.

- Each get up to two days of "innovation time" a month we can use to play with new toys or product ideas.

- Regularly attend conferences and community events, both as participants and contributors (we've recently run sessions at QCon London 2012, Software Craftsmanship 2012, and SPA Conference 2012).

- However, we're not perfect and not afraid to say so. We recognize we have many problems which need solving and a long way to go on our journey of continuous improvement.

Technologies We Use

Most of our stack is C#/.Net but we're using and investigating many other languages and technologies (e.g., Ruby, server side JavaScript, C++, Python). We'd be interested in candidates from any background as long as you have a keen understanding of Object Oriented languages. Here's a (not exclusive) list of technologies we currently use:

- C#, Ruby, JavaScript

- ASP.Net MVC, OpenRasta, Nancy, ServiceStack, Nhibernate, Windsor, StructureMap, NUnit, RhinoMocks, ReSharper, NDepend

- Cucumber, Rails, RSpec, Rake, Capybara, Selenium, Watir
- REST, OAuth
- Git
- MS SQL, ElasticSearch, Solr
- Mono, Windows, IIS, Nginx
- RabbitMQ
- TeamCity

We're also very keen on open source. We contribute to some of the technologies listed above as well as maintaining our own forks (+ publishing other things we'd like to share) on our GitHub account.

This job description was totally tailored to attract passionate and talented developers. They clearly state what they do, what they value, and what they expect from any developer joining their organization.

Passion is clearly their main criterion when looking for new developers and that is clearly stated in the "About You" section.

For them, technical practices like TDD, Behavior-Driven Development (BDD), refactoring, pair programming, and continuous delivery take precedence over specific technologies.

They are very clear and direct in saying they do not have architects, project managers, or middle management. Developers work directly with the product owners and stakeholders in a collaborative way.

Providing time for developers to practice and learn is embedded in their culture and also highlighted in the job description.

They describe what their technology stack currently is but they explicitly say they are investigating and are open to use other languages and technologies. As long as the developer has a good understanding of object oriented programming, they don't really care about the developer's background.

As part of the job description, they provide the link to their own GitHub account, which shows to developers applying for the role that they are serious when they say they care about open source.

Clearly the job description was written by great and passionate developers and not by HR.

Last but not least, they really proved they understand how great developers feel when they wrote: "For you it's more than a job."

A Job Is Not Just a Job

For great developers, their job is not just a job; it's also their hobby and their passion. They feel fortunate that they are paid well to do what they love. Since a job is far more than just a job, great developers will look for companies that think in the same way and can provide them with an environment where they can shine and have loads of fun.

Recommendations

Recommendations should be encouraged but not financially rewarded. Attaching a monetary amount to the recommendation system triggers wrong motivation—which invalidates the whole process. Good developers want to work with good developers and for them that is the only thing that matters. They see the recommendation system as an opportunity to bring in great developers and learn from them, which is great for the company and also for their own professional growth.

Software craftsmen understand that, by recommending another developer, they put their reputation on the line. When a software craftsman makes a recommendation, it is implied that the recommended developer is also a software craftsman, and that he or she shares the same passion, values, principles, and dedication.

Community Involvement

The best way for companies to hire talented developers is to be in contact with the wider community. Supporting user groups and technical communities is a great way to attract and approach great developers.

The chief technology officer of a small but profitable company in the financial sector came to one of the first Software Craftsmanship roundtable events we ran as part of the London Software Craftsmanship Community (LSCC). He came to demonstrate the company's testing framework, which is now open source. Months later the company became one of the LSCC sponsors, hosting one of our monthly meetings. It now also sponsors the London Scala User Group (LSUG).

It had a few advantages in sponsoring LSCC and LSUG:

- **Exposure to great developers:** Many were hired directly, saving them time and money.
- **Opportunity for their developers to learn for free:** Many of them attend our hands-on coding sessions, where we always pair-program and compare different solutions, and they also attend our Software Craftsmanship roundtables, where we discuss various topics in an open-space fashion.
- **Free technical advice:** Their developers have the opportunity to talk to other developers about better ways to solve their problems.
- **Cheap investment:** It takes just a few pizzas and their office space once or twice a month.

One of the great advantages of actively supporting the community is that we can spot talent and approach them directly. The same is true for the developers. They can analyze the culture of the company, the developers working there, the types of applications they work on, and how they work. Because user groups and technical communities meet on a regular basis, it is easy for both developers and companies to identify opportunities to work together.

For weeks, months, if not years, developers and companies have the opportunity to know and help each other. This closer contact is mutually beneficial—it can lead to business partnerships, employment agreements, networking, and a great deal of knowledge sharing.

DEFINING EFFECTIVE FILTERING CRITERIA

Relying on recommendations and community involvement is not always enough. Very rarely are good developers available, which means that sometimes we need to use the conventional channels, like job boards and job descriptions. When that is the case, we are back to our original problem: not enough time to interview.

Large organizations and reasonably well-known companies tend to receive many CVs every time they advertise a job position. As it is totally impossible to interview every developer, companies need to create filters in order to preselect the ones they feel have a better chance of satisfying their needs. The filter criteria used can be quite vague and nonscientific. HR or recruiters, when in charge of the filtering, will usually do it by a combination of keyword matching and some other random criteria like years of experience or academic background. When done by hiring managers, they analyze the candidate's previous experience, companies the candidate worked for, amount of time in each job, the sizes of companies and industries, and all the exaggeration written by the candidate when describing her role in each of the previous jobs.

Once I was recruiting for an investment bank. We were looking for an experienced developer to join our London team. The agencies and vendors working for us sent me some CVs and, at some point, I had more than 50 CVs that looked exactly the same. They all satisfied all the items in the investment bank job description—similar to the first job description described earlier in this chapter. We could not interview 50 developers because each interview may take a full day, if not more.

I started to think about the things I really valued about a developer and also what type of culture we were trying to create. We wanted passionate software craftsmen. Passion was the most important criterion, even when compared to technical skills and programming languages. I wanted people who were constantly learning, who took the time to try new things, who loved to share what they knew with others, and who were active in their communities.

Looking at all those CVs and with no idea how to select five or six for the interview, I pushed all the CVs back to the agencies and vendors and said, "I want you to find me passionate and talented developers." They asked me what was wrong with the CVs they sent. "I don't know. That's the problem. I can't measure passion from a black and white CV where the only thing that is in there is a huge exaggeration of how important they were in each job they had. They all use the same technologies and have many years of experience working for an investment bank, but that is not the most important criterion for me." Without understanding much of what I was talking about, they asked me for a job description. "There is no job description for this position. I just want you to find me passionate and talented developers." They kept pushing me to give them something, and I replied, "If you want keywords to match against a CV, I'll give you one: passion." The majority of them never got back to me.

Whichever filter criteria we apply, we will always filter some good developers out. If we say we want previous investment bank experience, we will filter out loads of talented developers who have never worked for an investment bank before. It would be the same if we asked for bachelors' degrees in computer science, experience with a specific framework, or a certain number of years of experience.

How can we make sure we are not filtering out good developers? The first thing is to define what a good developer means. This is totally context dependent. Different teams, with different cultures, developing different applications, will have different views of what a good developer means. I've had this discussion with many experienced developers over the years and not once were good developers defined according to knowledge of a specific technology, years of experience, or academic background. If a good developer is not measured according to that, why do we keep looking for these things or use them as filtering criteria?

In our case, our filter criteria were related to what we value the most: passion. We very soon realized we could not measure it just looking at traditional CVs, and that led us to start asking for different CVs. From that point onward, we would only accept CVs where developers had at least some of the following items: GitHub account, blog, open source contributions, technical communities and user groups with which they were active, summary of any pet projects, Twitter account, list of favorite technical books, conferences where they either gave talks or attended. From our perspective, even a passionate junior developer should have some of these items. This approach was good enough for us to identify the developers who were investing in their own careers outside working hours, which also indicates passion.

Although we know that some great developers may not have any of the things described above, the alternative would be to go back and interview every single candidate—which would make the whole selection process very expensive and maybe even prohibitive.

PROACTIVE RECRUITMENT

When we started Codurance, one of our first clients, an international consultancy company, asked us for a very unusual service. They asked us to help them to reshape their recruitment process and interview some candidates.

They were growing fast and had to recruit more than 70 developers to cope with their demand. They needed developers of all kinds: junior, senior, architects, permanent employees, contractors, and so on. They also needed business analysts, development operators (DevOps), and testers. They were hiring for many different new projects and needed developers skilled in various languages and technologies.

One of the reasons they asked us to help them is that they couldn't cope with the volume of interviews, and they were also not quite sure how to recruit all these developers. They needed to make sure they would get talented developers to join the company because the majority of these developers would work directly with their clients, developing bespoke software.

Before they brought us in, they were in desperation mode. They had no time to interview but had to fill all these roles in order to not lose new business opportunities. The problem is that when you are in desperation mode, you increase dramatically the risk of making mistakes, especially when it comes to recruitment. You end up lowering the bar and recruiting any developer who applies.

It took us some time, but we managed to help them to reshape their recruitment process, with much of the advice written in this book, and we managed to select some great developers for them.

We learned a big lesson: you should never allow your company to be in this situation. Recruiting when you are desperate will make you bring the wrong people to your organization and, although you may think that at least you were able to place these developers in projects, at some point these projects are going to end. Maybe they will end even before you expect, because your clients may be very dissatisfied with the service provided by bad developers. Besides damaging the reputation of the company, the company now has many bad developers *on the bench,* waiting for their next project.

At Codurance, we decided to be very proactive with our recruitment process. We decided not to wait until we had a paying client to start recruiting. We decided to recruit constantly. Finding great developers is very difficult and takes time; chances are that when you really need a good developer, you won't find one quickly enough. With this in mind, we constantly interview candidates for our apprentice and craftsman positions. The only difference is that we make our process specific enough so that only the types of developers we are more interested in will apply. This helps us not only to reduce the number of applications, but also to increase the success ratio.

During times when we are not ready to hire but still have applicants, we tell them at the very start of the recruitment process that we are not hiring straightaway. We suggest that if they want to go through the selection process and pass, they would be the first ones we would call as soon as we were ready. As part of our selection process, we ask developers to complete a code assignment that may take at least a weekend to complete. In order to convince them to go through the process, even knowing that we are not ready to hire, we promise to provide them with a very comprehensive review of their code. With this approach, applicants at least get some valuable advice on their code, and we can build a pool of talented developers who have passed our selection process, and we can call them when we are ready to hire.

SUMMARY

Companies can benefit a lot from engaging with local user groups and technical communities. It gives them a good chance to meet great and well-established professionals, as well as many young developers with huge potential.

Recruitment agencies should be used as a last resort. Due to their conflict of interest, they do not always care too much about their clients' cultures and values. Matching keywords in a job description to CVs is how they usually do their filtering. Their lack of understanding about software development and technologies makes them very poor talent scouts.

If a job description is needed in order to reach a wider audience of developers, make sure the job description clearly states your company's culture and values;

project details; expected responsibilities and technologies used (instead of required). Focus on passion instead of specific technologies and never use years of experience, academic background, certifications, or any other criteria that are not relevant to the job.

For a better predictability of future success, look for passionate developers because they are naturally open-minded and are constantly looking for ways to learn. They are also the ones who have a natural motivation to innovate and drive technical changes, instead of just waiting to be told what to do—which will keep the company stagnated. Due to their passion and the time they spend trying to get better, even if they are not so experienced today, they have a great chance to become great professionals in a very short period of time.

If you think your developers are not good, don't blame them. First, ask yourself why and how they were hired. Maybe your recruitment process is not working as well as you thought it was. As a company, don't think you are the only one applying filters and looking for the best people. Good developers are also filtering bad companies out and looking for the best ones.

INTERVIEWING
SOFTWARE
CRAFTSMEN

Interviews are a two-way street. Companies try to find developers who can help them achieve their goals, and developers try to find out if the hiring company is a good fit for their career aspirations.

As companies generally conduct multiple interviews as part of their selection process, it is vital that developers use the interviews to learn as much as possible about the hiring company. Choosing a new job is an important career decision, and it can also have a direct impact on our personal lives; we may be spending more time at work than we spend with our loved ones.

In this chapter we look at how companies and developers can identify whether they will have a productive partnership. We will then look at some interview techniques and describe how to interview software craftsmen.

A BUSINESS NEGOTIATION

As technology evolves, the need for software professionals increases. In order to have a competitive advantage, companies now understand that they must hire talented and passionate developers and, most important, pay them well. This is highlighted in an article in *InfoWorld*. The US Bureau of Labor Statistics projects a 30 percent job growth in the coming years, and CareerCast deemed software engineering the all-around best job for 2012.

During an interview, it is important to understand that we are not begging for a job. We are doing a business negotiation. On one side we have a company with needs and business goals. On the other side we have a software professional who could help the company to achieve those goals. Before signing any contracts, the most important aspect of providing a service, either as a contractor or a permanent employee, is to understand and measure the risks and rewards of that negotiation.

Every software craftsman has a reputation and anything that can damage that reputation must be considered a risk. An example would be to join a project that is way behind schedule, with dubious business value, command and control management, and in a company where developers are treated as factory workers—just following orders, coding against a pile of documentation, with no say in any technical decision, and with no contact with users and stakeholders. The chances of bringing a project like that back on track are close to none, meaning that the only thing a software craftsman will get out of it is frustration. A company like that is not ready for a productive partnership and must be discarded by a software craftsman. However, if the project is in trouble but developers have total autonomy to do whatever is best to save the project, working in close collaboration with the business, then this project can be a great opportunity for a craftsman.

A successful service provider is the one who understands that sometimes it is better to refuse a deal than to have a bad deal and that a good partnership is a partnership that is valuable for both sides. There is no reason to be working with bad partners, especially now, as the global demand for good software developers is so high.

IDENTIFYING PRODUCTIVE PARTNERSHIPS

Companies and developers are looking for the same thing: a productive partnership. However, during interviews, each side has a different perspective on what a productive partnership should be. Let's look at these different perspectives.

A HIRING COMPANY'S PERSPECTIVE

I've interviewed many developers over the years and, more often than not, when asking the candidates if they had any questions, the answer was no. On some occasions, I was so disappointed with this attitude that I decided not to hire them. As a mature hiring company, we expect to have partnerships with those whom we hire. We expect that the people working with us will question what we do, show us how we can improve, and contribute to our success.

If a developer doesn't ask questions about how we work, what we do, what we want to achieve, and what our main problems are, how can we be sure she will be asking questions when she joins the team?

Hiring talent means that we, as a hiring company, value their opinions and want their help to improve the way we work. If the developers' opinions were not important, there would be no reason to hire talent. Collaboration and empowerment are key for any successful team. The interviewer's job is to figure out if the candidate can collaborate well and be empowered. The number of questions (and also the types of questions) asked by an interviewee may be a good indication of how much this person can collaborate and contribute to the business. If the interviewee doesn't ask any questions about the work or about the company during the interview, it may be a sign that he is just looking for a job, regardless of which one. If the interviewee asks loads of questions, we can assume that she really cares about her career and finding the right company. Always favor candidates who ask questions. It doesn't mean they are better than the ones who don't ask questions but, at least, it shows they care enough about being in a place they will enjoy.

Here are some of the things we should pay attention to: how enthusiastic and passionate the candidates are when talking about technology, their previous projects and jobs, and their own achievements. How do they describe their failures? Do they take any responsibility for things that went wrong or do they just blame others? Have they done anything to turn an unpleasant situation around? Have they done anything in their previous jobs to improve the things they were complaining about? What sort of environment are the candidates looking for? Can we match their expectations?

Explaining the good, the bad, and the ugly about the company and the projects the candidate will be working on is essential, not just to hire the right people but also to keep them after they've been hired. It's important that the candidates know what to expect before starting the job.

Regardless of how we conduct interviews, when hiring talent, we should be looking for passion, ability to do the work well, and cultural fit.

A CANDIDATE'S PERSPECTIVE

It is vital that developers learn how to use interviews as an opportunity to understand more about the company and the people whom they will, potentially, be working with.

There are a few things to pay attention to: who is the interviewer? Is she a project manager, a developer, a team leader, or an architect? How many people are we being interviewed by? Is it a single-phase or multiphase interview process? What are the types of questions we are being asked? Is the interviewer following a script with predefined questions or just having a conversation? Are the questions specific or totally open? Is the interviewer more interested in binary answers to technical questions or more interested in knowing us better?

It's important to filter out all the potential exaggerations we may hear. Every company is great when we talk to recruiters, Human Resources, and interviewers, but paying attention to small details can help us see what the situation really is.

Our first hint that the management team does not trust developers, and that formal hierarchies govern the company, is when interviewers are managers, architects, and team leaders, instead of developers we would work with. That should be enough for us to question whether developers are empowered to make decisions or if a few people at *higher* positions make all the decisions.

Single interview processes always make me a bit worried. It seems that the company is in a hurry and cannot take the time to hire the right people. A multiphase interview process usually means that the company is interested in analyzing different aspects of the candidate's profile and are more serious about finding a more well-rounded professional.

Analyzing the questions asked during an interview can be very valuable and "educational." The questions asked generally represent what the interviewer values the most and what we can expect when we join the team. However, it is quite common to hear about interviewers who ask questions that are totally unrelated to the job offered. If we suspect that is the case, there is nothing wrong with asking how relevant the questions are to the actual role offered—as long as we do it politely and not in a confrontational way. It's important to observe how the interviewer will react and respond to this question. Some interviewers will be annoyed by the question. Some will be reluctant to explain, and some will not be able to explain at all. Some will just talk about it naturally and explain the reason for those questions. The interviewer behavior will show you how she reacts when challenged. Could you work with her? Would you feel comfortable to challenge her decisions?

If the interviewer is following a script—asking very specific and short questions, reading them, one after another, from a piece of paper—that shows that she is not willing to explore new ideas and engage in a debate. She already has a preconception of what a *good* developer should know. It also shows that she follows a *process,* even when it does not make sense or clearly is not the best approach. An interview conducted like that would make me think that the whole team may not be open to different ideas.

Judging developers by questions that have an exact answer—usually about APIs, tools, technologies—is the wrong thing to do. Having an open conversation about real-world and concrete scenarios, exploring different approaches and solutions, and, of course, writing code together, are the best ways to determine a candidate's experience.

When visiting one of our offshore teams, they invited me to be an observer in one of their interviews. The interviewer had a spreadsheet with a few questions and answers prepared, which he followed almost to the letter while interviewing the candidate. The questions were very specific and with an exact answer, not leaving any room for discussions.

It was quite robotic, I would say, with almost no real interaction between the interviewer and the candidate, besides the quick succession of short questions and answers. For each question answered, the interviewer would mark a cell on the printed spreadsheet. There was nothing there that could tell me if the candidate was passionate about his profession, or if he had the experience needed to do the job well.

When the interview was over, the only thing we knew about the candidate was that he was familiar with certain Java APIs and frameworks, but we had no idea if the candidate could use them well to write well-crafted code. Any inexperienced developer who had read a Java book, or studied for a Java certification in the past few months would have passed the interview with flying colors.

As we walked back to our desks, the interviewer asked me not to tell anyone about the questions he asked. He didn't want the questions to *leak*.

If we are scared that people will know what we are going to talk about during the interview, probably it is because we are doing it wrong. If the interview is composed of questions that any person could answer correctly after a quick search on Google, or after reading the APIs of a language or the documentation of a tool, the questions have absolutely no value in identifying good or bad developers.

Interviews like that show the lack of creativity and openness of the team. It also shows that, for them, there is just a small set of tools you can use to develop software.

GOOD INTERVIEWS

A good interview is like a good and informal chat between passionate developers. It's an exchange of information: a good debate about techniques, tools, challenges, and approaches to software development.

My first interview at an investment bank, the type of company I could swear I would never work for, was absolutely great. The interviewer said to me, "I've read some of your blog posts and I really liked the topics you covered. However, I don't agree with certain things you wrote and I want to discuss them."

We spent more than one hour discussing the things I had written, trying to find scenarios where certain things could or could not be applied, and the challenges related to some approaches, given different contexts. It was interesting to see the things that we agreed on, the things we didn't agree on, and, most important, the things that none of us had ever thought about before.

This was just my first interview, out of five, but after it I already knew I would like to work for that company and with the person interviewing me.

There is no way you can prepare for an interview like that. You either have the experience on the topics discussed or you don't. Googling for some stuff before the interview or reading a few articles won't be enough to prepare a candidate for an open conversation like that. And that's exactly the point of such interviews: figuring out how experienced the candidate really is.

THE RIGHT FOCUS

What are our core values? What are the key skills we need? What are the things we would like to do better? These are some of the questions we need to answer before we hire more people. If there is anything we want to change, improve, or adopt, the new people hired should be our allies in achieving that.

If we value Test-Driven Development (TDD), clean code, refactoring, pair programming, and Agile methodologies, they all should be part of our interview process. If we need to improve the design of our applications, we should test and hire someone who has great design skills. If we feel that our teams need an injection of passion, we need to hire passionate people.

Don't waste precious interview time talking about things that are not relevant. Focus on what is important and more valuable to the company.

MIND-MAPPING A CONVERSATION

One technique I find very useful when conducting interviews (or should I say conversations) is mind-mapping. I usually take a few pieces of paper and a pen, and I start the interview with a very open question. What is well-crafted software for you? What are the main challenges in a software project? In these examples, *well-crafted software* and *challenges* would be the root of my mind map.

Open questions like that tend to be answered with a list of things like maintainability, testability, readability, performs well, satisfies requirements, and so on. Each item in this list becomes a node, hanging off from the mind-map root *well-crafted software*. With that, we can start exploring one of the nodes and mapping the conversation against them, creating new nodes according to what is said— either by the interviewer or by the candidate. Whenever I'm happy with the conversation about one of the topics, I can easily go back to one of the other nodes that are hanging off the mind-map root. "We talked about readability, but you also mentioned testability. Could you expand on that?"

If the conversation deviates in a way that I don't judge very useful, I can look at the map and choose another node (topic) to explore. If I want to have a conversation about a completely different topic, I create a brand-new mind map on a different piece of paper, or another node under the root node.

If I want to be slightly more specific, because the conversation doesn't get to where I want it to, I then ask a more direct question: "What do you think about TDD?" This will lead to another interesting conversation captured by the mind map.

Once the interview is finished, I have the entire conversation mapped, which helps me to remember every conversation I had with each of the candidates.

PAIR-PROGRAMMING INTERVIEW

It is a huge mistake to hire a developer without seeing her coding. No technical interview is a replacement for a good pair-programming session.

There is a lot we can get from a pair-programming interview:

- How quickly the developer decides on which tests to write—that shows experience
- How familiar she is with the tools (the integrated development environment [IDE], language, testing and mocking frameworks, usage of shortcuts, etc.)
- Choice of names for classes, methods, and attributes
- How clean and expressive the code is

- How the developer reacts when the interviewer makes suggestions or comments
- Her thought process
- Her care in not just solving the problem but also how she is solving the problem

However, pair-programming interviews can be very tricky to conduct and choosing a good problem to work on can be quite challenging.

A common approach is to choose one of the various katas publicly available or to create our own katas. Katas are great when we want to test for TDD and general clean-code principles.

Another approach is to take an existing piece of code, from our own code base, especially a piece that is badly written and without tests, and ask the candidate to write tests and make it better. This is valuable for projects with loads of legacy code; it tests the real skills the candidate would be using if hired.

It is important to have realistic expectations when conducting pair-programming interviews. We need to remember that we, as interviewers, already know the problem domain but the candidate doesn't. We shouldn't expect that the candidates would get to certain conclusions or solutions straightaway. Once we know something, we tend to forget how much time we spent learning it.

If we provide the tools (computer, IDE, testing and mocking frameworks), we need to bear in mind that the candidate may not be familiar with them. This is not necessarily a bad thing. Every mainstream language has many testing frameworks and is supported by many different IDEs and text editors. It's common to see candidates getting stuck when they don't know the testing framework or IDE provided during the interview. Pay attention to how the candidate reacts to that. The expected reaction would be to have the candidate asking for help. Because this is a pair-programming exercise, the interviewer should do whatever she can to point the candidate in the right direction.

Whatever we do as an interviewer, we should never let the candidate struggle for too long. We should wait for a maximum of three or four minutes, and then make a few suggestions. The candidate is already under pressure, and making her struggle for too long will just make things worse. As long as we can mentally keep track of the points where the candidate struggled, we should help the candidate to show us what she can do.

Pair programming means pair programming and not standing over someone's shoulder and applying unnecessary pressure. That's not how we usually work with our colleagues and there is no point to behave this way with a candidate.

Once I interviewed a very experienced guy. On my machine I had Eclipse, JUnit, and Mockito (a Java mocking framework). He told me that he was more familiar with IntelliJ and JMock. "I never used Mockito, so at least I'll learn something today," he said with a big smile.

Quite quickly he became frustrated because he didn't know the Eclipse short-cuts. "I'm really feeling stupid using the mouse so often. It's really irritating me," he said. "What's the shortcut for running the tests?" I answered and he took notes on a piece of paper. He then started asking me about many other shortcuts and took note of them all. Fifteen minutes later, he had mapped, on a piece of paper, some of the basic shortcuts and started to feel more comfortable.

He also struggled with Mockito. "If you tell me what you want to do, I can type it for you," I said. "I want to mock this class and return this constant every time the public method is invoked," he said. I then wrote the code according to what he wanted to do. That was enough for him to understand how Mockito worked. By the end of the interview, he was using Eclipse and Mockito quite well.

The only thing I regret about that interview is that we were not fast enough to get back to him and he got a job somewhere else.

The interesting thing about this interview was that the candidate took the time to learn the Eclipse shortcuts and a new testing framework. We could have added JMock to the project but he was keen to learn Mockito. He showed me passion when he became irritated because he didn't know the shortcuts. He showed me he could learn new frameworks quite quickly—Mockito in this case. He was humble in asking me questions, showing me that we could easily work together as a team. We also had a few debates, but even when we didn't agree, I could feel that he had thought about the things he was saying. And, besides all that, his code was quite clean.

Bring Your Own Computer

Each candidate may feel comfortable with different tools and frameworks. Asking the candidate to bring her own laptop to the interview is a good way to see her working with her own favorite tools, and it can save precious interview time.

An interesting exercise is to ask the candidate to clone a project from GitHub—provided that the candidate can connect to the Internet—and then work on it. This approach can tell us a lot about the candidate. Is the candidate familiar with Git? Does she have it installed? How is her computer configured? Which tools does she prefer? Can she start a project quickly? Does she have all the testing and mocking frameworks installed and configured? Developers who write code outside working hours will always have all their tools installed and ready to go.

As we are interested to see the candidate's technique—how clean the code is, how she writes the tests, how she approaches the problem—it doesn't really matter which tools or languages the candidate will use.

TAILOR-MADE INTERVIEWS

Before interviewing any candidate, we should ask ourselves: what are our values? What sort of attitude do we expect from our colleagues? What are the essential skills for the role offered? The answers for these questions form the acceptance criteria we must use to hire someone. But that doesn't mean we shouldn't explore other topics. It's always good to verify how versatile the candidate is, as long as we don't reject a candidate for things that are not really important to us.

I was once contacted for an opportunity at a major newspaper in the UK. The role was for a server-side Java developer and the project had no user interface. The project seemed interesting and I was comfortable with the vast majority of the technologies listed. I decided to apply.

The interview process was composed of two phases: an online multiple-choice test and an interview with the project manager or team leader. That was a very bad start because I believe online tests are stupid and totally inefficient. On top of that, as I wouldn't be talking to any of the developers during the selection process, there would be no way for me to judge their knowledge, core values, and the real situation of the project. No, I don't trust managers and HR to give me this information.

The online test was 30 multiple-choice Java questions, randomly selected. Out of the 30 questions, 14 (46 percent) were about Swing and Java Applets—old and horrible technologies that were totally irrelevant for the job. From the code examples, I noticed that the questions were based on a very old version of Java—clearly they had not been updated for years. I had never used Applets before and I couldn't even think why someone would use that crap. As far as I know, Applets were not being used in any of their applications.

A couple of hours after I finished the online test, the HR department called me. They said the team was still deliberating whether they would call me or not for a face-to-face interview, because I had scored 87 percent on the test (26/30) but the team would only interview candidates who scored at least 90 percent. "Not a problem at all," I said. "I'll help them with their decision. Please tell them I don't want to continue with the process."

The preselection process is extremely important. That's where you filter candidates according to your core values. Judging candidates by online multiple-choice tests on totally unrelated technologies is definitely not how you do it.

TAKING A PUNT

Once I interviewed a candidate in his early twenties. He had two years of experience and was still working for his first employer. His CV didn't have any mention of TDD or Agile—things that are quite common in a CV these days. His CV was quite boring, with almost nothing in it, besides two years of experience at a single company. It was a CV that I wouldn't usually pay much attention to. However, there was one line there that really made me curious. He had been a member of a Linux user group since he was 16 years old.

I invited him for the interview and, as we spoke, he told me that he was working for an organization where Agile and Extreme Programming practices were *not allowed*. However, he also mentioned he was trying to do TDD as a pet project. "How many pet projects do you have?" I asked him. "Five," he said. We then spent the rest of the interview talking about his pet projects: the technologies he used, his approach to TDD on the projects, challenges, things he would do differently, and so forth.

Although he didn't have much experience in the technologies we used and had basic TDD skills, I could see how passionate he was to try new things. He was using his own time to learn things that he could not do during working hours. He was a classic example of a guy who, given the right environment and opportunity, could really shine and become a great developer.

We were looking for more experienced developers but something told me that I could not let him go. One year after he joined our team, he became one of the best developers we had.

When interviewing, we should look for talent, attitude, passion, and potential, not knowledge of specific technologies.

HIRING FOR AN EXISTING TEAM VERSUS HIRING FOR A NEW TEAM

Recruiting the first developers for a new project is slightly different from recruiting for an existing project.

When recruiting for an existing team, I look for passion, positive attitude toward the way we work and our core values, and a good foundation in software development such as TDD, refactoring, clean code, and design. Everything else—specific languages, frameworks, and tools—is secondary. I know that if the candidate has a good foundation, she will learn whatever technologies we use in no time.

When recruiting the first developers for a new project, besides the passion and a good software development foundation, we should aim to have at least two (maybe one if a small project) experienced developers with a good track record of delivering projects. Dealing with the client's bureaucracy, business pressure, production issues, and stakeholders' management are things that cannot be learned while coding a pet project or in our spare time. These are things that we just learn when we are actively involved in delivering software for real customers.

Medium to large projects—deployed in a real production environment—need experienced developers with loads of scars on their backs to minimize the pain of bringing a project to life. For the first developers in a brand-new project, besides passion and potential, we also need to look for real-world experience and a good track record. We also need technologists (developers who are familiar with many different technologies and tools like databases, build tools, scripting, virtual machines, and whatever else may be needed for the project) and not just specialists (developers who know just a few tools really well, like a programming language or certain technical practices like TDD).

PRE-INTERVIEW CODING EXERCISES

Asking candidates to submit some code before the face-to-face interview is a great way to preselect candidates. However, we should give them time. Don't ask candidates to submit the code a few hours after giving them the requirements. At this point in the selection process, the focus is to analyze the best code the candidate can write according to a given set of requirements and not how fast they do it. Small time frames will make the candidate rush to solve the problem instead of focusing on writing well-crafted code.

One approach is not to set a time frame at all. Just let the candidates submit the code whenever they are ready. However, this approach is more suitable for larger companies that are constantly hiring or for small companies that are keen to build a pipeline of good candidates over time.

Another approach is to tell candidates when we will start evaluating the code submissions. Assuming we have a few CVs in hand, we can send the requirements to all the candidates at the same time and tell them that in one week we will start looking at the code submissions. However, this one-week period is not a deadline; it's just the date we will start evaluating the submissions. The first candidate to have an acceptable submission will be invited to the next round of interviews. If no one is hired, we keep accepting submissions. Although one week sounds like a reasonable amount of time, I prefer to give candidates an interval of time that contains at least two weekends.

Let the candidate choose the language and tools. At this stage, we want to see if the candidate can code well, regardless of the language. Even if we are hiring developers to work with Java or Ruby, the important thing is what techniques are applied to solve the problem and not the language or frameworks. Looking at submitted code is a far better way to filter candidates than looking at CVs or conducting phone interviews.

There will be cases where some candidates will decide not to go forward with the selection process because they don't want to spend too much time writing code for a job they might not even get. In a way, that's a good thing. At least we know that the ones who decided to submit their code are keen to work for us and are taking the selection process seriously.

EVERYONE SHOULD KNOW HOW TO INTERVIEW

Interview techniques are a skill we should master, both as interviewers and as candidates. However, this is a skill that is very rarely taught. Usually companies have a few senior developers who conduct all the technical interviews. Although that seems to make sense, and may work for a period of time, it is not sustainable. A strong team is a team where each developer can conduct interviews, making sure he or she will find the talent the team expects.

Experienced developers should always take less-experienced developers to the interviews with them. Watching more-experienced developers interviewing will help them to conduct interviews in the future. Over time, they can switch roles. The less-experienced developer will be the interviewer, and the most-experienced developer will be the observer.

Pair interviewing and rotating interviewers is a good way to keep everyone involved. Being able to interview and select new developers to join the team gives existing developers a great sense of empowerment and team spirit. It gives them the certainty that they are in control of their own project and of who is going to work with them.

DEVELOPERS MUST INTERVIEW DEVELOPERS

I've seen how frustrated developers were in companies where they could not choose their own teammates. It's very frustrating when, all of a sudden, our manager comes to us and says, "Guys, this is Steve Stranger. He is joining the team today."

Good developers don't hire bad developers. They will try to find developers who are even better than they are; they know how important it is to have a great team—not just for the benefit of the company but for their own benefit as well.

As a company, it is essential that you have the developers conducting the interviews. As a candidate, if developers do not interview you, consider finding a job somewhere else.

SUMMARY

We can learn a lot from a company, team, and individuals just by paying attention to how they interview. We can learn how hierarchical they are. We can learn if they are bureaucratic and strictly follow a process. We can learn how much they care about software development and how developers are treated. We can learn how much trust there is between management and the development team.

When looking for a job, software craftsmen look for far more than just a project with cool technologies and a good salary. They look for a productive partnership and a job that makes them happy to wake up every morning and go to work.

INTERVIEW ANTI-PATTERNS

Paying attention to every detail during the selection process is one of the best ways to get insights into the culture and values of the hiring company. Experienced and talented developers are very selective about the clients they want to work with. On top of the financial offer, autonomy, mastery, purpose, productive partnership, talented and passionate people, and a good working environment are some of the things they will consider before accepting any offer. How they are interviewed and, most important, the people who are interviewing them can be decisive factors in them accepting the job.

In order to attract software craftsmen, as an interviewer it is important to know what to avoid when conducting interviews.

In this chapter we cover many interview anti-patterns that should be avoided if you want to attract software craftsmen to your organization.

DON'T BE A SMART-ASS INTERVIEWER

Don't try to make yourself look smarter and better than the candidate. Don't intimidate the candidate by putting her in a tough situation just for your pleasure. Don't try to impress the candidate with your job title, responsibilities, and skills.

Don't talk to the candidate as if you were the most powerful person in the world. Simply put, don't be an ass.

Don't try to look smart by asking tricky and irrelevant questions. Experienced and talented developers will notice it straightaway and won't be very inclined to work with you.

When recruiting for talent, you should be looking for a partner, a person who can join your team and help you to be better, and not a submissive developer who just follows your orders blindly.

Just be honest and humble. Treat candidates like fellow professional developers, and conduct the interview as if you were having a great technical conversation with someone you respect. Most important, listen to the candidates and keep your mind open. You may actually learn a few things.

DON'T USE BRAINTEASERS

Avoid stupid questions that are totally unrelated to the job. How many golf balls can you fit into an airplane? A clerk at a butcher shop stands 5 feet 10 inches tall and wears size 13 sneakers. What does he weigh? The ability to answer these stupid brainteasers has nothing to do with writing well-crafted code, being a good team player, or having a professional attitude. Brainteasers are a total waste of time, as Google interviewers finally realized after using them for a long time. At least for them, better later than never.

DON'T ASK QUESTIONS TO WHICH YOU DON'T KNOW THE ANSWERS

Googling for questions and answers to ask candidates before the interview makes no sense. If you, as an interviewer, are not sure about the questions and respective answers, they are probably not very important to the job. If you are good at your job, you will know what is important and what is not important.

Don't try to trick the candidate with confusing or misleading questions. If we don't do that to our colleagues, and we even get mad when people do it to us, why would we do it to candidates?

DON'T TRY TO MAKE THE CANDIDATE LOOK LIKE A FOOL

Once I was invited to interview for a very well-known telecom company. They were interested in me because I had worked for telecoms before and I had been recommended by a very senior person there.

Two people cointerviewed me: a director and a lead architect, whom—if hired— I would be reporting to. The director started the interview talking about general things, trying to get to know me better, asking about things that I liked and disliked in software projects. We quite rapidly ended up talking about Agile, autonomy, and collaboration. A few times during those first 15 minutes, the director turned to the lead architect and said things like, "That's what I was trying to tell you before. I like this stuff."

Based on the conversation and body language, I noticed that the director and I could work well together. However, the lead architect was not happy at all. He then interrupted the conversation and asked me to explain bits of the architecture I had designed and implemented in a previous project. I immediately stood up, went to the whiteboard, and started explaining the high-level architecture and roughly how one of my previous systems worked. After I finished, the lead architect looked at the director, then back at me, and with disdain he said, "That looks too simple. It's not a real architecture." I could clearly see contempt in his attitude.

I took a deep breath and counted until 25. From that point on, I knew I would not be able to work with the lead architect. "Thank you. I'll take it as a great compliment. This *simple* architecture today is responsible for providing the service for more than 20 million subscribers in three different countries. I'm glad we never needed anything more complex than that." That was the beginning of the end. If the lead architect didn't like me before, he now hated me.

The director still tried to bring the interview back on track but it was clear to everyone that the partnership would not happen. I then put an end to that awkward situation, explaining to the director that there was no point in continuing the interview. I thanked them for the opportunity and left.

DON'T BLOCK THE INTERNET

I've heard about interviewers who don't allow candidates to use the Internet during coding activities. "That's a good way to measure whether the candidates really know what they are doing," they say. I wonder what would happen to these interviewers if they didn't have access to the Internet at work. Do they really know everything off the top of their heads? Can they really develop systems without ever searching for anything online? I doubt it.

Being able to research solutions and better ways to solve problems is an essential skill for any software developer. Removing Internet access just doesn't make sense. If the interviewer thinks that his interview would be jeopardized because the candidate could find the solutions on the Internet, she should probably change her interview.

DON'T CODE ON A PIECE OF PAPER

Asking candidates to write code on a piece of paper (or on a whiteboard) is a very stupid idea when it comes to interviewing developers. I don't think interviewers should ask candidates to do anything that they can't do themselves, or that doesn't reflect the reality the candidate will face if they get the job. Should the candidate write tests and refactor the code on the piece of paper, too? Should the candidate tear the paper in smaller pieces and rearrange them as she gets more understanding about the problem?

There is a difference between being a teacher in high school—asking students to produce algorithms in pseudocode—and hiring a professional software developer. When hiring professionals, we should look for developers who master their tools and techniques and who can produce well-crafted code through testing and refactoring. We should look at real code produced with real tools and not some scribbles on a piece of paper or whiteboard.

DON'T USE ALGORITHMS

Which coding exercise should we give to candidates? Although this sounds like a very reasonable question, the question we should be asking instead is: what are the things we value the most?

Many interviewers choose algorithmic exercises for their coding interviews. However, not many of them work on systems where a deep knowledge of algorithms is necessary. "I'm checking the candidate's ability to solve problems," they say. While this is a fair point, interviewers can achieve the same results by using exercises that are closely related to the reality of their projects.

The vast majority of the problems I've seen in different systems over the years were not related to how algorithms were written. The most common problems were lack of tests or, at least, good tests; bad design; low cohesion and tight coupling; lack of refactoring as new features are introduced; a constant change of requirements; anemic and deficient domain models, and so on. Those were the real problems I've seen the most. By nature, algorithms are procedural and better implemented in a functional style. We don't create classes or model the business domain when implementing an algorithm.

If the main problems we have in our system are not about algorithms, we should not use them in our coding interviews. We should focus on giving candidates exercises where they need to design a solution and express the business domain. If we need developers with good skills in Test-Driven Development and design, we should use exercises that reflect that.

However, if our application is all about algorithms, then, of course, we should definitely test for that. The point here is not about using or not using algorithms for our coding interviews—it's about testing candidates according to the things we value and to what is important for the project.

DON'T CONDUCT PHONE INTERVIEWS

Phone interviews are only needed when the preselection process is poor. Many companies conduct them before inviting the candidate for a face-to-face interview. The purpose is to verify whether the candidate can satisfy the minimum set of requirements for the job.

Although they serve a purpose—avoiding wasting time on much longer face-to-face interviews—I find them impersonal and sometimes quite mechanical. Phone interviews tend to be quite dry, with a sequence of questions and answers, with not much time for a proper conversation. The reason is because the interviewer is usually in a rush to ask the questions she needs to ask in order to decide if she will or will not invite the candidate for a longer interview.

For non-native speakers, having a phone interview can be very challenging. Because they can't see the other person, there is a large chance they won't understand every single word the interviewer is saying. They may also struggle to express themselves when they cannot use their body language, paper, or a whiteboard.

Save a phone interview for when it is the only option—interviewing candidates who are located in different countries—and always favor a face-to-face interview.

SUMMARY

Finding good developers is difficult and time-consuming. If we are investing time to interview, we should make it count. Using brainteasers or making the candidate look like a fool or feel inferior are good ways to make good developers not want to work for or with you. Coding without the Internet or on a whiteboard or on a piece of paper is pointless and annoying. What we really want is to see a developer at her best. We want to pair with her, using good tools and producing something. We want to see tests, refactoring, and good naming. We want to have a nice conversation and see if we can work together well. We want to feel how it would be to work with that person.

There is a huge demand for good developers and if we want them to join our company, we must learn how to interview them properly. We also need to remember that developers are not the only ones being interviewed. Good developers are also interviewing companies and they will exercise their option to reject the bad ones.

THE COST OF LOW MORALE

Low morale can be one of the main reasons for a software project to fail. Low morale could bring a whole company to a halt. In this chapter we will discuss the cost of low morale and how it can be harmful to projects and companies. We will end the chapter describing how software craftsmen can be helpful for injecting some passion into a team of unmotivated individuals.

From this chapter onward, I will assume that the process used by you and your team is based on a combination of Agile processes and disciplines. By Agile process, I mean that you work in a cross-functional team, have a quick daily catch-up with all team members to discuss what you are doing and how things are going, work in short iterations, and are empowered to estimate the work and decide what you want to work on according to the priorities. I'll also assume that you have a unified backlog, prioritized by someone responsible for the product (the product owner), and developers are responsible for testing the application.

THE AGILE HANGOVER: LOW MORALE

The vast majority of the companies I worked for in the past ten years have gone through some sort of Agile transformation. And with almost no exceptions, a few years after their Agile adoption, many of these companies realized that their software delivery capability was still very poor. This realization is what Mashooq Badar and I call *the Agile hangover*.

A common problem we find in all these companies is low morale. We often hear people complaining about their colleagues, managers, architects, clients, and how uninspiring their jobs generally are. "The whole thing is a mess," a developer told me. "Although managers keep talking about this five-year plan, no one really knows exactly what needs to be done and still we have loads of people that are not directly involved with the project, dictating what developers can or cannot do. We have different people, from different departments, asking us for *urgent* features, quite often conflicting with each other. We have no idea why we are doing certain things, but people giving us requirements are normally too busy or refuse to explain them in detail. And the few times we tried to suggest a better way of working, nobody listened." This is a situation that I've seen time and time again in medium and large organizations. Although less common in smaller organizations, I've met many developers who were also not very happy to be there for similar reasons. They felt they were not being treated as skilled professionals who could contribute not only code but also ideas to make the company better.

Adopting Agile should be synonymous with empowering people, embracing change, improving collaboration, focusing on the things that are really important, understanding the value of each piece of work, and knowing why we are doing things. Agile should be synonymous with doing things right, improving communication, delivering value to customers, shortening the feedback loop, and working effectively as a team. A true Agile organization can easily provide what knowledge workers need the most to enjoy their jobs: autonomy, mastery, and purpose.

After working with so many Agile teams over the years, I noticed that many developers on those teams were not really motivated and proud of their jobs. "You know, it's just my job. I just work here." Why is it so common to work with people who don't enjoy their jobs? Why is it so common to see unhappy developers, working like zombies, just waiting for the clock to hit five o'clock so they can go home? Why don't our colleagues care about doing the best they can for the project and for the company they work for? And what about ourselves? Are we really motivated and enjoying our jobs?

As discussed in Chapter 2, although Agile transformations had a very positive impact, shortening the feedback loop and improving visibility, they did very little to make developers better. Old-time developers were still quite resistant to change the way they worked, and they were not so keen to collaborate with other developers. "I've worked for this company for ten years and I know what I need to do. I don't need to write tests. I won't make silly mistakes. I know this application inside-out." Newcomers and younger developers struggle to have their voices heard; for them it may be very difficult to challenge more senior developers.

Agile coaches had very little success improving developers' technical skills; very few Agile coaches can actually sit down with developers and write code. Developers quite quickly learned not to listen to Agile coaches when they talk about Test-Driven Development (TDD) and all the other Extreme Programming (XP) practices. "This guy comes here talking about TDD, pair programming, and all this nonsense, but what does he know? Can he sit down with me and show me how it works? Can he look at our applications and explain to us how we can make them better? Can he lead by example? We don't need another person telling us what to do."

The sad reality is, for certain companies, the outcome of their Agile adoption was developers mechanically following a new process, but still developing software exactly how they were before. If they were not motivated before, they were certainly not motivated after, either.

THE COST OF EMPLOYING 9-TO-5 DEVELOPERS

When asking passionate developers about what to do with 9-to-5 developers, the first thing that comes to their minds is *fire them all*. I must confess that I really need to make an effort not to think this way. Although I believe that in the majority of cases that would be the right thing to do (conveniently ignoring the laws that might prevent us from doing that), that should not always be the case. The reason is that I don't really think it is possible to precisely measure passion. Different people enjoy different things and express their passion in various ways.

Lack of passion is not what really bothers passionate developers; what frustrates them is to be held back by other developers when they are trying to improve their applications and the way they work.

An international media company once contacted the consultancy company I was working for. They were looking for a developer to join their team and I was the *lucky* one. My role was to help them develop a new replacement system for a 14-year-old internal system they had, written in a proprietary technology, similar to Oracle forms. The company that developed the technology went bust and very few unskilled developers remained to support the application—when things are not going well, the best developers are always the first ones to go. The project to build the *new* system had started almost three years before I joined. The team was composed of a "technical" project manager (with very little experience as a developer), a very well-paid contractor (totally useless, working on his own— God knows on what), a permanent developer (who had no idea of what was going on), three consultants (just interested to stay there for as long as possible without doing much), and a business analyst (who had been hired to try to understand what the old system did). The head of the IT department—the person responsible for the project—barely knew how to switch her computer on. People on the project very rarely talked to each other, and for months, I'd never seen any of them going out for a drink after work. To make things even worse, that project was not a priority for the business; they were still using the old system.

After the initial three years of procrastination, the business finally realized that their money was not being well spent and started putting pressure on the consultancy company (us) that they had hired; the three other consultants were also from the consultancy company I was working for. That was the situation when my company sent me there. "Go there and sort that out," I was told.

As it happens to every passionate developer joining a new project, I was ready to make an impact. And there I went, full of energy, to try to bring the project back on track. For the first two weeks, although painful, I tried to only observe and learn, gathering information to make informed suggestions. In our *daily* stand-up meetings, when we had them, very rarely would we see the whole team there. Backlog? Well, they had some stuff on the wiki with no estimations or prioritization. Iterations? Well, sort of. There was this notion of working on stuff every two weeks but no one was really bothered if things would be delivered during the iteration or not. The majority of the *stories* and *tasks* were *ongoing* tasks. "This feature here will probably take around six weeks to be developed. I'll let you guys know when it is done," some developers used to say.

For the first couple of months I tried to bring some order into the chaos. I tried to organize the backlog and run planning sessions and retrospectives. I tried to know more about each person, organizing team lunches and drinks—just one or two people came to them. I tried to motivate the other developers, inviting them to pair with me. Maybe we could even try to do this new thing called TDD. "What's the point of that? Sounds stupid." I then tried to propose improvements in the process and also in the code, but the only comments I got back were, "Sorry man, I don't think it's going to happen. I have no interest to rush or make things better. In fact, I don't really care. And for your information, the client doesn't care either. This is just a job. I have a life and I don't want to get stressed out thinking about this stuff. Just relax."

I was the only one writing tests. I had the hope that maybe at some point some of them would enjoy working that way and would start doing it as well. It never happened. What happened instead was that they would change the code and break all the tests. When I went to speak to them, they would say, "We told you that this stuff is a waste of time. The project manager and the business analyst are useless; they don't really know what they want. Let them test the system. If they complain about something, we fix it."

For eight months I tried. I tried in many different ways to make people care. I tried to make them at least have a small degree of pride in what they were doing. At some point, I was so frustrated that I decided to completely isolate myself. I picked up a few features that were fairly independent and started working on my own; I had the hope that at least I would feel better if I could deliver something useful. But it didn't work. The only thing I achieved was more frustration and more arguments with some members of the team.

As a last resort, I decided to escalate the issue and talk directly to the head of IT. She was not too bothered either. "I've supervised quite a few software projects in this company. Trust me. Software projects are always complicated and take a long time to be delivered. It's just the nature of the beast."

This story does not have a happy ending. I asked the consultancy company I was working for to find me another project—I would leave the company otherwise. My consultancy company escalated the problem to people above the IT department and replaced almost the entire team; my company later took full ownership of the project and delivery process. The head of the IT department disappeared—many said she was fired. The project took seven years to complete and cost more than ten million pounds. Looking back, our rough estimation was that the same project, with full support from the business, a team of five talented and passionate developers, and with a good business analyst, would have taken between 18 and 24 months to complete, costing less than two million pounds. Eight million pounds, five years: that is what passionate and talented professionals could have saved for the company—money and time that could have been much better spent on new initiatives and improvements in other areas of the business.

In projects like that, it is almost impossible for a single developer to change the world. Certain projects need a bigger intervention, where external experts need to be brought in and take control of the project for a period of time.

Fortunately, not all projects and companies are like that.

CONSTRAINED BY LACK OF MOTIVATION

Every company has problems. Every single employee, without much effort, could easily come up with a big list of things they wished were better. But, if employees know what needs to be changed and how things could be improved, why don't they do anything about it? Here are the most common reasons, in no particular order:

- They don't feel they are empowered to do it.
- They don't want to be the ones pushing it.
- Nah! Too much hassle.
- They don't believe that things could be changed.
- No one agrees on what the better thing is.
- They don't care. It's *just* a job.

The reason why many companies fail when trying to improve the way they work is low motivation. There is no way we can change an organization when people are not motivated and don't care about their jobs. Before trying to convince people to work in a different way, ask yourself: are they motivated to do a good job? Do they really care about improving the way they work? Are they constantly trying to get better at what they do? Do they even believe in or like what the company does?

INJECTING PASSION

Embedding software craftsmen in a team, either hiring them permanently or bringing on external craftsmen for a period of time, is the most efficient way to motivate existing developers. One of the differences between regular developers and software craftsmen is that software craftsmen are on a mission. They are on a mission to make things better, to deliver value to their clients, and to inspire people around them. They are not afraid to lead the way and drive changes. For software craftsmen, striving to always do their best is just a natural state of mind.

There is nothing more annoying for a developer than having a manager or an architect dictating what she should do. Instead of just telling others what to do, software craftsmen can sit down and pair with other developers, sharing their knowledge, experience, and passion. Besides getting the work done, they are always keen to act like mentors to many other developers. Software craftsmen are always talking about software and are willing to share the things they are doing to better themselves.

While working for an investment bank, my job was, among many other things, to inject some passion into the development teams. There were quite a few smart developers there but not many of them were really excited about their jobs. They were coming to the office, doing what they were asked to do, and going home. Although they were in the middle of an Agile transformation, they still had loads of bugs in their systems, they were deploying software into production only two or three times per year, and they brought very little innovation to their department.

We've done many things over the three years I was there but, since this is not a book on Agile transformation and organizational change, I'll just focus on some very simple ones that ended up having a very good result.

One of the first things we did was to hire a few craftsmen to join us. The advantage of bringing a few more craftsmen to the team was that they became our allies not only to fix technical problems but also to inject passion and bring innovations.

We were using Scrum and at the end of our daily stand-up meeting, we started asking: "Has anyone learned anything since our last stand-up meeting?" In the first week just another developer and I would answer yes and then describe something we read in a book or blog post, or some technology we tried the night before, or some code we had written. As weeks went by, more and more developers became motivated to learn more and share in our daily stand-ups. We started sharing blog post links, videos, and books. All of a sudden, more and more conversations about software, technologies, methodologies, practices, and possible solutions to some of our problems became common during lunch and coffee breaks. This was possible because the old developers could see the enthusiasm and expertise the new craftsmen had and they wanted to be part of it.

I once bought a copy of *Seven Languages in Seven Weeks* by Bruce A. Tale and started going through the first language (Ruby) and I mentioned it a few times during our stand-ups, coffee breaks, and pairing sessions. At some point two of the developers asked if they could join me when I was ready to start the second language (Prolog). We then agreed that we would meet every Wednesday at 12 P.M. and spend our lunch doing that. After each session, we were excited and would talk about it. More and more developers got interested and at one point we had 12 developers coming to the sessions and some of them decided to run talks and hands-on sessions in some of the languages.

Things like that completely changed our environment. Developers were excited about technology again and were keen to get better. They were all far more inclined to pair-program and try new things. Many innovations were brought to our department, many technical problems were fixed, the number of bugs reduced dramatically, everyone embraced TDD, and we started deploying to production far more often. The change in the general mood was so great that even product owners, project managers, and production services noticed. They were far happier to work with the developers as well. They could feel how much developers cared about the quality of what they were doing, not only because they cared about the company, but mainly because they were enjoying themselves. They were having fun. What before was a boring department in a large organization was now a cool group of people working very efficiently, always striving to get better.

SUMMARY

Low morale can destroy a company. Unmotivated people have no energy to create and bring innovation. They have no motivation to do a good job and take responsibility. But people are not normally like that; they *become* like that. Some companies do a very good job in beating the passion out of people. The good news is that low morale can be reversed over time if we have good support from management. Embracing Agile processes and ideology is essential for providing the right environment for improving morale, but when it comes to developers, we need more than that. Managers and Agile coaches have a very low chance of motivating developers because they are not close enough to them. I don't mean sitting next to them and talking to them multiple times a day. I mean sharing a career, a passion. The best person to motivate a developer is another developer. A good developer. A software craftsman. A developer whom other developers can look up to, who can inspire them. If you want to bring passion and motivation to a development team, make sure you bring in a few craftsmen to join them.

CULTURE OF LEARNING

No change can be made effectively if the people involved are not motivated or don't really care about their jobs. Over and over again I've seen managers trying to define strategies to make the organizations more efficient. And there they would go, with their PowerPoint presentations, telling everyone how great that change would be. They would also say, with a big smile, what everyone had to do to comply with the new policy. "From now on, developers must do Test-Driven Development [TDD]. Delivery teams must *do* Agile. Everyone is now expected to follow our new process." Developers would just ask themselves: "What does she know about writing code? Could she sit down and pair with us? Does she understand the details well enough to tell us how we should work?"

But let's not underestimate a manager's ability to make things worse. To make sure people would comply with the new (and imposed) way of working, managers would make them part of people's objectives and bonuses. However, when it comes to software development, this approach can lead to disastrous consequences.

In this chapter we discuss many different things we developers can do to create a culture of learning. All the things described in this chapter have been used in large global financial companies and also in a few smaller companies in various industries, with positive results in all of them.

WRONG MOTIVATION

There was a time when a very well-known investment bank hired the consultancy firm I worked for. They had a very specific requirement: "We want some developers that can retrofit unit tests to our code base." The consultancy then asked me to be one of these developers. I was really caught by surprise but, as I was on the bench, I couldn't really say no. To make things even weirder, the client wanted us to do it from our own office. Something was not quite right: normally companies in the financial sector are paranoid about security, never allowing their code to be accessed from outside their premises.

For a few months some colleagues and I wrote unit tests for the existing code without ever speaking to any of the developers who wrote it. The client was very clear: "You just need to write the tests. Your target is to bring the test coverage up to 70 percent. Once you reach that, you just need to keep maintaining it above this mark." On many occasions, we had no idea if the code had a bug or if the strange behavior we found was actually the desired behavior. We also had no idea if the existing classes and methods made any sense in the overall design and solution. We tried to talk to the developers but that was not part of the deal. They were always too busy and not interested in talking to us.

To make things even worse, the developers working for the bank were not keeping the tests up to date as they made changes to the code. And, of course, they were not writing new tests either. Every single time we updated our machine with the latest version of the code, we would find that many of our tests were broken.

After a few months of blindly retrofitting tests, without having a clue if the code itself was fit for the purpose, we managed to keep the test coverage above 70 percent. A few weeks later, the company was happy and terminated the contract.

Sometime after the project was finished (if we could call that a project), we asked our managers what that project was really about. Apparently, as part of their targets for the year, some technical managers had to bring the test coverage of their applications up to at least 70 percent. As it was part of their targets, their bonuses would be directly impacted if they didn't achieve that. So they just outsourced it.

Looking back, knowing what I know today, I feel that what we've done was immoral. Our consultancy company shouldn't have accepted that type of work. I should have said *no* to that. We would have helped them more if we had told them that what they were asking was not just wrong, but also dangerous. Some people would trust those tests. Some people would think that the system was reliable and could be deployed into production. Bad tests are worse than no tests at all. The retrofitted tests, at best, would guarantee that the code was working according to what we, external developers with no context of the business, understood. However, if the classes (or the application flow) had a bug, we wouldn't know, and now we had created tests that would perpetuate that behavior. If the tests are passing, the code must be correct, right?

At the end of the day, the client knew that what they were doing was wrong, but they only cared about the bonuses. At least we learned a lesson: we will never change an organization by forcing people to adopt a new process or different practices. Instead, we should create a culture of learning, where people can find their own motivation to make things better.

CREATING A CULTURE OF LEARNING

Creating a culture of learning is one of the most efficient ways of injecting passion into a company. Not many developers have been exposed to environments where their senior colleagues were constantly looking for ways to improve themselves. Many developers started their careers in places where senior developers didn't like what they were doing or were not motivated enough. Due to a lack of good role models, junior developers are led to believe that software development is not an exciting career and, like their seniors, they soon start planning how to become managers or architects; they believe that this is their natural career progression. These young developers, as they join our industry, have to deal with so much crap and unnecessarily complex code produced by their seniors that, for them, creating presentations on PowerPoint and spreadsheets on Excel seems far more attractive than writing code.

On the other hand, if the same junior developers had been brought up in an environment where their seniors were always trying to find ways to get better at what they do, getting excited every time they found a better way to do things or learned something new—truly aspiring to become software craftsmen—these developers would have enjoyed their professions. With highly motivated developers who have fun doing what they do and who are constantly looking outside their own cubicles, companies could benefit immensely from all the innovations and efficiencies they would bring.

However, instead of having managers trying to impose how, when, and what developers should learn, companies should empower developers to create their own culture of learning. If imposed, it becomes obligation, which in turn may lead to lack of interest. Let developers decide how, when, and what they want to learn. With this freedom, developers have a much better chance of creating and embracing a culture of learning. The better the developers are, the more innovative and agile the company can be. If the company becomes a place where developers are happy, many other good developers will be attracted to it.

Let's explore some of the things developers can do to create such an environment.

START A BOOK CLUB

Pick a book and tell your colleagues you will start reading it. Tell them what the book is about and check if anyone is interested in having a discussion about it once a week at lunchtime—or any other suitable time slot. If at least one other developer is interested, you are ready to start.

If no one is interested, ask the other developers what sort of book (or subject) they would like to explore. Make a list with the suggested topics, pick the one that the majority is interested in, do some research, and present them with a small list of books on the topic. As a group, choose one of them and schedule the first meeting.

If no one is interested, start reading the book you want, but take the time to share what you are learning during informal conversations. Maybe some of the developers who initially were not interested will change their minds and join you.

HAVE A TECH LUNCH (BROWN BAG SESSION)

Ask your team if, once a week, they would like to have lunch together while talking about technical stuff. The meeting doesn't need to have any structure; you decide what you want to talk about when you get there. Although it could be beneficial to discuss improvements to the project you are working on, don't make this meeting about work. Make it about learning. Make it about different technologies, approaches, techniques, books, or whatever else people want to share and discuss. Let people do short presentations if they want to. If you think that some of the ideas discussed could be used to improve the project you are working on, schedule a proper time to discuss it.

Tech lunches are very easy to set up because there is no preparation or organization needed. You just need a placc and people bringing their own lunches. I recommend using a meeting room instead of a coffee shop or restaurant; it saves time and you can use whiteboards, flip charts, and projectors if you want.

HAVE GROUP DISCUSSIONS (ROUNDTABLES)

Divide a wall or whiteboard in two. One side is for lightning talks; the other side is for topics to be discussed in a group. Hand Post-Its and pens to all the participants (or spread them on the table). Ask participants to write down the title of the lightning talk they want to give (five minutes for the talk, two minutes for questions) or the topic they want to discuss as a group.

Start with the lightning talks. People giving lightning talks can just stand up and speak. They can use the whiteboard or projector if they want to, of course. Make sure you control the time. If there are too many questions after the talk is finished, interrupt when time is up and move the lightning talk Post-It to the group discussions side. Tell everyone that they will have the opportunity to discuss that topic further if they want to.

Once the lightning talks (if any) are over, move on to the group discussion topics. Read the first card out loud and ask whoever wrote it to give a 30-second explanation about what she wants to discuss. Do it for all the cards. Once all the cards are explained, check if you can merge any similar topics into a single discussion; make sure people collaborate and are happy about merging the topics. Once this is done, start reading all the topics again, but this time ask people to raise their hands if they would like to discuss the topic. Write down next to the cards (or on the cards) the number of people interested in the topic. If there is a clear winner, ask the person who proposed the topic to start the discussion. Before the voting, tell people that they should try to vote for a single topic but if they are really undecided, it is OK to vote for more than one topic.

If there are two or three topics that have almost the same amount of votes, you can do one of the following:

- Take the two most-voted topics and split the people in two groups (you will need to have another room available).
- Take another vote but only on the most-voted topics.
- Propose to discuss one topic for the first half of the meeting and the other topic for the second.

After 45 minutes (or 30 if you don't have much time), interrupt the discussion and ask if people want to switch topics or carry on discussing the same topic.

Switch Projects for an Iteration

Within a company, it is common to have different development teams working on different applications or in different parts of the same system. After a period of time, projects fall into a routine; some of the initial technical challenges have been solved and the biggest design decisions have been made. However, as projects evolve, very rarely do previous decisions get reviewed. As developers become comfortable with their tools and design decisions, they also stop looking for better ways of doing things. Boredom takes over.

Assuming that developers are constantly pairing with each other, we can solve this problem by providing an opportunity for developers to switch projects for at least a full iteration. Pairing with developers from different teams exposes developers to different technologies, techniques, and ways of working and thinking. Having different people joining an existing project, even if for a small period of time, makes the members of the team rethink their problems and solutions and explain why things are done the way they are. This may bring a few positive effects:

- **Validation of the decisions:** The new person, after understanding the context in which the decisions were made, can confirm that it was a good decision.
- **Knowledge sharing:** The new developer learns how certain problems can be solved.
- **Improvements:** The new developer can propose better ways to solve those problems.
- **Collective learning:** After discussing the current solution and sharing knowledge with each other, the existing members of the team and the new developer can come up with a better solution.

Periodic exchanges can greatly improve motivation, spread innovations across projects, and break knowledge silos. These periodic exchanges don't need to be limited to developers. The Scrum master of one team can swap places with a tester from another team.

Switch Projects for a Few Hours

As a variation to the approach just described, we could have developers working with different teams for just a few hours or days. Developers can organize the switch themselves. They just need to walk to the other team's location, sit down with one of the developers, and pair with her for a couple of hours.

I once worked for a large organization where all the software developed in our department was written in Java. Over time, different teams started adopting Gradle as a build tool, and Spock as a testing framework, instead of Maven and JUnit. The team I was working with decided to use Scala and a commercial in-memory data grid instead of Java and Oracle in one of our new projects.

Being able to freely walk over to another team and ask if we could pair with someone for a few hours every other week was a great way to expose many of us to the different technologies. At the moment of this writing, one of our teams is already migrating to Gradle and Spock, and another team is strongly considering Gradle.

CONDUCT GROUP CODE REVIEWS

Group code reviews are another very interesting way to create a culture of learning. It's amazing what we can learn just debating with colleagues whether a piece of code could be improved or if it could be used as an example that should be followed. If done right, group code reviews can bring the whole team together; everyone feels responsible for the decisions of what constitutes quality for them.

Although I value group code reviews, it is important to get it right. But what does "get it right" mean?

- Comments should never be personal.
- It doesn't matter who wrote the code.
- Never look at the commit history during a group code review. Focus on changing the future, not on dwelling on the past.
- Comments should be objective and constructive. The focus is on how to make the code better and not to say why it sucks.
- Sometimes having a facilitator helps. Her role is to make sure everyone speaks and that there is no fingerpointing.
- Don't expect to make a lot of progress. If developers want to spend a lot of time discussing a single issue, let them do it.

HAVE HANDS-ON CODING SESSIONS

Hands-on coding sessions are sessions where developers get together to write code. The facilitator will choose an exercise, normally a kata, and add some twist (constraints) to it just to spice things up. The main objective of a hands-on coding session is not to finish the exercise; the focus is to practice writing the best code we can possibly write and challenge ourselves. Here are some suggestions to run a good hands-on session:

- The facilitator must be familiar with the exercise; she would have done the exercise herself at least twice before the session.
- Developers work in pairs, preferably with a person that they never paired with before.
- As a rule, TDD is mandatory, unless stated otherwise by the facilitator.

- All developers should work on the same exercise; this makes the retrospective more relevant and focused.
- The facilitator should walk around and help developers; normally he or she should ask challenging questions, not give them the answer or direct suggestions.
- The facilitator should run a small retrospective at the end, where all developers can share what they've done, how they've done it, and what they've learned.
- Developers thank their pairs when the session is over.

Hands-on sessions are very helpful for injecting passion into our teams. It creates an opportunity for developers to learn from each other, and it brings a bit of fun to the workplace.

I strongly suggest you follow the suggestions above if you plan to organize regular hands-on sessions. They serve as a base for all of the very successful hands-on sessions organized by the London Software Craftsmanship Community (LSCC) and also the ones we run internally in our companies.

A few other important points for running a hands-on inside companies:

- Don't make it about work. The focus is to practice and learn in a safe environment.
- Allocate two hours for the session: one hour from the company's time and one hour from the developers' own personal time (i.e., 4 to 6 P.M. if the working day finishes at 5 P.M.). This way we have a mutual commitment to creating a culture of learning.
- Be prepared to run the first few sessions yourself. Very rarely will other developers put themselves forward to run the first sessions. Make sure you run them in a very informal and friendly way so the others get encouraged to run future sessions.

Favor Technology-Agnostic Thinking

Try running technology-agnostic sessions. Although it is always easier to run technology-specific sessions, if developers are not interested in the technology, they won't come.

When running technology-agnostic sessions, developers are in control of which technologies they want to use, which will make the session far more enjoyable for them. Choose a kata, add a few constraints (you cannot use an else statement, you cannot speak to your pair, you need to commit your code every two minutes, you need to use a tell-don't-ask approach, you need to write acceptance tests first, etc.), and let them choose which languages and frameworks they want to use.

Technology-agnostic sessions encourage variety. There will always be a pair trying to use a new language or framework. The retrospectives become more interesting and informative, because different pairs will talk about the challenges they had while using the technology they've chosen.

START INTERNAL COMMUNITIES OF PRACTICE (CoP)

Once you have a few regular sessions going, invite the developers who come more often to the sessions to help organize the sessions. Try to meet regularly to discuss future sessions and share the load of the organization and facilitation of the CoP. Keep it open and democratic so everyone can participate.

You just need two people to start a community, internal or external. That's exactly how LSCC, the largest Software Craftsmanship community in the world, started. Internal communities also start like that. You just need two people meeting regularly to attract more people over time. Just make sure people are aware that you are meeting and how much fun you are having. Share what you are learning during informal conversations over coffee or lunch. In no time, more and more developers will be joining you.

Just a word of caution: don't focus on growing the community. Focus on having fun and running good sessions. The growth will come naturally.

ENCOURAGE PET-PROJECT TIME

If you or anyone else on the team has a pet project, or wants to start a pet project, make it known. There is nothing more rewarding for a developer than having a good pet project to work on. You are your own boss. You decide what features to work on next, how you want to do it, and, most important, there are no deadlines.

Passionate developers love to have a playground where they can try many new ideas, technologies, and techniques. Ask around. See who has a pet project or is interested in starting one. Make the introductions and organize some time where developers can work on their own thing. If it is not possible to do that during working hours, try early in the morning, lunchtime, or evenings.

ENGAGE WITH EXTERNAL TECHNICAL COMMUNITIES

Although we covered many ways to establish a culture of learning in our organizations, we shouldn't stop there. Why limit ourselves to our small group? Check if there are any technical communities or user groups in your town. Invite your colleagues to go to their meetings. Get involved. See how you can contribute.

Exposing yourself and your colleagues to so many passionate and amazingly talented developers from the external communities can be a great way to motivate you all. In addition, participating in external communities can give you and your colleagues many ideas of what to do in your own internal CoP.

WHAT IF OTHERS DON'T WANT TO JOIN IN?

Different people, on different projects, in different companies, behave in different ways. Persuading people to change their behavior and to care about something is no simple task. Some will even say that it is impossible. If you think you are going to change an entire organization with your enthusiasm and the knowledge you got from a few books, forget it. That's not going to happen. However, you can help *some* people to (re)discover their passion and how great it is to be a developer.

You don't need to change every person to make the organization more effective or a better place. That's where the majority of the attempts to create a culture of learning fail. Attempting to change the whole organization (or the whole department, or the team) in one goal will bring frustration for those leading it. Frustration leads to lack of motivation, which in turn will make us give up. Don't let that happen.

The following sections provide advice that can help aspiring software craftsmen to create a culture of learning.

BE AN EXAMPLE

"It's really annoying," complains a developer. "I would love to do TDD but no one else in my team wants to do it." This is an excuse, not the attitude of a software craftsman. How can you persuade people to do something if you don't do it yourself? The most efficient way to inject passion into a team, and help them embrace different ways of working (or different technologies), is to lead by example. Many developers are not comfortable working in different ways, even if they feel that it could be a good idea. Having someone who is not necessarily experienced but has enthusiasm leading the way may be what is needed to ignite a whole team.

FOCUS ON THOSE WHO CARE

Not everyone will be moved by your enthusiasm and willingness to change. Focus on the ones who are willing to change. Pair with them. Write tests and review each other's code. Engage in good conversations; share ideas and information. Have fun with them. Once a few people are having fun, working well together, and using different techniques and approaches, more people will want to join.

DON'T FORCE

Forcing developers to attend any of the learning initiatives will just make things worse. Keep sending them the invitations (as you do for all the developers), making sure that they feel welcome to join in whenever they want. Never let people who don't want to be in the sessions compromise the fun that people who want to be in the session expect to have. If people don't want to participate, that's OK. At least they are not discouraging others to participate in future sessions because of a bad experience.

Don't get disappointed or angry with developers who don't want to join in. Keep your own motivation up, regardless of how many people turn up. As one of the open space guiding principles says, "Whoever comes *is* the right people."

DON'T TRY TO CHANGE EVERYONE

If you are on a team of ten where no one is doing TDD or pairing (or whatever else you want the team to do or adopt), and after a few months three or four started doing it, be happy about it. You don't need to change everyone. Big improvements can be made by just a small number of people.

AVOID CONSENSUS DELAYS

Trying to reach a consensus of when and where to run the sessions can be one of the biggest reasons not to have the sessions at all. Although we should always try to accommodate everyone, sometimes we just need to say: "Guys, John and I will be in the meeting room every Wednesday at 12:00 P.M. playing with Scala [or whatever other technology]. You are more than welcome to join us."

Many times I've seen teams discussing for weeks, trying to reach consensus. Sometimes it is just not possible to accommodate everyone. "I go to the gym at this time," says one. "Wednesdays I work from home," says the other. Just pick a day and run the session.

DON'T ASK FOR AUTHORIZATION

You don't need authorization from your boss to learn and practice on your own time. This is true in many companies, even during working hours if you don't ask. You just need to be responsible. No sensible manager will complain when she realizes that the team is practicing and trying to get better.

Find an empty room and have the meeting at lunchtime, early in the morning, or late in the afternoon. Just keep a healthy balance between your learning activities and the things you promised you would deliver. Be sensible.

DON'T COMPLICATE

"Our office layout is not suitable for group activities. Our meeting room does not have a projector. We don't have Internet access. What about our teams in other locations? How can we include them?" These are common complaints I hear from developers who are trying to create a culture of learning at their workplace. Because many of these problems cannot be resolved quickly enough, the sessions never happen.

You don't need any of that. If your office space is not good enough, go to a coffee shop. If you don't have Internet access, ask people to install whatever they need to install on their own laptops before coming to the meeting. If some of your teams are in different geographical locations, have the different teams running local sessions.

Aim for sessions that don't require too much organization or preparation. If you choose to have a group discussion, there is nothing you need to do besides booking a room and emailing everyone; the people attending the meeting can choose the topics when they get there.

Establish a Rhythm

The secret to having a healthy community, and keeping the sessions going, is to have a rhythm. It is much easier for people to come to the sessions regularly if they always know when and where the session is going to happen. "Our open space will be every Wednesday at 5 PM in the board room." Regular meetings are also much easier to organize. Find a meeting room and schedule a recurring meeting inviting everyone. Just make sure you find someone to run the meeting when you are not in the office. It is important that meetings happen even if you are away.

It is not difficult to bring a culture of learning into an organization. The only thing needed is a passionate developer willing to start it. Stop finding excuses and be this developer.

Summary

Creating a culture of learning is not only a manager's or Agile coach's job. It's everyone's job, including developers. Lack of time or an appropriate place for learning is not an excuse. Even with no support from management, developers can easily create a culture of learning, an environment where they can learn and share with each other. Don't have a place? Go to your local coffee shop. Don't have time? Use your lunchtime or do it before or after working hours. It's not possible to do it every day? Do it once a week.

Despite what many companies or managers think, creating a culture of learning is cheap and easy. Hire passionate developers and provide them with a good environment and support, and they will figure out many different ways in which they can learn, share, and bring innovation and quality to the company.

DRIVING TECHNICAL CHANGES

How do I bring technical practices to my team? How do I convince my team to do Test-Driven Development (TDD)? How do I convince my manager to let us do pair programming? How can I introduce another language or framework in my current project? These are questions that always pop up during conversations with other developers. Over the years I found that convincing other developers to adopt technical practices and tools or change their attitude was far harder than convincing managers. Many developers suffer from what Kent Beck calls *adolescent surety*. They think they have the secret formula for delivering great software and nothing else is worth considering.

From developers to managers and architects, learning how to deal with them is essential when driving technical change. In this chapter we look at different types of skeptics and how to convince them to be more open to different ideas.

IDENTIFYING SKEPTICISM PATTERNS

The first thing that any software craftsman needs to do before trying to change the culture of a team or trying to introduce new practices, tools, or processes is to identify the different types of skeptics she is facing. Terrence Ryan, in his book *Driving Technical Change,* defines the categories that skeptics of technical change tend to fall under: the Uninformed, the Herd, the Cynic, the Burned, the Time Crunched, the Boss, and the Irrational.

- **The Uninformed:** The main reason why they don't use certain tools or practices is lack of awareness. They simply don't know that certain tools or practices exist. Because of our natural tendency to fear the unknown, when new ideas are presented, they are usually rejected without much consideration. Developers in this group usually don't spend much time reading books or blogs or trying to understand what is going on outside their cubicle.

- **The Herd:** They feel they are not experienced enough to make certain decisions; they lack confidence and leave the decisions to *smarter* and *more-experienced* developers. They also think they are not allowed to do certain things just because no one else does them. However, they could easily adopt certain practices or tools if someone else pushed for it. Developers in this group are usually followers, not leaders.

- **The Cynic:** They like to argue and are constantly trying to prove that they are smarter than everyone else. They will question everything we say, transforming minor details into major issues, just to undermine what you are saying. Sometimes it's not personal—previous events may have made them so frustrated that they just can't see the upside of anything anymore. Developers in this group believe that *looking smart* is more important than *being smart*. One of the reasons for them not to adopt certain practices or tools is that they don't want to expose their own weaknesses; they believe their seniority status may be threatened if they show that they don't know how to do something. For them, it is easier to find ways to undermine and avoid new ideas than expose themselves and try them.

- **The Burned:** They tried a certain practice or tool in the past and it didn't work for them. Since they haven't had a good experience, they don't want to try it again. In the case of TDD, for example, if they didn't have anyone with experience on the team, it is safe to assume that they had problems. Probably their tests were very long and difficult to write. Maybe some of their tests were taking too long to run. Maybe they were too brittle. These are common problems inexperienced developers face when adopting TDD. Since they had a bad experience, they will not be so keen to try the same thing again.

- **The Time Crunched:** They are always busy and never have time for anything. Developers in this group are usually very shortsighted and unable to see the real cost of things. They don't have time to do things right but they have time to do the same things over and over again. For them, if we take TDD as an example, writing tests will take too much time—it is an extra thing they need to do. But they just can't see the amount of time that is being spent manually testing the entire system, debugging, and fixing bugs. They also don't understand the cost of developers having to be meticulously careful when changing the code without tests, and worst of all, not making any significant improvements for the fear of breaking the system. The only thing they see is that they don't have time to change the way they work.

- **The Boss:** If the boss is not a technical person, she probably won't understand what you are talking about and will fail to see the advantages of what you are proposing. The boss has management problems; you have development problems. Instead of "creating tools to automate something," you need to say "reducing ongoing project costs." Instead of "making code more maintainable," you should say "deliver the project faster." If the boss is an ex-developer, one who stopped writing code ages ago, you may have an even bigger problem. "When I was a developer, we never needed TDD and we always delivered." Yeah, right. Very few technical managers were actually great developers in the past, and even fewer were actually promoted because of their software development skills; they would disagree with this statement, of course. If they still write code, they may sometimes be perceived as Time Crunched.

- **The Irrational:** The worst type. All the other types of skeptics base their opposition to new ideas on premises that, although not necessarily correct, are at least rational and logical. As long as the skeptic has a rational and logical premise, we can reason with them, and eventually come to a sensible conclusion. But not the Irrational. They will swing from one premise to another as they get defeated. "This will cause performance issues. Automated tests are never better than humans. I heard the framework has security issues." One after another, they will raise irrational points against our proposal, and as soon as we defeat their point, they will bring up another point that is even more irrational than the previous one. It doesn't matter what we say. They just won't accept whatever we are trying to propose. Maybe they just don't like us. Maybe they already have one foot outside the company and don't want to create more work for themselves. Maybe they have too much on their plates and just don't want to hear about any changes right now. It's very difficult to know.

Unfortunately, throughout my career, I've identified a few more categories and named them. Let's have a look at them.

- **The Indifferent:** The Indifferent simply doesn't care. Developers in this group don't necessarily go against anyone or anything; they are simply indifferent. The problem is that indifference leads to lousy implementations of good ideas, transforming those good ideas into very bad ones. For example, bad tests are worse than no tests. If you allow bad tests to proliferate, your whole TDD crusade can be jeopardized. Besides bad TDD adoption, other examples can be found in companies where Agile *didn't work.*

- **The Wronged:** This is a dangerous type. Developers in this group think the company has wronged them. They usually feel they are underpaid, or never had the recognition they deserved, or are being unfairly treated. They usually don't like the company and never miss an opportunity to badmouth it. In extreme cases, they may do things that can harm the project they are in just for the satisfaction of quietly saying, "I told you so. You got what you deserved." Their presence on a team can be extremely destructive, contaminating other developers. And worst of all, they don't resign. They just stay there waiting to be fired so they can press charges against the company.

- **The Inept:** They just don't get it. They are more aware than the Uninformed but they are not able to see things clearly. Their thoughts are fuzzy, and their opinions are based on distorted facts and half-baked ideas—usually someone else's ideas. Developers in this category see software development only as a job, and even when they try, it is clear that this job is not for them. "TDD is not good. I heard that if we want to *do* Agile, we should do things as quickly as possible. When a client complains, we change it. Tests are anti-Agile because we will need to write more code and that is going to slow us down" (sigh).

- **The Ivory-Tower Architect:** Besides the Irrational, this is the worst type of skeptic for a software craftsman to deal with. They think they know it all. They are smarter than any developer. They think they are at the top of the food chain. Ivory-Tower Architects usually haven't written a single line of production code for years (useless proofs of concept that have no resemblance with reality do not count). They like to say they are responsible for every technical decision, but very rarely are they held accountable for any of them.

If things go well, they get the credit; if not, they blame the development team that didn't follow their *clear instructions*. If it is not their idea, it's probably not a good one. Since they don't write code, they feel the constant need to prove why they are needed. Their favorite pastime is to browse the Internet looking for new acronyms. They read the marketing material of expensive technologies, create nice PowerPoint presentations, ask junior developers to write prototypes, and convince managers that developers should follow whatever they recommend. They believe that their job is to define the technology stack for projects even before the business and development team agree on what really needs to be done.

- **The Insecure:** They are worried about being replaced or losing their status. They are usually found in organizations in which their core business is not technology, in an environment where almost no one above them is capable of judging how good (or bad) they are. Since they are the only technical people in the organization, they are known as "the IT guys," the *wizards* who solve all the business problems, from configuring the printer to writing some code. The Insecure are average developers who fear that, one day, their customers will realize that they are not so great. They see software craftsmen as a threat and will do whatever they can to discredit them.

- **The Fanboy:** They are totally devoted to a single subject (or point of view) in a fanatic manner, often to the point where it can be considered an obsession. Developers in this group are the ones who dedicated a long time to learn and become a specialist in one particular thing—usually a tool, language, or framework. Because this is the only thing they know well, they believe it is a silver bullet, rejecting all other possible alternatives. But their obsession is not always about a particular tool or framework. Sometimes their obsession is about a particular design technique, methodology, or process. If they happen to disagree with what you are proposing, which is very likely, be prepared to have very heated debates for extended periods of time.

BE PREPARED

There are a few things you must have if you really want to change things around you. The most important one is courage. You cannot be afraid to engage in heated debates with managers, technical leaders, and fellow developers; certain discussions are unavoidable and you need to be prepared for them. You must be brave and say everything you think, no matter what. Honesty and transparency are core values for any software craftsman. You also need to be confident. You will never be able to convince anyone to do anything if they don't feel that you know what you are talking about.

Encourage simplicity. Your idea or proposal must be simple and clear. Organize your thoughts before proposing anything. Make it very easy for people to understand; use examples whenever possible. The ability to communicate well is key if you want to have your ideas accepted.

Speak the same language. Depending on which changes you are proposing, you may need to speak to developers, managers, architects, sponsors, product owners, business analysts, or any other person who can be affected by them. Learn how to speak their language. Don't try to talk about details of your code or frameworks with managers or product owners. Instead, tell them about the benefits that your proposal has for the project: reducing maintenance costs, more reliable and frequent releases, and so on.

Do your homework. Make sure you understand what you are talking about. Research, try, and practice. Think about what questions the skeptics would ask, and make sure you have an acceptable answer before you speak to them. If your proposal has any drawbacks, mention them before anyone else does. If you feel that there are areas where you don't know enough, be clear about that. Being clear about the drawbacks shows that you thought hard about the problem and increases your credibility.

Be respectful. Don't treat people as if they were stupid. Disrespect and aggression will immediately put people in a defensive mode, making the task of convincing them almost impossible.

Learn how to listen. You may have a very good idea of how things should be done, but make no mistake, you are not the only one with an idea. Everyone has an opinion and sees the same problems from different angles. Probably, there are many things you are not even aware of. Listen and digest what everyone has to say before you make any judgment.

WHERE DO WE START?

After a short period of time in a new project or organization, ideas for improvements start popping into our heads like popcorn in a microwave oven. And once we start identifying all the different types of skeptics we may face, it is not hard to imagine how difficult it will be to push our ideas forward. So where do we start?

ESTABLISH TRUST

We can't change anything if people don't trust us. As a developer, the best way to build trust (with fellow developers, delivery managers, or clients) is by consistently delivering quality software. The trick here is to understand what quality software means. For other developers on the team, that may mean the design we've chosen, how we've named our functions, whether we've written meaningful and readable tests, and whether there are no duplications—that is, if the code is easy for them to maintain. For delivery managers, quality software may mean software that satisfies the requirements, has no bugs, and was delivered on time. For clients, it may mean software that is in production, making them money, saving them money, or protecting their revenue.

Although essential, consistently delivering quality software is not enough to build trust. You won't change anything if you stay quiet inside your little cubicle waiting for someone to recognize that you have something interesting to say. You need to expose yourself. You need to be visible. You need to demonstrate how passionate you are and how much you care about the project and about what you are proposing. People are far more inclined to follow someone who is passionate about something than someone who doesn't exhibit any passion.

But showing your passion is not enough either. Above all, to establish trust, you need to be good. People need to feel that you can do it. They need to feel you can lead them.

Gain Expertise

When proposing changes, we always tell our teams (including managers, product owners, etc.) that the future would be a much better place if we did the things we are proposing. Whatever these things are—adopting a new technology, changing the design of an application, changing our process, or adopting TDD—they have an initial cost. Skeptics will immediately say that it is too risky, it will cost too much money, or it will take too much time.

Before proposing a new technology, make sure you really understand it. Play with it, build something with it, talk to experts, and compare it to other similar technologies. Make sure you can do what you need to do with it and, above all, that you can teach it to others. There aren't many people out there willing to use their spare time to become an expert in a new technology or to master a new practice. However, that doesn't mean that they don't want to learn them. You can speed up their learning curve if you go through the learning curve yourself and teach them.

In gaining experience, you can inform the Uninformed; the Herd will join you, since they feel you know what you are talking about; the Cynic can be disarmed if you answer questions with confidence and demonstrate a deeper knowledge. The more knowledge you have, the easier it will be for you to understand what happened to the Burned. With this understanding you can identify where they went wrong and address their concerns. Gaining expertise gives you more ammunition to engage in discussions with the Ivory-Tower Architect and the Fanboy. And if it all fails, you will have more knowledge than you had before, which makes you a better professional. For a software craftsman, this is a win-win situation.

LEAD BY EXAMPLE

When it comes to driving technical changes, especially if the change is about attitude and practices like TDD, nothing will help you more than the ability to lead by example. There are certain things for which you cannot just find a manual online, read it, and start doing it. TDD is one of these things. Software design, clean code, planning iterations, inspiring people, coping well with pressure, establishing trust with customers—whether managers, business, or external clients—are not things that you can just point out a few Internet links to your team and expect them to be good at. Certain disciplines and practices take years to master, or at least a few months until we can reach a point where we are reasonably comfortable with them.

Developers may reject certain practices because they are *too difficult* to master or to become comfortable with. Managers, on the other hand—worried about deadlines and productivity drop—use "our lack of expertise" as an excuse not to support and promote certain practices.

We can help developers to overcome their initial fear by sitting down and writing code with them. Developers will feel much more comfortable adopting a practice if they know they can count on us to pair with them. From a manager's perspective, she will have nothing to complain about if she feels the team (or at least a few individuals) has the skills, can keep a constant velocity, and deliver code with the same (if not superior) quality.

If you want your team to behave in a certain way or adopt a technology or practice, first make sure that you can do that yourself. Leading by example will help you to deal with the vast majority of skeptics—they would have a hard time rejecting your proposals if you could successfully demonstrate your technique and mentor them.

CHOOSE YOUR BATTLES

"If I had the power, and could work without anyone disturbing me, and could hire and fire whoever I wanted, I would change this entire organization in a very short period of time." This is something that crossed my mind many times during my career. However, this is a very naive, inefficient, and potentially self-destructive feeling. And above all, forget it; it's not going to happen. A one-man army won't win a war, so choose your battles carefully, one at a time.

After a few weeks working for an investment bank, I had a big list of things that I wanted to change. The items on the list varied quite a lot in terms of the effort required to tackle them. I wanted to change some small pieces of code here and there, throw away and rebuild entire applications, fire and hire people, reduce the number of bugs, increase software quality, change the way we dealt with off-shore teams and vendors, reduce bureaucracy, and many other things. The list was huge. Some of the changes could be done quite quickly, in a day or two. Others would take months, if not years. Trying to do everything at the same time wasn't just impractical but also impossible.

One of our primary goals was to change the culture of our department, so the first thing we changed was our recruitment process, making sure that any new person joining our teams would already be aligned to the culture we wanted to have.

The second thing (that happened almost in parallel with the first one) was to introduce TDD and pair programming to our teams. This was a long battle, not only with some developers, but also with a few delivery managers. It took us almost one year to be comfortable with it and to notice a big improvement in our systems. Entire proprietary black-box testing frameworks, which had had years of investment, were thrown away and replaced with open source alternatives.

Certain changes had to be done before others. We had to wait for some changes to be in place so we could start tackling bigger design and architectural issues, restructuring our applications, introducing new technologies, changing our process, and many other things.

Before driving all these changes, we had to consider the impact of those changes, speak to a lot of people, and prepare ourselves for the tough questions from the most varied types of skeptics. In order to choose our battles well, we had to weigh which changes were most important. The criteria can be a bit fuzzy, quite often driven by gut feeling and experience, but we tried to put some thought into it. Certain changes would bring us a lot of benefits in a very short period of time. Others would prevent us from being burned in the future. We also had to weigh the types of forces we would be fighting against, and who our major supporters would be. In a highly political and bureaucratic environment, being able to write well-crafted code is definitely not the only thing you need in order to drive changes.

You don't get to change the software development process of an organization, large or small, if you don't prepare yourself for it. Don't fight all the battles; they are not all equally important. Concentrate your efforts on what really matters, prioritizing the battles that will bring you more value faster.

ITERATE, INSPECT, AND ADAPT

One of the easiest ways to avoid big confrontations is to propose gradual changes. Instead of saying, for example, that from now on everyone should follow the new design you are proposing, you can suggest that in the next sprint, you and another developer will choose a story and try a new design. After the story is finished, and demoed to everyone, the team can decide if they want to adopt the new design.

It is important to include people in the decision-making process and provide a feedback loop mechanism where everyone has an equal say. We can use the *iteration boundary trick:* "Let's try this approach for one iteration and then we revisit." Once people feel they are included in the process, they will be far more inclined to collaborate than to fight against each other. Proposing gradual changes reduces the amount of resistance and minimizes the risk—changes are done gradually, iteration by iteration, with a well-defined feedback loop. Another advantage of using this approach is that the majority of the skeptics, with the exception of the Irrational, will be disarmed. "Let's just try it for one iteration, in a small part of our software. We can then have a discussion around something more concrete and, if you don't like it, we revert it. There is nothing decided (yet)." No sensible person would go against that, especially when this discussion happens in front of the whole team.

FEAR AND INCOMPETENCE

Fear and incompetence are two of the culprits of bureaucracy and politics inside companies. Have you ever wondered how certain people managed to become a CTO, CEO, manager, architect, or team leader? Have you ever been in a situation where everyone knew that the solution was wrong or inefficient, but no one wanted to tell the boss or escalate the problem? Have you ever become frustrated by having to follow stupid procedures just because they were the organization's "policy"? How many times have you had to deal with an ill-defined architecture designed by someone who is not even part of the development team? And how many times did you remain silent about that?

Fear. Incompetence. The fear of losing our jobs. The incompetence to develop good solutions and convince our team to do something better. "I knew that it was wrong but I could not say that. He's the boss. He is the person who has the power to promote me." Fear. Incompetence. The fear of expressing our opinion and being professional. The incompetence to change things around us and fight for what is right.

Only incompetent people fear losing their jobs. Incompetents and cowards prefer to play political games and hide behind someone else's mistakes, so they can get their promotions. "If I make my boss happy, I'll get promoted. I don't care about the company, I care about my bonus." This is selfish, unprofessional, and immoral.

Professional developers, real software craftsmen, have ethics, a code of conduct. Software craftsmen are in control of their jobs and careers. They don't need to play political games to be promoted—they know they will never struggle to find a job in a place where they are valued.

If you want to change things around you, don't fear. Prepare yourself, practice, read, study, and be the best you can be. Regardless of what happens, always speak the truth. The only advice here is just be careful not to be an asshole.

How Do I Convince My Manager?

The simple answer is you don't. It's easier to ask for forgiveness than to get permission. Just go there and do it. When it comes to technical practices, why would your manager care anyway? Managers want projects delivered on time, on budget, and with no bugs, and they want to make stakeholders and clients happy. Who cares if we use TDD, if we pair, or have continuous integration? Besides us, no one.

If we asked our managers, "Does the code need to work? Is it OK if we introduce bugs every time we touch the system?" what would their answer be? "Sure, go ahead and write the worst code you can possibly write. That's what we hired you for. Screw the users. They can call and complain if they are unhappy." If your manager says that, make sure you call the nearest mental hospital or find another job.

We are expected to deliver quality software. We are expected to deliver good solutions. So, when it comes to TDD, pair programming, continuous integration, or any other practice you think can help you to achieve that, just do it. Don't ask for authorization. Don't ever put a task card on the board called "unit testing." A unit test is not a task. You cannot say that a coding task is done if you still have a pending "unit test" task for that code. Don't split coding tasks into two tasks: one hour to code this service class and another hour to write unit tests. They are not separate tasks. In this case, you just have a single two-hour task to implement a service class that works. Testing, regardless of which type, is part of the coding task and not a separate thing.

Whatever you do, make sure you deliver value to your customers. Be transparent and honest about your progress but, unless they ask, don't keep highlighting all the minor details about how you are implementing your code—it's not important. I'm not saying you should lie or hide anything. I'm just saying that telling your manager that you will take a specific amount of time to refactor your code or write unit tests is totally pointless. Who cares? What is important for managers is when you are going to be done, and by done we mean provide code that works according to the business specification and is in production (or ready for user acceptance testing [UAT]). Tests and refactoring are part of any coding task. The more technical details you expose, the more managers feel they should micromanage you.

How Do I Convince My Team to Do TDD?

Introducing a new framework, tool, or design approach is hard. Telling other developers that they should change the way they work in order to produce better code is even harder.

Asking for help is a very good way to introduce TDD without much friction. Choose the most enthusiastic developer on the team and ask her if she could help you with your task. Explain to her what the task is about, and then ask her if she would like to try TDD to implement it—just for an hour or two. If she says that no one else does it, tell her that it doesn't matter. "Let's just try it anyway, just for fun." And that is your chance to show her how awesome TDD, or any other technical practice, is. Share with her that great feeling of seeing the red bar turning into green. Show how awesome it is to be able to refactor the code without the fear of introducing a bug. Take the opportunity to Ping-Pong (a TDD style where one developer writes the test and the other writes the code to make it pass, switching roles every time a test passes); offer her the keyboard and ask if she wants to write the next test. Make sure you have fun together.

Introducing TDD to someone who is eager to learn it is quite easy. Even if you are not very good at it, you can learn it together. On the other hand, it can be very tricky to introduce TDD to someone who is skeptical about it. In this case, I suggest that you make sure you are comfortable with TDD before trying it. The last thing you want is to have a skeptical developer, after pairing with you, thinking that TDD is too hard, takes too long, and hence not worth it.

Developers are creatures of habit and are generally very opinionated. You cannot just go there and tell them what to do. The most efficient way to introduce a technical practice is to lead by example. Ask them to pair with you and show them how you do it.

FACING THE SKEPTICS

We started the chapter talking about the categories that different skeptics may fall into. By now, we have already discussed the most important things we need to know and do in order to deal with almost all of them. There are just a few other things we should know.

Practicing in our spare time, preparing ourselves, and being able to demonstrate our technique can take us a long way when driving changes. We can easily inform the Uninformed, shepherd the Herd, convince the Cynic, understand where the Burned went wrong and reason with them, and reduce the team's learning curve, which addresses the Time Crunched's concerns.

Being able to communicate well and at the right level is also important. If you want to bring the Boss to your side, speak her language. Don't bring up developers' problems. Raise the conversation to her level. Improving productivity, reducing cost, increasing revenue, meeting deadlines, reducing the number of bugs, keeping a steady and predictable velocity, and satisfying business requirements are the things the Boss will care about. If you want to change something, think about how this change would affect some of the things the Boss cares about.

Ignore the Irrational. Besides a huge amount of stress, there is nothing to be gained discussing issues with Irrationals. Focus on people who are willing to have a rational debate and are keen to know more about what you have to say. Irrationals are irritating people and there is a huge chance that the rest of the team will ignore them as well, regardless of whether they agree with what you are proposing.

Make sure you include everyone in the decision-making process. Don't impose your opinion. Instead, propose that the team use iteration boundaries to try to inspect new things. Make sure you are not seen as a threat to anyone's job. Your objective is to make things better, not to become the Boss or claim the credit for all the improvements. You need to establish that you are a developer like any other developer on the team. With this established, hopefully no developer will fall into the Insecure category.

Sharing your passion, leading by example, being honest and transparent, exhibiting confidence, and teaching what you know are the best ways to gain the trust of people around you. You end up becoming a role model, a person whom people want to follow and listen to. This behavior can bring the vast majority of sceptics to your side, including the Indifferent, the Inept, and the Fanboy.

THE IVORY-TOWER ARCHITECT

The Ivory-Tower Architect will probably be the most difficult skeptic to deal with. There's a natural clash of values and ideas of how things should be done. While a software craftsman would consider following a more Agile approach to software development, the Architect will try to push for a big upfront design, trying to define the technology stack and general architecture even before understanding the business problems we are trying to solve. The Architect normally imposes the technology and the design of the solution on the development team but does not sit down with the team on a daily basis to code and understand how her decisions are affecting the project.

The Ivory-Tower Architect is usually in a position of authority, having the responsibility to look after a department or even a whole company. She may draw individual applications as little boxes in PowerPoint presentations but she won't understand all the details of each one of them. Because the Ivory-Tower

Architects are not part of any development team and don't write code, they never feel the pain caused by their ill-defined architecture decisions.

Responsibility versus Accountability

Ivory-Tower Architects feel they are responsible for all the decisions and think that developers are just a bunch of coders implementing their vision. Technical debates with Ivory-Tower Architects can be soul-draining.

Although the Ivory-Tower Architects may have the responsibility for creating the *IT vision* for the company or department, they very rarely are held accountable for their decisions. If, for some reason, something goes wrong, they can easily say, "I gave clear guidelines." Usually, these guidelines are a few PowerPoint presentations or diagrams drawn on Microsoft Visio, random links from the Internet, or small proofs of concept that don't reflect the reality faced by developers. "We probably should hire better developers. They can't understand the one million pound in-memory data grid I chose. It's written on the website that many companies use this product. It must be good." With a closer relationship to the business, and being able to use the developers as scapegoats when things go wrong, Ivory-Tower Architects become responsible for the solution while the developers are the ones who are accountable for it. Maybe, in the example above, the application built by the developer never needed an in-memory data grid.

Although we should always push for productive conversations, some Ivory-Tower Architects are not open to that. They see developers as mere coders that should do whatever they are told. But one way to get our point across is to make Architects accountable for their decisions. If we have no say in the technical solution, then it is fair that we are not held accountable for it either. Some may call it passive-aggressive. I call it a last-resort measure.

Once, while I was working for a large organization, the relationship between the team and the Ivory-Tower Architect got tense. After months dealing with bad architectural decisions, bureaucracy, unnecessary complexity, frustration, and loads of arguments, here is a conversation I had with the Ivory-Tower Architect:

"Who **authorized** you to use this web framework? Why are you not using the other one I recommended?" said the Architect.

"Because the other web framework is not a good fit for our project. Also, I didn't know I needed your *authorization* for choosing a framework. I thought that the development team was responsible for that," I said.

"What do you think I'm here for? I decide which frameworks and libraries are used in all the projects."

"Ah, OK. I didn't know that. I thought your role, as an enterprise architect, was to look after the information flow within the company, and how all the applications collaborate in order to satisfy the business needs."

"I'm responsible for the whole technical solution. From the vision to the implementation, including frameworks and libraries."

"Our product owner said that the business is still trying to figure out what the requirements are. In order to help them, we decided to keep our code base to the bare minimum, enabling us to change the code almost as fast as they changed their minds. This will provide them with a quick feedback loop and help them to decide what they want."

"How are you planning to achieve that anyway?"

"The first thing we did was to put our continuous integration in place. Once our local changes are merged into the repository, our continuous integration server runs all the tests. If all the tests pass, the application is deployed into the UAT environment. This happens multiple times a day. The business guys then can just refresh their browsers (as many times a day as they want) and they will see our changes. This way they can see how the system is working and make up their minds about what they want to change or add to the system. This is one of the ways we found to help the business."

"That's good, but that doesn't mean you should use whatever frameworks you want. You should follow our guidelines."

"So I assume you understand all the functional and nonfunctional requirements of our application in order to prescribe the technology we have to use. Even when the business itself doesn't."

"I don't need to. I know that the in-memory data grid we bought and the web framework I'm recommending are good for all applications we have and should be used by everyone."

"That's great. I'm sure they are good. But are you going to write code with us as well? I'm sure we could benefit a lot from your experience using all these tools and frameworks. However, I still think that we are in a much better position to choose the tools that will make us more productive and provide a fast feedback loop to the business. The choices we are making only impact the internals of our application and not the external world. That means it doesn't change how our application communicates with other applications and its role in the entire ecosystem."

"Well, my role is to standardize the technology stack. This allows us to have people fungibility. [I had to ask what that meant. I didn't know the word. It meant that people could be easily substituted.] Not everyone is a super *coder* like yourself." There was something in the way he pronounced *coder* that made me feel inferior.

"People fungibility? That makes sense," I said calmly but in an ironic tone. "You are saying that instead of choosing the right tools for the job, we should choose the tools that low-skilled developers can deal with. Instead of trying to hire better developers or train the existing ones, the approach is to lower the bar and sacrifice quality. Sure, I'll explain that to the business."

"You are putting words in my mouth."

"Sorry, that was not my intention. I probably misunderstood. Could you please tell me exactly what you meant, and how a person that is not directly involved in the delivery of the project could be choosing the tools and frameworks used by the team? I understand you see each application as a small box in an ocean of small boxes. Why exactly do you care how each box is implemented? Shouldn't you just care about how these boxes talk to each other, and the responsibilities they should have?"

"Like it or not, that is my role," he said angrily. "I get to choose the technology stack for all projects. If you want something different, you need *my* authorization for that. This is *my* responsibility."

"OK. Got it. That's not a problem at all," I said calmly. "I'm gonna go back to my desk and send an email to all the stakeholders, project managers, business analysts, and every other person involved in the project, copying you, of course, saying that we will be stopping the project for some time. During this time, I'll tell them that you will be going through all our Maven repository and checking if we are allowed to use all the libraries we chose. We will also be waiting for a full list of approved technologies. Once we have this list, we will make all the changes to our software so they comply with your recommendations. As this may take a few weeks, if not months, I'll ask the stakeholders, sponsors, and product owners to speak directly to you, in case they want any business changes to be done during this period. As they are the people paying for the project, I'll ask them to talk to you about any delays and problems that may be caused by the technology choice."

With a worried look, the Architect tried to cut me off and say something, but I continued. "I'll also tell the production services guys [the people responsible for maintaining the application in production], and the business guys, that once we do all the changes and our application is 100 percent compliant with your guidelines, any urgent problems in production should be directed to you. As you are making the decisions on the technology, we assume you understand the technology better than any other person in this organization."

"Hey, hold on a second. You cannot do that. You are on the project, not me. The development team is responsible for delivering the solutions," he said nervously.

"Let me see if I understand. You are responsible for the decisions but the development team is accountable for them. If the project goes well, you get the credit since you gave the *directions*. If the project doesn't go well, we will be accountable for it." That was an interesting notion of fairness, I thought to myself. "Sorry, but I can't work like that. In my view, a professional should be accountable for her own decisions. I'm more than happy to take all the heat if something goes wrong, but only if we, the development team, make the decisions. I'm giving you two options: either the development team makes all the decisions and takes full responsibility for them, or I'll go back to my desk and send the email saying to everyone that you are accountable for all the technical decisions, hence the first point of contact in case of any problem." And with an angelic face I continued, "So, what do you want me to do?"

"I think you are being too radical. Of course you can experiment with technologies and choose the ones you think are better. There is no need for all of that. I just said I want to approve it."

"I'm sorry if it came across that way. But my position remains. I'm happy to explain our technical decisions to you and whoever else may be interested in them. I'm happy to write about it on our internal wiki, explaining the rationale behind our decisions, and the tools and libraries we compared before making each decision. I also understand that our application lives in a huge ecosystem composed of many other applications. We are happy to comply with whatever guidelines you may have when it comes to integrating with the outside world. However, I just want to make it clear that we don't want to come here and ask for your approval when it comes to how we are going to build our application. So, again, what should I do?"

"Make sure you document all your decisions," the Architect said, trying to hide his desire to kill me, "and keep me posted."

After this discussion, we were free to make our own decisions without any external influence. The business was extremely happy because we could implement what they needed very quickly and it was bug-free. We were happy because we felt we were delivering real business value and our efforts were being appreciated by the business. A few months later, some people in the senior management of the company assigned the Ivory-Tower Architect to other projects in a different department. They said that our department didn't need him anymore.

Real software professionals understand that responsibility should always come with accountability. If you want to be responsible, be prepared to be accountable. If you are accountable, make sure you are also responsible for the decisions. Ivory-Tower Architects are usually scared of their own decisions, hiding behind bureaucracy and politics in order to succeed in their careers. If you want them out of your way, try to make them accountable for their decisions.

THE WRONGED

The Wronged is another very difficult type to deal with. They are not against you; they are against the company. They feel as if they've been treated unfairly, but instead of resigning, they just hang in there, moaning, complaining, and doing a very poor job. There is not much we can do about it besides trying to make them excited again. I never had much success in resolving the situation in a satisfactory way. This is the type of problem that can't really be solved by another developer. The best thing is to treat the person well, do our best to integrate the person with the rest of the team, but also escalate the problem when needed.

SHOULD WE REALLY CARE ABOUT ALL THAT?

Besides all the technical skills, a software craftsman is also a role model for less-experienced developers. Software craftsmen are not afraid of being honest and transparent. They don't lie or deceive their customers, hiding problems to make them happy. Software craftsmen don't say what people want to hear; they speak their minds. Software craftsmen take responsibility for their actions and are not afraid to fight for what is best for the project.

As a software craftsman, you cannot deliver value to your customers if you work on a dysfunctional team or environment. Delivering value to customers is not just about writing code. It is about delivering a full solution to their needs. To deliver a full solution, especially in certain types of organizations, just writing well-crafted code is simply not enough.

SUMMARY

Driving technical change is hard. Very hard. To be successful, we need to understand how to deal with all the different types of people we will need to interact with and convince along the way. These people are not stupid; they just have a different opinion and different reasons for believing what they believe. Their opinions may be based on previous experiences, access to information you don't have, lack of confidence, or even fear.

Being good at what we do, being able to communicate clearly, and, most important, being able to establish trust are essential skills for any developer willing to drive changes. Understand who you are speaking to. Understand the reasons for each person's thinking. Prepare yourself. Be brave. Drive.

15 PRAGMATIC CRAFTSMANSHIP

There is an assumption that quality takes time. Managers and developers believe they need to choose between expensive well-crafted code that takes a long time to write or cheap average code that is delivered faster. Unfortunately, cheap average code that is delivered faster usually triumphs over well-crafted code.

In this chapter we bust the myth that quality is expensive. We will also discuss, with examples, what pragmatic craftsmanship really means.

QUALITY IS ALWAYS EXPECTED

I've yet to meet a person who wouldn't want quality if quality were inexpensive or if quality didn't need to be considered as a trade-off for something she judged more important at some point in time—like time to market or cost. No manager or client expects bad-quality software. Regardless of what they say, they will always expect high quality. Even when developers tell them many times that quality will suffer if they want to keep the costs down and deliver things faster, they will nod in agreement but they will still expect quality.

The main problem is this big and wrong assumption that cheap and average code is good enough—maybe in the short term, but never in the medium and long term. For a company that usually aims for average code, more often than not, average means very poor. As the big ball of mud grows, cheap doesn't remain cheap: the number of bugs increases, time to develop new features increases, and conversations about rewriting the entire application become more frequent. But managers and project sponsors don't see that. They are not developers. For them, software development is a service just like any other service they pay for. And like any other service provider, developers are expected to deliver quality. They are expected to deliver good value for money.

Think about yourself when buying a service. Imagine you are hiring a building company to do an extension to your house or to renovate your kitchen. You want to know how much it is going to cost before they start the project. At the very least, you expect to get a very well-educated guess and price range. You want to know how long it is going to take. You also want it to be cheap. And, most important, you want to use the extension or your new kitchen as soon as possible. What if the builders told you that, to be quick and cheap, they couldn't guarantee quality. "If you want us to do what you are asking us, you *may* have some problems in the future." What would you do? If you rushed to say you would choose quality over time and price, think again, because usually that is not the case. Unless you are very rich and are not living in the house where the work is going to be done, you will want it to be done quickly, cheap, *and* with quality.

Now let's assume you really need the work to be done in your house but you have a limited budget. If the building company told you that you would need to pay a lot more for the quality you wanted, or that the project would take two or three times longer, what would you choose? Within budget, but with low quality, or over budget with high quality? Either way, you would be screwed.

There are many circumstances that may make you swing between keeping quality high, even if you need to pay a premium for it, and keeping quality low and having the service done cheaply and as soon as possible. Maybe you are on a tight budget or you need to sell the house quickly. Maybe you and your wife are having twins and you need the extension before they are born. Perhaps you don't live in the house but you need a new kitchen so you can rent it out as soon as possible. Or maybe you are planning to stay in that house for a long time and are looking to make it as comfortable and functional as possible, regardless of how much time it takes.

Regardless of which decision you make, even if you choose the low-quality one, you will always hope for quality. You will always hope to not have any problems with the service you paid for. And that is exactly how managers and clients think when paying for a software project. They may decide not to pay for quality and ask for a quick and cheap solution, but deep inside, they will always be expecting quality and won't be happy if they don't get it.

But what if quality didn't cost more? What if a quality service didn't take much longer to be done? What if the difference in cost and time between a quality service and a nonquality service was so small that, in the grand scheme of things, it wouldn't make any difference? Would anyone still choose a low-quality service? I doubt it.

BUSTING THE "EXPENSIVE AND TIME-CONSUMING QUALITY" MYTH

Software craftsmen embrace Extreme Programming (XP) practices and Agile principles. In a project developed by software craftsmen, the client will have working software from day one. If the production environment, due to regulations or internal policies, is not readily available, software craftsmen would deploy working software on any machine available to the people involved in the project.

Completing a new feature means that the feature is deployed into production or a production-like environment if the company is not ready to release the software publicly. A team of experienced craftsmen is able to deploy multiple times a day. As software craftsmen aim for continuous integration and delivery from the outset of a project, the assumption that quality software takes longer to be released to production is totally unfounded.

Software craftsmen master their practices—Test-Driven Development (TDD) is second nature and not something that slows them down. Typing has never been a bottleneck in any software project. For anything that is more complex than just a few lines of code, software craftsmen can test-drive code as fast as other developers can write code without tests, if not faster. Because every feature is test-driven, applications developed by craftsmen will always be entirely covered by tests, making discussions around the ideal percentage of test coverage totally irrelevant.

A big suite of automated tests in a reasonably large application, when done by craftsmen, is executed in a few minutes, if not seconds, making the delivery of features much faster than when done without tests. There are no extra steps: features can be continuously deployed into production without manual testing. The increase in speed of delivering features becomes even more evident as applications grow: there is no time wasted manually testing the application and fixing existing bugs. Applications developed without tests demand longer cycles of manual testing as they become bigger, making continuous deployment totally impossible.

"Well, but that is not our experience," says a project manager or a developer. "We were far slower when the development team tried pair programming and TDD." I'm sure that they are not lying about this, but we cannot say that these practices are bad because they slowed developers down. What we can say instead is that developers are slower than normal while learning any new technical practice; they are out of their comfort zone. When comparing experienced software craftsmen who have mastered these practices with experienced developers who don't use the XP practices, I don't think there is much of a difference for small pieces of code, but there is a massive difference for larger problems. The bigger the application is, the faster software craftsmen will be, when compared to developers who don't use XP.

Given the option, assuming developers wouldn't be slowed down by the XP practices, would any stakeholder choose not to have them applied? I doubt it. Learning and mastering practices takes time and can be costly, but that doesn't mean that the practices are bad. Instead of ignoring the practices, we should focus on shortening their learning curve by hiring experienced software craftsmen who could join the team and mentor existing developers.

Do We Need to Test-Drive Everything?

A pragmatic answer would be "no." However, I don't like extremes and I try not to use words like *always* or *never* when talking about things we should or should not do.

"But what if we have a small market window to deliver this," some TDD skeptics say. "What if we are still trying to figure out what we need to do and want to explore different options? What if we just need to hack something quickly so we can show it to potential investors or try out the market?" say the startup guys. These are some reasons I don't like to use words like *always* or *never*. Context is important when choosing your tools and practices. However, what bothers me is that only developers who are not proficient with TDD would ask these types of questions. They are the developers who focus purely on delivering something without any understanding of the mess that they are leaving behind.

Experienced XP developers, including myself, find some discussions around TDD a waste of time; TDD doesn't slow experienced developers down. Period. Experienced XP developers test-drive things because test-driving things is not a big deal. As a rule, I test-drive all my code. Very rarely, when I find a situation where the effort of having an automated test would not pay off, I don't write the test—the very few times it has happened, it was usually related to some user interface behavior.

Developers who are proficient with TDD would never say that TDD was the main reason why they could not finish something in time or that they didn't write the tests because they didn't have time. Before ruling TDD and other XP practices out, make sure you understand them and are good at them.

Imagine you have some DIY work to do in your house. You want to replace your carpet with laminate flooring. Or you want to add a new phone extension to another room and you need to switch some cables around. Surely you can do that. But who would do it faster and with better quality? You or a professional who does this type of service on a daily basis? If you are not a DIY type of person like me, probably the professional would do it much faster and with a much superior quality. However, if you decide to become a professional in this area, over time, doing these things over and over again, you could probably do it even better and faster than other professionals in this area. And that is exactly the same with technical practices like TDD.

REFACTORING

Refactoring for the sake of refactoring is a waste of time. Unless you have nothing else to do, there is no point in opening a piece of code that you don't need to change and spending days refactoring it. The Boy Scout rule says "leave the campground cleaner than you found it," not "clean the whole campground until it is so clean that you could lick the floor." Although it would be nice, that's a pure waste of time and not very pragmatic.

When working with legacy code, we should always leave at least the area of code we changed cleaner than we found it. Whenever I need to add a new feature to the code, I usually study the code a little bit and refactor it (if needed) so it can accept the new feature more easily and gracefully.

Refactoring the code *before* adding a new feature is a good idea when the impact on the code is significant. Before adding any feature I ask myself: is the code ready to receive this new feature? How many places do I need to change in order to add this new feature? If the answers to these two questions are "no" and "many," I will first refactor the code to prepare it for the new feature. I change the code in a way that would make it easy to simply slide the new feature in, without opening (or changing) existing behavior, minimizing the impact the new feature will have on the code. I would refactor my code in a way to make it compliant with the "open/closed principle" (OCP) first, and then add the new feature.

When there are no significant changes to the system, I just start writing the new code I need, and I do a series of small refactorings while I'm doing it—using the refactoring step inside the TDD lifecycle (red, green, refactor). First I make it work, and then I make it better, all in small increments.

Improving your system with small but constant refactorings, justified by necessary changes to the system, is a good and more pragmatic way to improve an application.

THE "ONE WAY" OF DEVELOPING SOFTWARE

The main mission of the Software Craftsmanship movement is to raise the bar of software development. Software Craftsmanship communities and prominent figures in the Software Craftsmanship movement try to raise the bar by promoting a different software development mindset and ideology. They also promote a set of technical practices that they currently judge to be the best ones to be used.

For developers starting on their journey, while they still don't have enough experience to make good judgments, we recommend that they follow the practices we advocate. However, as they move forward in their careers and gain more experience, they should try to discover better ways of doing things, exploring alternatives, trying them in real projects, and sharing their experiences with the rest of the community.

Good practices and processes are good until we find better ones to replace them. That's the same for programming languages and tools. That's the same for building things like cars, electronics, and almost everything else. Back in the 1990s, the Rational Unified Process (RUP) was a great alternative to waterfall development. Scrum became a much better option years later. After more than ten years since the Agile summit, and all we've learned during this period, different alternatives are being discovered and tried out. That's called evolution.

As craftsmen, we should not believe that TDD and all the XP practices are the best practices we will ever have. At this time, they are the practices we use and advocate but that doesn't mean we should stop looking for ways to improve. The day we convince ourselves that there is just one way of delivering software—in other words, that there is just one set of practices we should use—is the day that we will stop evolving. Being dogmatic about certain technologies, practices, or tools, without understanding the context we are in, is not Software Craftsmanship. A software craftsman has a large toolset and can choose the most appropriate tools and practices for the job.

Don't rush to call people unprofessional just because they don't use certain practices. Ask them what practices they use instead and then compare the benefits their practices have over the practices you use.

HELPING THE BUSINESS

It's common to be on a project where the business doesn't really know what they want. It's common to have a situation in which they are still trying to figure out what makes sense for the project—speaking to clients (internal or external), and trying out different solutions. Any Agile coach would say that in order to help, developers should engage in conversations with the business, ask questions, and propose solutions. Be part of the team. Sure, that goes without saying, and it should happen in any situation. But there is far more we can do.

I was once on a project where the business and the IT department were being pressured by auditors to create a solution to assess the risk associated with their financial operations. It was a big program, where new systems were being created and integrated with many existing ones.

The problem was that, at a macro level, everyone knew what the goals were. However, at the detail level, things were very fuzzy and complicated. The challenge was not just related to the natural complexity of the requirements or systems involved; it was also related to how the organization was structured. Refining requirements in a product backlog refinement (PBR) meeting was not just about prioritizing and defining acceptance criteria for user stories. Certain discussions could lead to a change in how the business operated. Deep knowledge of certain parts of the organization, alongside its politics and bureaucracy, was essential in those discussions. This was a situation where developers struggled to contribute ideas.

When the business is still trying to figure out what they want, and the only things they have in mind are ever-changing, half-baked ideas, the best way to help is to put something in front of them as soon as possible. We should be able to change the code almost as fast as they change their minds, giving the business an opportunity to visualize their ideas and also to get feedback from the people who will use the application.

A SIMPLE AND QUICK SOLUTION

Quick doesn't mean dirty. The problem I mentioned above was related to an internal web application we were building. As part of the acceptance criteria of each user story, we drew mockups and agreed on the expected behavior with the business. That worked well for a while but the mockups didn't really give them the experience of using the real software—mainly because of the rich user interface behavior we wanted for certain features. They wanted to play with the real application in a safe environment, then demo it to sponsors and users in other parts of the business. They also wanted to go live every month or so, so people could start using the application.

Some of the features were simple, but others not so much. The back-end solution, which had to be compliant with a bunch of rules and nonfunctional requirements, was far from trivial to implement. Each feature was composed of a few user stories, which all had to be completed in order to be meaningful to the users. The problem was that neither the business nor the users knew how things should work at the detail level. Reducing scope, which means having fewer features, did not make sense in this case—we didn't have a big deadline we had to meet and we could release new versions of the application reasonably often. Thin vertical slices, with fully functional features, would take too long to give the business the feedback they wanted. They wanted to see quickly if the solution as a whole would make sense—how all the features would fit and work together.

We then proposed a quicker solution. Let's build all features, with the respective web pages, as view-only (pages where users could not change the data displayed) and with all data stored in memory. The data, which were in many cases production data, would be read from files at startup and stored in data structures in memory. We would build the vast majority of the pages as read-only, just displaying the data and providing the appropriate behavior (navigation, AJAX calls, rich behavior, styling, etc.). This would give users a much better idea of how the application would work. We then enabled a few pages to actually change data (inserting, deleting, and updating), but just in memory. Nothing would be persisted. If the application went down, the data would be lost. Basically we built the real application without physical persistence, without all the auditing that was needed for any application inside the bank, and without all the compliance with nonfunctional requirements.

With this approach, we were able to build a functional application quite quickly, deploying new versions multiple times a day to our user acceptance testing (UAT) environment. Product owners and business analysts had the opportunity to very quickly look at the application and ask for changes. Because we incrementally built a thin *horizontal* slice of the application, our code was extremely simple to change—there were no data migration scripts or complicated domain logic.

After some time, we all had a better idea about how the system should behave. We discovered which web pages would be used more often and, bit by bit, we started adding database persistence and the appropriate business logic. We went live with many read-only pages, and just a few pages where users could actually change data. For changing the data that could not be changed by the users (read-only pages), we would prepare new data files with the desired change, bounce the application, and the data would be loaded into memory.

The whole application was test-driven. We didn't abandon our practices just because we were "spiking." We were all very experienced TDD practitioners, and because typing was not a bottleneck for us, TDD didn't slow us down. In fact, it made us go faster due to the large number of changes we had in a short period of time. Although we were spiking, we didn't want bugs to be in there. The versions deployed into UAT were also used for demos to clients. Bugs, while spiking, could have made us discard a good solution.

Over the period of one year, we had one small bug in production and just five small bugs in UAT, which were fixed very quickly. There were times where the complexity of requirements and features slowed us down, but never the unit tests. Tests helped us to release often and quickly. Tests helped us to make sure that even half-baked ideas from the business would work correctly, according to their expectations. Changing the code every time they changed their mind was easy as the code was simple, well crafted, and fully tested. We could quickly be sure that a change in one place in the code would not break other parts of the code.

The point here is not about vertical versus horizontal slices. The point here is not about when we should write tests or not. The point here is about helping the business to figure out what they need, and the best way of doing it is to be able to change the code almost as fast as they change their mind—without breaking anything. In order to achieve that, in the project I described, TDD, continuous integration, and pair programming were essential for us.

The problem is not the amount of unexpected changes in a software project; the problem is our inability to cope with them. Well-crafted software is a means to an end, where the goal is to provide value to our clients. In a project of any significant size, well-crafted code makes us go faster and with better precision.

Software Projects Are Not about Us

As professionals, we need to understand that a software project is not about us and our egos. The I-know-what-I'm-doing-and-I-don't-need-to-write-tests attitude is selfish and arrogant. Even if that were true, the project is not about you. It's not about one or two great developers. We need to think about who is going to maintain the software when we leave. We need to think about how difficult it will be for the company to keep evolving that software. If the value we add to a project is conditional to our continuous involvement in the project, it's not value. It's a point of failure.

Great versus Mediocre

Passionate developers love writing code. They enjoy creating complex solutions in order to keep themselves interested in the job. Sometimes they create complex solutions just because they are bored—the business-related features are just too dull. They are proud of all the architecture and all the design patterns they create and use. Back in the 1990s, creating complex and cryptic code was a sign of seniority. You were considered *senior* when you could write code that no one else could understand. "I have no idea what this code does. The guy who wrote it must be really good." The good news is that we were wrong about that and now we know it.

Any stupid developer can make things work. What distinguishes great and mediocre developers is *how* they make things work. Great developers write simple code that satisfies the business requirements, and less-experienced developers have no problem understanding it. Solving the problem with a simple and elegant solution is far harder than solving it with a complex and overengineered one. I believe that all the horrible legacy code out there is more than enough proof of that. Great developers even go beyond simple and short solutions; they strive to solve problems without writing any code at all. The best line of code is the one you don't write.

Well-crafted code is simple, small, testable, easy to understand, and most important, does the job. Code is the main source of bugs and pain. The less we write it, the better.

FOUR RULES OF SIMPLE DESIGN

Before thinking about architecture, design patterns, generic solutions, or anything else, as a rule, a software craftsman will always try to write code that satisfies the "Four Rules of Simple Design," as defined by Kent Beck:

1. Pass all tests
2. Clear, expressive, and consistent
3. Duplicates no behavior or configuration
4. Minimal methods, classes, and modules

Over the years, many people reworded these four rules (or elements). I personally prefer J. B. Rainsberger's version:

1. Passes all tests
2. Minimizes duplication
3. Maximizes clarity
4. Has fewer elements

There is a lot of debate about the right order (in terms of importance) of these elements. As J. B. Rainsberger defines it, if we assume that software craftsmen usually practice TDD, rule number one is just stating the obvious, hence it can be ignored. If we strive to minimize duplication (second rule), we would naturally have fewer elements, hence the fourth rule becomes irrelevant. With that in mind, we end up with just two main rules:

1. Minimizes duplication
2. Maximizes clarity

I would always favor clarity over duplication, so as a guideline, in order to achieve a simple design, I focus first on good names and nice abstractions that represent business concepts. Then I focus on removing duplications, which usually leads to a highly cohesive and loose-coupled code. When removing duplications, new structures emerge, which forces me again to maximize clarity, and then again to remove duplications. I stay in this cycle, working in very short iterations, until I'm done. This cycle was first described by Rainsberger as well.

Combined with the knowledge of Domain-Driven Design and the SOLID principles, this approach is normally enough to achieve well-crafted code without polluting the code with loads of design and architectural patterns.

Design Patterns

Back in the 1990s, I would not dare to write a single line of code without first consulting one of my favorite books: *Design Patterns* (a.k.a., a GoF, or Gang of Four, book). That led to totally overengineered and convoluted solutions, where everything was designed to be generic. "What if a different implementation is needed in the future? What if the requirements change in the next five years? What if Godzilla destroys the entire city while fighting King Kong? What if the orcs kill Frodo?" Everything had to be generic. Everything.

Look at all the legacy code we see out there today. It is far easier to identify the design patterns used by the developers than the actual business features they were trying to satisfy. Generic code is a great thing, but it doesn't come for free. The more generic the code is, the more complex it becomes.

With the adoption of Agile and XP practices, mainly TDD, we went from writing generic and future-proof code (if such a thing existed) to writing specific code that satisfied our immediate need. This was a big shift in perspective and also a source of many complaints from the Ivory-Tower Architects: "These XP guys are irresponsible. We will pay a big price in the future when it comes time to maintain this code. Of course the code should be more generic. We will need to rewrite everything. They are throwing away decades of valuable knowledge."

Refactoring to Patterns

It turns out that these Ivory-Tower Architects are not entirely wrong. They are wrong to say we should keep doing a big design up front (BDUF), but they are right to say that we should not throw away decades of knowledge.

Proficient TDDers very rarely use design patterns from the outset. We write our tests according to the business requirements, and we write enough code just to satisfy the tests. This usually leads to a very specific, but much simpler, solution to the problem. Just enough code is written, not more. We use the refactoring phase from the TDD lifecycle (red, green, refactor) to make sure all duplications are removed and the domain is appropriately expressed in code.

Let's say we had a system where one of the features was to calculate the salaries of permanent employees. This feature was test-driven and specifically written to satisfy the original requirement. After a few months, the business decides to employ contractors, and we now have to implement a feature that calculates their payments. That is when, before creating the code to satisfy the new feature, we would refactor and redesign the existing code creating a payment strategy abstraction; adjust the existing code (related to permanent payment) to use the new abstraction; and create the new contractor payment strategy that can now be easily added to the code. This way, we can do "just-in-time" design, making sure the code is prepared (redesigned) to gracefully receive the new features.

There is a price to be paid every time we introduce an abstraction or, in other words, a level of indirection. Before, the code could easily be read sequentially (no indirections, single payment strategy). Now it is a bit harder—it is not straightforward to understand which payment strategy is being used at runtime. We would need to look at some configuration or factory classes. Now that we have two payment strategies, we can justify the added complexity of the code.

Introducing abstractions early, with no justification other than "we *may* need it in the future," is what makes applications so complicated. Since we don't know which part of the system will change or evolve, we end up introducing abstractions (complexity) everywhere. We think we are being smart, trying to prepare our applications to grow and change in every single direction. But that is not smart; it is stupid.

There will be a few parts of the code where the effort of introducing abstractions earlier will pay off, but for all the rest of the code base, those abstractions will just cause unnecessary pain. The pragmatic approach would be to only introduce abstractions when they are really needed. This will help us to keep the overall complexity level down. Obviously, a system with low complexity levels is always easier to maintain and evolve than a system with a higher complexity level.

Design patterns are, and should always be, part of our toolkit. However, that doesn't mean we should always use them. When we are refactoring the code to introduce necessary layers or abstractions, we can then go one step further, potentially refactoring the code to an appropriate pattern that is commonly used to solve that type of problem. Instead of choosing your favorite set of patterns and then trying to make your problem domain fit into them, focus on solving the problem via small refactorings, guided by the elements of simple design and SOLID principles. Then, if you feel your solution is almost the same as the one defined by a design pattern, consider going one step further and refactor your code toward it. Generic code, although more extensible, is more complex than specific code. Instead of always striving for generic code, write code that is specific to the problem you are trying to solve and make it generic just when you have a reason for that.

I still remember the early days of my career. "We have a new application to build? Awesome. Let's define the architecture for it. What patterns should we use this time?" We would then spend days discussing *the architecture.* "Cool, looks great. Now let's speak to the businesspeople and figure out what problems we are trying to solve." Teenagers, huh?

CRAFTSMANSHIP AND PRAGMATISM

Craftsmanship without pragmatism is not craftsmanship. A craftsman's primary focus is customer satisfaction. Besides quality, time and cost are part of this satisfaction. Code cannot be considered well-crafted code if it doesn't provide value.

It's vital that we understand what our customers are trying to achieve with a software project. There are many reasons some projects need to be done quickly, including proving that it is a viable business; convincing investors to invest, or benefiting from a market opportunity. Other projects have more long-term goals. Different projects demand different approaches. However, regardless of how big or complex the project is, a craftsman will always produce quality code. Quick doesn't mean dirty. Large projects don't mean BDUF or overengineering. Clean and well-crafted code is important—it gives us the ability to quickly and safely make changes according to the business needs. One of the best ways we have to help the business to achieve their goals is to be able to change the code almost as quickly as they change their minds.

SUMMARY

Quality is not expensive. The lack of skills is what makes well-crafted software expensive. TDD doesn't slow developers down. Typing is not a bottleneck. Learning and mastering a new skill, practice, or technology is.

Regardless of what managers and product owners say, they all expect quality. They would always choose quality if they didn't need to trade it off for something else, like time and money.

Our job as craftsmen is to lower the cost of quality to a point that it is not a concern anymore. For that, we need to master our practices and be pragmatic. We need to understand the value that certain practices bring in different contexts. When dealing with craftsmen, clients should never pay more for quality.

A CAREER AS A SOFTWARE CRAFTSMAN

Being a software developer is awesome. Look around you. Almost everything that is man-made today has software behind it. The chair you are sitting on comes from a factory that uses software. TVs, refrigerators, and cars all have software running inside them. The food you eat is connected to software—if it were not for the many companies using millions of lines of code in their systems, food from so many different suppliers and countries wouldn't arrive at the supermarkets. Software saves lives—many of the advancements in medicine were possible because of software. Transport, communications, entertainment, sports, everything has software behind it. Software enables businesses to succeed and charities to help people in need. Software enables us to have a global view of the world. Software provides support for the authorities and volunteers to help people, minimizing suffering after natural disasters. Software helps to prevent injustices, assists law enforcement, and helps to bring water, electricity, and communication to remote parts of the world. Software also gives us cold beer and hundreds of channels in our TV boxes. Software unites families and friends that, for one reason or another, live miles apart from each other. How can we not be proud of that? How can we treat our jobs as "just a job"? How can we not care when we know that what we do is so important, sometimes even essential, for our own lives? Software developers are essential for the evolution of the world we live in.

In this last chapter we will discuss what it is to be a craftsman and how to have a successful and fulfilling career.

BEING A CRAFTSMAN

Passion. That summarizes it all. Software craftsmen are passionate about software development and their profession. They are passionate about solving problems with simple solutions. They are passionate about learning, teaching, and sharing. Software craftsmen are passionate about helping the software industry to evolve; sharing their code; mentoring young developers; sharing their experiences via blogs, books, talks, videos, and conversations; and being active in technical communities. Software craftsmen are humble, always ready to learn from more-experienced developers, and eager to help the less experienced.

It is no secret that the demand for software is only going to grow in the next few decades, making our society even more dependent on it. In order to cope well with this demand, software craftsmen feel they have a social and moral obligation to prepare the next generation of craftsmen, making sure our industry becomes more mature and more professional.

Being a craftsman is more than being a good developer who writes code well and delivers business value. It's a lifestyle. It's a life where we choose to do things well, to be the best we can be. It's a life where we are prepared to make some sacrifices to learn and help others to learn the craft. It's a life of continuous dedication to the art of writing code. It's a constant search for better and more efficient ways to deliver value through software.

Being a craftsman means to be curious and experiment with new things. It means not to be dogmatic about tools, languages, or frameworks. It means to be pragmatic, always looking for simple solutions and using the best tools for the job. Although not dogmatic about them, a craftsman must master a good set of tools, languages, and frameworks.

True software craftsmen focus first on solving problems, not on writing code. However, when they do need to write code, they focus on writing quality code—code that is testable, easy to understand, and easy to maintain.

A craftsman is never missed for the wrong reasons. No other developer will miss a craftsman because of the mess she left behind or because she was the only one who could understand the code she wrote. A craftsman is missed for the right reasons: insightful contributions, enthusiasm, knowledge, and, most important, being a great colleague.

HONESTY AND COURAGE

Honesty and courage are essential qualities of a software craftsman. "Well, but that is valid to everyone," you say. Surely, but by honesty and courage I mean saying "no" to clients when we think it is necessary. I mean being honest and courageous enough to tell our clients that what they are asking for is unrealistic and is not going to work—even if we know they will be annoyed by that. I mean telling our clients they are making a bad decision. We need to tell our clients that we are not going to commit to, or be responsible for, something that we don't feel is right.

However, simply saying "no" is also not a craftsman's attitude. A "no" should always be followed by a "but." "This will not work, *but* maybe we could try this other thing instead." Or, "There is a big chance we are not going to meet the deadline, *but* maybe we could reduce scope, doing the most important features first, and release the rest as soon as we can." Or even, "Sorry but what you are asking for is not going to happen within the time frame you expect. I would advise you to speak to the stakeholders and then call a meeting so we can all discuss the alternatives. I cannot commit to what you are asking because I know that the risk is too high."

The career of a craftsman is built on honesty and courage. A craftsman never hides anything from customers. Craftsmen and customers are in a partnership, where honesty, courage, and full transparency are key.

CAREER PROGRESSION

I once worked with a few teams in Eastern Europe—my mission there was to disseminate the Software Craftsmanship ideology and attitude, and also to introduce the teams to Extreme Programming (XP) practices. Besides helping developers to get better at writing code, one of my main goals was to inject some passion into the teams and help them to create a culture of learning.

While working with them, I asked, "What are your career aspirations? Where do you want to be in a few years' time?" After two or three minutes of silence, and a bit more encouragement from my side, one developer said, "I want to become an architect." Another said, "I want to become a manager." Other developers said team leader, head of department, product owner. No one said, "I want to still be a developer." I was sad. "Why not a developer?" I then asked them. After an awkward minute of silence, with a strong accent, one of the guys said, "Here, if you are still a developer when you are over 30, you are considered a failure." Some developers lowered their heads, and the rest just nodded silently. More silence. "I'm 35," I said loudly, "and I'm very proud to be a failure."

From that day onward, things changed. The developers seemed happier. Free. They were enjoying what they were doing, pairing with each other, making a good effort to write tests first, trying to make their code read well, running internal sessions, really trying to get better at writing code. They realized that you can have a successful career (and a lot of fun) doing what you love.

Unfortunately, that was not a situation I encountered only in Eastern Europe. I've seen similar situations in Asia, Brazil, and also in a few companies in the UK and US. We still have companies that treat developers like second-class professionals, who are there just to type stuff on the keyboard. Developers, on the other hand, think that this is how things work, and they do their best to *move up* in their careers, away from development, so they can be treated as real professionals.

Fortunately, this mentality is changing. There are many companies out there that recognize how important software developers are for their businesses, and they offer excellent packages to attract the best ones. Today, every company is a software company, and companies that fail to understand that will struggle to be competitive in the future. Companies that fail to recognize developers as high-skilled professionals will never have craftsmen working for them.

DIFFERENT LADDERS

Every profession has a career ladder. Software development is no different: we start at the bottom and move upward as we become more experienced.

Climbing up the software development ladder does not mean becoming a manager or an architect. This is not a career progression; it is a career change. The skills needed to become a great manager or architect are not necessarily the same ones needed to become a great developer (and vice versa). Developers who, for one reason or another, decide to take roles as managers or architects are not climbing up the software development ladder; they are switching ladders.

ROADS AND MILESTONES

There is a huge difference between following a career within a company and following your own career as a software craftsman. A successful software craftsman carefully plans her career; she usually looks for opportunities where she is going to learn the things she wants to learn in order to become a better professional. Different people have different aspirations, and these aspirations change over time. Looking ahead and planning the next steps is key for a successful career.

For many developers, looking for a new job means, "I will offer my current knowledge and time in exchange for the highest salary I can get." That's very shortsighted. For professionals who are interested in long and successful careers, a job is far more than that. It's a constant investment in their careers.

Besides the things we are paid for, we should also invest all our dedication, passion, commitment, and knowledge we acquire outside working hours to make our workplace a better place—a place where everyone can learn and thrive. Investing in making our working environment better means creating more opportunities for enriching our own careers.

I never focused on doing just what was specified in the job listing. I never said, "That's not my job." In fact, I don't think I ever looked back at any job description or contract after being hired. I always tried to offer more, to do more, and to make sure everyone around me would become better. I always tried to help as much as I could, regardless of what my role or position was. This is what I consider my investment. It was an investment not only in my job, but also in my individual career. But, as we would expect from any kind of investment, I wanted a return. At different moments of my personal or professional life, and at different jobs, what I wanted as a return on my investment varied. Exposure to certain technologies or industries; experience with different types of projects; opportunities to develop different skills, play different roles, and have different types of responsibilities; or even having more money were all things that at some point in my career I wanted as a return. Money was never a priority though—good software professionals will always have money enough to have a decent life. During my time in each job, I did my best to provide as much value as I could—*I wore the company's t-shirt,* as we say back home—and I got my return back.

I changed jobs a few times during my career, spending on average two years in each company. There were a few exceptions though. There was one company where I stayed for almost five years, and another company where I stayed for just three months. In the one where I spent just three months, although I was working with lovely people, I realized in the first couple of months that the job was not aligned with my career aspirations, so I did all of us a favor and resigned.

Throughout my career, I chose each one of my jobs very carefully. I never sent a whole bunch of CVs to many different companies with the expectation that at least one of them would make me an offer. I was focused. I always knew exactly what type of company I wanted to work for. And even when I had to face reality, when I was told I was not ready or good enough for that type of job, I took my time, prepared myself, and then tried again. Each job helped me to move forward with my career. Each job was a very important step in the very long ladder that is my own career—my long road to mastery.

This should not be confused with "CV building" though. CV building is when, while working for a company, developers force the use of a technology or a methodology that is *not* fit for the purpose just because they want to have it on their CV. This is not only wrong, but also unprofessional.

BUILDING OUR CAREERS, ONE JOB AT A TIME

Before I choose a job, I ask myself the following questions:

- What do I want for my career?
- What is the next step to achieve that?
- Is this job aligned with my career aspirations?
- How much value can I add to this company?
- What is the return on my investment?
- How long (roughly) will the duration of my investment be?
- How would this job help me to get to where I want to be as a professional?
- In this job, will I have autonomy, mastery, and purpose?
- Will I have a productive partnership with my employer, where both sides will be happy with the value they are getting out of the deal?

NOTE
The questions above are completely unrelated to the type of contract I had. I was a permanent employee for the vast majority of my career, so this is not exclusive to contractors or consultants.

Knowing the answers to all these questions, before starting employment, is almost impossible. We only get some of these questions answered after we start our employment. But that doesn't mean we shouldn't try to get these answers upfront. As I mentioned in previous chapters, the interview process is a two-way street, and we should use it to get as much information about the employment as possible before we commit to it.

So, the question is: why have I resigned from such carefully chosen jobs? If my employers could offer me exactly what I was looking for when I joined, why have I left? There are quite a few reasons for that. Over time, my career aspirations changed. My personal life changed. Some of my employers changed. Things changed. When things changed, I spoke to my employers, and within their own limits, they were able to give me all the things I was looking for. Some employers sent me to different projects or departments; others gave me opportunities to try new things. Some employers gave me more responsibilities, and some even gave me pay raises and promotions. However, there were times when they could not offer me what I was looking for. There were times when, without straying away from my own career aspirations, there was not much more I could offer. There were times when I wanted a bigger change: I wanted to work for a consultancy company; have my own startup; work for a global company with distributed teams; live abroad; have a position where I could make changes that would go beyond a single development team. When I had my first daughter, I wanted to reduce the amount of time I was spending away from home while working on projects. At different stages of my career or personal life, I wanted different things, and my employers could not always offer me that. With maybe one or two exceptions, all my employers were great, but at some point, we had to go separate ways.

I see my career as a very long, uneven, and curvy road. At the end of the road, there is the Promised Land: mastery. However, this road also has roadblocks, hidden dangers, confusing signs, and many junctions leading to other roads. Sometimes it is very difficult to know when, where, and whether we took the right or wrong turn. Going for too long in a single direction may make it very hard, if not impossible, to go back to where we were and take another route. Weather conditions do not always allow us to see too far ahead.

After a few years working as a professional software developer, I thought I was really getting great at it. I thought I was getting closer to becoming a master. But as I started meeting more and more developers, outside of my close circle, I realized how far away I was from it. I realized that I was not traveling fast on a German Autobahn like I thought I was. Reality showed me that I was in fact traveling very slowly on a Brazilian countryside road. I was so far away from mastery that I could not even see it anymore. I was disappointed, and it took me a while to recover from that. That was when I realized that I had to do something about it. I had to take my blinders off and seek opportunities where I could learn and evolve.

Each job is a milestone, a step in a ladder. Each job should take us farther on our journey, so they should be chosen very carefully. The amount of time we should stay in a job can vary enormously—it can be from a few months to many years. My advice is to stay in a job for as long as it remains aligned with our individual career aspirations. Whenever a job starts to diverge from our career aspirations, the partnership with employers gets weaker and less beneficial for both sides.

Whenever we feel we are not moving forward, we are not learning or enjoying ourselves anymore, we should move on. Loving the company and our colleagues is not reason enough to stay in a job. People move on, companies move on, and so should we. Looking for a job that is more aligned with our career aspirations is a favor that we do to our employers and to ourselves. Companies benefit from unhappy people leaving their jobs; it creates opportunities for them to bring in new people, with fresh ideas and more energy and the willingness to challenge the status quo and do a great job. From experience, I believe that a staff turnover of 15 to 30 percent a year is very healthy for a company. New people with new ideas help the company to remain up to date, competitive, and fresh.

WHAT IF WE DON'T KNOW WHERE WE WANT TO GO?

At first, this sounds like a silly question, but in fact, it happens to everyone. We don't always know where we want to go or what we want to do next. Sometimes we are just confused. Lost. It takes a lot of courage to admit that, but when we do admit that to ourselves, things get better. Once we accept we don't know where we are going, we can be more focused and objective in finding our way. That certainly happened to me. In fact, it happened three times in my career. There is just one thing you can do when you are in this situation: open yourself up and meet people. Get out of your shell and open as many doors as you can. Start attending community events. Start contributing to open source initiatives. Engage in conversations in mailing lists. Look for people who can inspire you. Go out there and show people who you are and what you can do. You will see that there is a whole world out there, full of amazing people, and with opportunities you never considered before. This exposure will help you decide where you want to go next. I personally know quite a few stories from developers who met in technical communities and later started their own companies, found great jobs, or changed their careers completely.

JOB DIVERSITY

Software development is a very diverse profession, and successful craftsmen usually have very broad experiences. Being a software developer in a startup and building games for mobile devices is very different from being a developer building enter prise applications for a global investment bank. Developing a mass-market product is very different from developing internal software. Developing frameworks and tools is very different from building bespoke business applications. Developing rich web applications is very different from developing applications with no user interface. Although you can argue that all software should be treated as a product—internal users or other systems are also your clients—that is not always the case. Building an embedded system for a car is not the same as having thousands of unknown users using your application in ways you never imagined before. Although many of the good coding practices apply in many different types of software, the whole environment is different. People are different. The relationship with clients or users is different. The amount of pressure developers are under in certain projects can be very different. For certain applications, a bug in production can cause huge damages (millions of dollars in fines, or even endangerment of human lives), while in others, a bug in production may not be a big deal (some users may get a bit annoyed but they will get over it soon, when the bug is fixed).

Working for a consultancy company can be a good way to get exposed to different types of projects and environments. I'm not saying this is the only way, but it is definitely a very good way. A consultancy company has many different clients and can provide you with many different opportunities. As you move from project to project, you may have opportunities to work with different technologies, different types of software, different types of companies, different team dynamics, and different tools and processes. You may have all these opportunities while still working for the same employer. On top of that, you can increase your network, which can be very handy as you move forward with your career as a craftsman. Working on various types of projects prepares a craftsman for the future; it makes you a very versatile and experienced professional, opening many different doors that can lead you to places you never considered before. Life as a consultant is not for everyone, but this is something to consider, mainly early on in your career. Working as a consultant for a few years can give you a lot of experience, exposure, and options, making it easier for you to decide where to take your career in the future.

But what about being a specialist in an industry or sector? No, there is nothing wrong with this either. You can still be a great and very specialized craftsman. Specialists are needed and essential in many types of projects and industries. However, exposure to different environments and types of projects may give you more ammunition to come up with better solutions in the area in which you decided to specialize. Moving from project to project, experiencing different environments, companies, industries, technologies, and approaches to software, is what I would consider to be the craftsman's journey.

THE MISSION

Software craftsmen are on a mission. They focus on bettering themselves, constantly investing in their own careers, and learning, teaching, sharing, and delivering value to every single client. But this mission is not just about clients—that's just one part of it. The real mission of a software craftsman is to make a contribution to raise the bar of the software industry, with professionalism, passion, and care. Software craftsmen are more than just ordinary developers who are hired to do a job. Craftsmen focus on helping other developers to get better at their craft and to be proud of what they do and who they are. The goal is that, one day, the quality and success rate of software projects around the world will be at a far higher rate than they are today.

Being a software craftsman is about more than just waking up in the morning, going to work, and getting paid to do some *stuff*. Software craftsmen wake up in the morning to make things better and to change the world we live in. Being a software craftsman is far more than writing well-crafted code or being a software developer. It's a lifestyle—a commitment to excellence. Embrace it. Be proud of the role you play in the evolution of our society.

CRAFTSMANSHIP MYTHS AND FURTHER EXPLANATIONS

I've had many discussions about Software Craftsmanship over the years, and it seems there are still a lot of myths and misunderstandings related to the terminology used by the Software Craftsmanship movement. Even inside different Software Craftsmanship communities, there are some differences of opinion about what certain things actually mean.

Unfortunately, this is not an easy problem to solve. Myths and misunderstandings are unavoidable, especially when a specific topic becomes popular, and many people around the world get involved in it. It has happened before. It happened to Agile, to Scrum, Kanban, programming paradigms, management styles, and many other things. Due to the vast diversity of our industry, and the many different personal experiences and biases, it is no surprise that we have so many different opinions about Software Craftsmanship.

In this appendix, I try to clarify many of these misunderstandings and myths. My opinions are based on personal experiences, my heavy involvement in the Software Craftsmanship movement, and many conversations I've had with many other professionals that I greatly respect. Some of these professionals are deeply involved in the Software Craftsmanship movement, while others never really wanted to associate with it; for one reason or another, they don't agree with or like some of the things that came out of the Software Craftsmanship movement.

SOFTWARE CRAFTSMAN VERSUS SOFTWARE DEVELOPERS

Every craftsman is a developer but not every developer is a craftsman. Contrary to what many people think, this has nothing to do with seniority or skills. The difference is more about the attitude each developer has towards his or her profession. Although any developer could call herself a craftsman, saying you are a craftsman doesn't make you a craftsman. Similarly, saying that you have certain values means nothing if you don't behave according to those values at all times. The values you have are defined by your actions, not your words.

I've met quite a few developers that prefer not to call themselves craftsmen. They don't want to "label" themselves and don't really care about this whole "craftsmanship thing." However, their professional attitude, the care for what they do, the practices they use constantly, the dedication they have towards improving themselves, and the respect they have for their clients makes them craftsmen, like it or not.

Being a craftsman doesn't mean you are superior or better than any other developer. When a developer calls herself a craftsman, she is just stating the values and professional attitude she has. But that doesn't mean that developers who don't call themselves craftsmen don't have the same values or attitude.

ELITISM

Quite a few times I've heard that the Software Craftsmanship movement is an elitist movement. I must confess that I was really surprised when I first heard that. From my experience, the Software Craftsmanship community is one of the most inclusive communities I've ever seen. It embraces developers from all sorts of backgrounds and levels of experience. All the sessions promoted by the communities are about sharing knowledge and learning from each other, and every single developer out there is more than welcome to join in.

But as happens every time you have a large group of people, there's always a small minority of individuals that may not behave according to the values of the group.

APPRENTICE, JOURNEYMAN, AND MASTER

To be honest, I don't really like this part of the metaphor and that's the reason I barely mentioned it in the book. In reality, terms like "journeyman" and "master" are very rarely used within the Software Craftsmanship community. They are just metaphors, and ones that we don't care too much about.

The relationship between "mentors" and "apprentices" is used far more often, and represent far better what we believe.

A common misunderstanding is to think that developers who call themselves "craftsmen" are also calling themselves "masters." I personally have never seen a single example of that. The interesting thing about this metaphor is that the critics of Software Craftsmanship talk about it far more often than the software craftsmen themselves.

MASTER CRAFTSMAN

This is a title that a very experienced software craftsman may have *inside* a company that is based on the Software Craftsmanship principles and values. However, this doesn't make the master craftsman a master craftsman for every single craftsman out there.

No one calls herself a "master," but some professionals may consider other professionals as "masters" in certain disciplines.

I have a lot of respect and admiration for quite a few professionals inside and outside the Software Craftsmanship movement. They are people who taught me a lot and inspired my career. For me, and maybe only for me, they are "masters."

NARROW FOCUS

Another very big misunderstanding is to think that Software Craftsmanship is about TDD and "beautiful" code. Some very uninformed people, mainly from the Agile community, have made comments that software craftsmen are shortsighted and have a very narrow focus. I hope that the content of this book helps to explain that Software Craftsmanship goes way beyond TDD and well-crafted code.

Lean, Agile, and Craftsmanship are totally aligned and have similar values. They all focus on providing value to clients through transparency and short feedback loops. The major difference among them is that their practices and disciplines are best applied in different spheres of an organization.

CRAFTSMANSHIP VERSUS XP

Craftsmanship is an ideology. XP is a methodology. An ideology is about values, attitude, and behavior. A methodology is about practices that solve specific problems.

XP is also based on values (simplicity, communication, feedback, respect, and courage), but it is more commonly known for its practices.

Craftsmanship focuses on professionalism. However, a professional attitude is totally related to the practices we use, and currently, the majority of these practices are XP practices.

ATTACHMENT TO PRACTICES

Software craftsmen are not attached to practices. They are attached to the value that those practices give them. For the vast majority of projects, XP practices have proven to be the practices that provide more value to clients and developers, and that is the reason why Software Craftsmanship advocates them.

Our industry is in constant evolution and we are always trying to uncover better and more efficient ways to deliver software. Practices are chosen according to the value they bring, and whenever we find practices that could give us more value than the XP practices, we are more than happy to adopt them.

AGILE COACHES AND MANAGERS

While reviewing this book, I noticed that I was quite tough, verging on unfair, with Agile coaches and managers. For a technical author, when expressing an opinion about a specific subject, it is not always easy to put down into words all the implied knowledge and personal experiences we have which serve as a context for that opinion.

I've had the pleasure of working with some great Agile coaches and managers. Their professionalism, knowledge, and ability to deal with tough situations (business or people-related), were second to none. Unfortunately, I've also worked with many Agile coaches and managers who were totally useless, or at best, not very good at their jobs.

Due to their positions, power, and influence, their decisions can damage not only projects, but also an entire organization. Working under bad managers and being advised by bad Agile coaches can destroy the motivation of a team, causing a lot of frustration, and even make the best people leave the company.

In many parts of the book, when referring to Agile coaches and managers, I was thinking about all the bad ones I met or worked with, and not the few good ones.

Agile coaches and managers are very important and needed in some organizations, and I have a lot of respect for great professionals, regardless of what type of work they do.

SOFTWARE APPRENTICESHIPS

Some people have asked me why I didn't write about software apprenticeships. For a Software Craftsmanship book, this is a very fair question. When I started writing this book, it was my plan to cover software apprenticeships as well, but there were a few reasons that made me decide not to. The main reason was that software apprenticeship is a huge topic, with many different people and companies doing it in a completely different way. Although I have my own strong views on the subject (we have a software apprenticeship program at Codurance), I felt that the topic would take a big chunk of the book and it would end up deviating it from its core message. However, it is still my plan to write about it in the future. Maybe in another book or a series of articles.

THE PROBLEM WITH METAPHORS

A metaphor is a figure of speech that describes a subject by asserting that it is, on some point of comparison, the same as another, otherwise unrelated object. Metaphor is a type of analogy and is closely related to other rhetorical figures of speech that achieve their effects via association, comparison, or resemblance.

Using metaphors is a common, and quite often, very easy and efficient way to explain or describe something. The problem is, when taken out of context or too literally—usually by people who don't know enough about the original context in which the metaphor was first used—all sorts of misunderstandings and myths are created. I hope this book will help to make things a bit clearer.

Index

testing and fixing bugs, 83–87
unit test task card, 86–87
using time wisely, 87–88
Time requirements
and quality of code, 209–211
for recruitment interviews,
122–123
Toyota, becoming Agile, 17–18
Trade, Software Craftsmanship as,
25–26
Training. *See* Culture of learning; Professional development
Trust, driving technical change,
191–192
Trust indicators, in recruitment interviews, 140
Trying to change everyone, 180–181
Twitter, for professional development,
47

U

Uncertainty about career path, 231
The uninformed, 186
Unit test task card, 86–87
Unit testing and fixing bugs, 83–87.
See also Testing and fixing bugs
Unrealistic deadlines
anecdotes, 61–64, 65–68, 71–74
enlightened managers, 74–75
"I'll try." equivalent to "Yes, I will
do it." 69
learning to say no, 64–68, 69–70
professionalism, 68–70
saying no, with options, 70–74
saying yes to avoid disappointment,
69

V

Value through practices, 98–104
Values

Agile Manifesto, 12–13
Software Craftsmanship Manifesto,
32–37

W

The Wandering Book, 28
Well-crafted software, 32–33
Working software
but also well-crafted software,
32–33
code is like a garden, 79
code quality *vs.* time per feature,
80
craftsmen are like gardeners, 81
dealing with bad code, 79–81
frequent deliveries, 78
as measure of progress, 78
over comprehensive documentation, 12
technical debt anecdote, 82–83
Work-life balance, 56–60
The wronged, 188, 204–205

X

XP (Extreme Programming), history
automated testing, 99–100
C3 (Chrysler Comprehensive Compensation) payroll system,
96–97
continuous integration, 101–102
pair programming, 102–103
practices and values, 97–98
refactoring, 103–104
TDD (Test-Driven Development),
100–101
test first, 100
value through practices,
98–104
XP (Extreme Programming), in an
Agile transformation, 19

Made in the USA
Columbia, SC
13 January 2020